Communications in Computer and Information Science   2889

Series Editors

Gang Li, *School of Information Technology, Deakin University, Burwood, VIC, Australia*

Joaquim Filipe, *Polytechnic Institute of Setúbal, Setúbal, Portugal*

Zhiwei Xu, *Chinese Academy of Sciences, Beijing, China*

Rationale

The CCIS series is devoted to the publication of proceedings of computer science conferences. Its aim is to efficiently disseminate original research results in informatics in printed and electronic form. While the focus is on publication of peer-reviewed full papers presenting mature work, inclusion of reviewed short papers reporting on work in progress is welcome, too. Besides globally relevant meetings with internationally representative program committees guaranteeing a strict peer-reviewing and paper selection process, conferences run by societies or of high regional or national relevance are also considered for publication.

Topics

The topical scope of CCIS spans the entire spectrum of informatics ranging from foundational topics in the theory of computing to information and communications science and technology and a broad variety of interdisciplinary application fields.

Information for Volume Editors and Authors

Publication in CCIS is free of charge. No royalties are paid, however, we offer registered conference participants temporary free access to the online version of the conference proceedings on SpringerLink (http://link.springer.com) by means of an http referrer from the conference website and/or a number of complimentary printed copies, as specified in the official acceptance email of the event.

CCIS proceedings can be published in time for distribution at conferences or as post-proceedings, and delivered in the form of printed books and/or electronically as USBs and/or e-content licenses for accessing proceedings at SpringerLink. Furthermore, CCIS proceedings are included in the CCIS electronic book series hosted in the SpringerLink digital library at http://link.springer.com/bookseries/7899. Conferences publishing in CCIS are allowed to use our online conference service (Meteor) for managing the whole proceedings lifecycle (from submission and reviewing to preparing for publication) free of charge.

Publication process

The language of publication is exclusively English. Authors publishing in CCIS have to sign the Springer CCIS copyright transfer form, however, they are free to use their material published in CCIS for substantially changed, more elaborate subsequent publications elsewhere. For the preparation of the camera-ready papers/files, authors have to strictly adhere to the Springer CCIS Authors' Instructions and are strongly encouraged to use the CCIS LaTeX style files or templates.

Abstracting/Indexing

CCIS is abstracted/indexed in DBLP, Google Scholar, EI-Compendex, Mathematical Reviews, SCImago, Scopus. CCIS volumes are also submitted for the inclusion in ISI Proceedings.

How to start

To start the evaluation of your proposal for inclusion in the CCIS series, please send an e-mail to ccis@springer.com

Tadashi Dohi
Editor

Software Engineering and Development

7th International Conference, ICSED 2025
Bangkok, Thailand, October 29–31, 2025
Proceedings

 Springer

Editor
Tadashi Dohi
Hiroshima University
Hiroshima, Japan

ISSN 1865-0929   ISSN 1865-0937 (electronic)
Communications in Computer and Information Science
ISBN 978-981-92-0201-0   ISBN 978-981-92-0202-7 (eBook)
https://doi.org/10.1007/978-981-92-0202-7

This Springer imprint is published by the registered company Springer Nature Singapore Pte Ltd.
The registered company address is: 152 Beach Road, #21-01/04 Gateway East, Singapore 189721, Singapore

If disposing of this product, please recycle the paper.

Thaweesak Yingthawornsuk	King Mongkut's University of Technology Thonburi, Thailand
Tzung-Pei Hong	National University of Kaohsiung, Taiwan
June Tay	Singapore University of Social Sciences, Singapore
Apostolos Xenakis	University of Thessaly, Greece
Constantinos Constantinides	Concordia University, Canada
Grigorios Kyriakopoulos	National Technical University of Athens, Greece
Man Fung Lo	University of Hong Kong, China
Cuauhtemoc Lopez Martin	Universidad de Guadalajara, Mexico
Malcolm Munro	Durham University, UK
Riccardo Sisto	Politecnico di Torino, Italy
Marina Mongiello	Polytechnic University of Bari, Italy
Daniel Lucrédio	Federal University of São Carlos, Brazil
Anas AlSobeh	Southern Illinois University Carbondale, USA
William Chu	Tunghai University, Taiwan
Yulia Kumar	Kean University, USA
Mohd Aliff Afira Bin Hj	Sani, Universiti Kuala Lumpur, Malaysia
Fadi Abuamara	Shenandoah University, USA
Leau Yu Beng	Universiti Malaysia Sabah, Malaysia
Tomasz Hachaj	AGH University of Krakow, Poland
Richa Sharma	Commonwealth University of Pennsylvania, USA
Zichao Li	University of Waterloo, Canada
Basava Gudivaka	Raas Infotek, USA
Dinesh Kumar Reddy Basani	CGI Inc., Canada
I-Ching Hsu	National Formosa University, Taiwan
Yung-Pin Cheng	National Central University, Taiwan
Tz-Heng Hsu	Southern Taiwan University, Taiwan
Shang-Pin Ma	National Taiwan Ocean University, Taiwan
Venkat Garikipati	Innosoft, USA
Guman Singh Chauhan	John Tesla Inc., USA
Rajababu Budda	IBM, USA
Huang-Wen Huang	Tamkang University, Taiwan
Hao-Tsung Yang	National Central University, Taiwan
Kannan Srinivasan	Saiana Technologies Inc., USA
Venkata Surya Teja Gollapalli	Centene Management LLC, USA
Chun-Feng Liao	National Chengchi University, Taiwan
Morakot Choetkiertikul	Mahidol University, Thailand, Taiwan
Ching-Long Yeh	Tatung University, Taiwan
Rahul Jadon	CarGurus Inc., Boston, USA
Visit Hirankitti	King Mongkut's Institute of Technology Ladkrabang, Thailand

Contents

Language Modeling and Semantic Analysis

Software Design and Intelligent Program Development

On the Comparison of Dynamic and Static Unsafe Objects Identification in Rust Programs

Shaowen Li[1(✉)] and Hiroyuki Sato[1,2]

[1] The University of Tokyo, Bunkyo City, Japan
`li-shaowen879@g.ecc.u-tokyo.ac.jp`
[2] National Institute of Informatics, Chiyoda City, Japan

Abstract. Rust offers C/C++-level performance while enforcing memory safety through compile-time rules such as ownership and lifetimes. When these rules prove too restrictive, programmers can annotate regions as *unsafe*, bypassing static checks and re-introducing the risk that erroneous or malicious code corrupts otherwise safe memory. Ensuring runtime isolation therefore hinges on accurately locating every memory object an *unsafe* block may touch. This paper proposes and prototypes two complementary identification algorithms: (i) a dynamic scheme that tracks pointer provenance at runtime, and (ii) a static scheme that analyzes a value-flow graph built from LLVM IR. We evaluate both techniques on widely used Rust crates, highlighting trade-offs in precision and coverage.

Keywords: Memory safety · software security · software engineering

1 Introduction

Unsafe programming languages like C and C++ have long been the standard for systems programming due to their low-level control over memory, but their lack of built-in memory safety leads to frequent and costly bugs [6]. Rust addresses these issues by enforcing memory safety at compile time using ownership and lifetime rules, allowing it to prevent memory leaks and concurrency errors without runtime overhead [20]. Rust's type system also helps eliminate common errors like *null* dereferencing and manual exception handling, contributing to its growing adoption in major projects such as the Linux kernel [13] and Mozilla Firefox [15]. Rust ensures safety through a combination of static and dynamic checks. While static analysis enforces unique ownership and safe borrowing, dynamic checks are used when static reasoning is insufficient [16]. To support low-level operations and foreign function interoperability, Rust provides the *unsafe* keyword, which allows programmers to bypass compile-time checks when necessary [1,5]. Although essential for flexibility and performance, *unsafe Rust* reintroduces risks by disabling static protections, making it critical to accurately identify and monitor its interactions with memory.

T. Dohi (Ed.): ICSED 2025, CCIS 2889, pp. 3–17, 2026.
https://doi.org/10.1007/978-981-92-0202-7_1

```
fn main() {
    let mut buffer: [char; 4] = ['a', 'b', 'c', 'd'];
    let secret_token = ['s', 'e', 'c', 'r', 'e', 't'];
    unsafe {
        let ptr = buffer.as_mut_ptr();
        *ptr.offset(4) = 'N';
    }
    /*
        secret_token becomes 'Necret'
    */
}
```

Listing 1: Out-of-bound access from unsafe code overwrites secret data in safe code.

Rust requires unsafe code to be enclosed within an *unsafe* block, but this syntax provides no runtime isolation. Code marked as *unsafe* is exempt from the compiler's safety checks and may introduce memory vulnerabilities, especially when interfacing with foreign functions written in unsafe languages. Such code can overwrite memory allocated by safe code, as shown in Listing 1, undermining Rust's compile-time guarantees [17]. To address this, researchers have proposed isolating memory used by unsafe code from that used by safe code [2,12,14]. These approaches partition stack and heap memory into separate regions, limiting unsafe code's ability to access safe memory. Hardware-based protections like *memory protection keys (MPK)* [19] can further enforce these boundaries at the architectural level.

The effectiveness of memory isolation depends on accurately identifying unsafe objects. Prior work follows two main approaches: (1) manual annotation using macros or APIs and (2) automated analysis of memory accesses by unsafe code. As manual approaches depend on programmer expertise, they are beyond the scope of this paper. We focus on automated identification of unsafe objects and compare static and dynamic methods. For dynamic analysis, we extend the Rust interpreter Miri [9] to track *pointer provenance* and identify memory accessed by unsafe code during execution. For static analysis, we construct a value-flow graph from LLVM IR to trace pointer origins at unsafe operations. Our methods are designed to handle aliasing, casting, and field-, context-, and flow-sensitivity. While we do not propose a new isolation mechanism, the outputs of both analyses can be integrated with existing systems [2,8,12,14]. We evaluate both techniques on widely used Rust crates and offer insights for system designers.

We summarize the contributions of this paper as follows:

– An implementation of a dynamic unsafe object identification algorithm leveraging pointer provenance using Rust MIRI interpreter.

- An implementation of a static unsafe object identification algorithm on a value-flow graph constructed from LLVM IR emitted by the Rust compiler.
- A comparative evaluation of the analysis results from the static and dynamic approaches on popular Rust crates.

2   Related Work

Recent efforts to improve unsafe object identification in Rust have explored hybrid dynamic analysis pipelines, such as the one proposed by [3], which combines fuzzing, sanitizers, and symbolic execution using Miri. This pipeline aims to uncover memory safety violations by generating diverse inputs at scale and then validating violations on specific paths using Miri's interpreter for MIR. The approach shares the same foundation as our dynamic analysis method, which also relies on Miri to detect undefined behaviors at the MIR level. However, this method complements Miri with external fuzzing and runtime instrumentation to expand its path coverage, while our approach uses targeted test inputs to isolate and trace unsafe objects. On the static analysis side, TeaDsa provides an alternative to SVF by adopting a unification-based pointer analysis that reduces alias over-approximation and improves analysis speed [11]. While both TeaDsa and SVF aim to conservatively approximate memory behaviors, our use of SVF emphasizes field- and flow-sensitive analysis at the LLVM IR level to trace unsafe object propagation. Compared to TeaDsa, SVF offers more general-purpose alias information, but at the cost of higher computational overhead and potential false positives. Together, these comparisons underscore the trade-offs between precision, scalability, and Rust-specific semantic handling across different approaches to unsafe object identification. Our implementation builds on established research in memory safety and hybrid program analysis. The static analysis via SVF follows the tradition of alias analysis and conservative memory modeling, prioritizing soundness despite potential false positives. In contrast, our dynamic analysis with Miri reflects a growing interest in lightweight symbolic execution for IR-level precision on exercised paths. These methods illustrate the classic trade-off between scalability and precision. By comparing them in the context of unsafe object identification in Rust, we contribute to the broader effort to balance static coverage and dynamic precision in systems language analysis.

3   Dynamic Unsafe Object Identification

The raw Rust MIR compiled from the source code is fed into MIRI virtual machine for interpretation. The key data structure is an allocation table maintained by the MIRI machine which associates each allocation with a unique ID. In this section, we explain how the orignal MIRI implementation can be augmented for tracking unsafe memory objects.

3.1   Pointer Provenance and Allocation Tracking in MIRI

Rust's ownership model and lifetime tracking eliminate many errors at compile time, but issues in *unsafe* code remain unchecked. To detect such runtime undefined behavior, Miri tracks memory operations using *pointer provenance* and an allocation table. This table covers all memory types, including heap, stack, and globals, enabling Miri to monitor pointer usage across the entire program. Pointers are more than raw addresses; *pointer provenance* refers to their origin and validity. A pointer is valid only within its allocated region (spatial validity) and before deallocation (temporal validity). Pointer arithmetic and dereferencing must respect provenance to avoid undefined behavior. Figure 1 illustrates how Miri tracks provenance using an *allocation ID*, a 64-bit identifier indexing a global memory map. This map stores metadata such as memory type, size, alignment, and mutability. A pointer in Miri consists of its provenance and an offset, and operations are checked to stay within these bounds. The model assumes pointers are not fabricated without provenance, as such cases typically reflect external memory management.

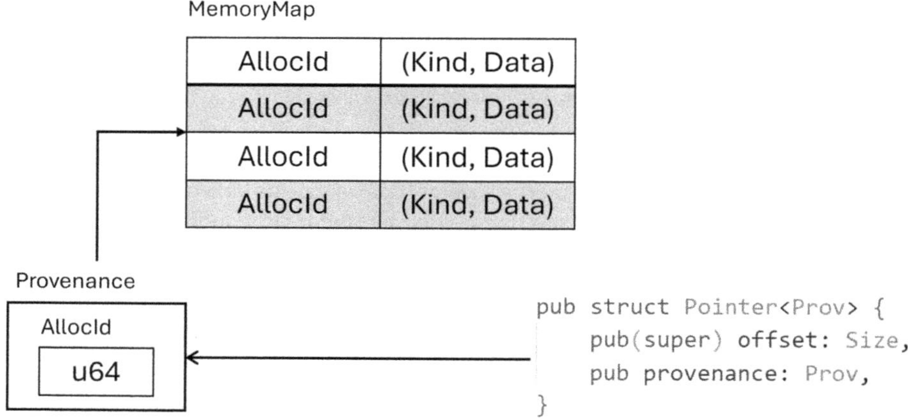


```
pub struct Pointer<Prov> {
    pub(super) offset: Size,
    pub provenance: Prov,
}
```

Fig. 1. Representation of the internal structure of a Rust pointer in the Miri engine, which is defined as `Pointer<Prov>`. The pointer consists of two main components: an offset of type Size (an alias for u64), which encodes the byte offset from the base of the allocation, and a provenance field of type Prov, which represents the allocation identity (AllocId). The AllocId uniquely identifies memory allocations during interpretation and is used by Miri to track pointer origin and enforce provenance-based aliasing rules. This abstraction allows Miri to distinguish pointers not only by their numerical value but also by their allocation context, which is essential for detecting undefined behavior such as use-after-free and type-punning violations in unsafe code.

3.2 Identification Process

MIR is a control-flow-graph-based intermediate representation (IR) with simplified operations. Miri follows the control flow and emulates the effects of operations on its internal state. Each control-flow block consists of statements and an optional terminator, which determines the transition to the succeeding block. Statements and terminators are associated with safety properties, making it straightforward for Miri to determine whether it is interpreting an unsafe statement or terminator.

Table 1. Classification of Rust MIR (Mid-level Intermediate Representation) statement types based on their usage and potential effect on program safety as interpreted by Miri. Each statement corresponds to a specific kind of operation on memory, variables, or control flow. The "Safety" column indicates whether the statement is considered semantically safe in terms of memory safety and pointer aliasing when interpreted by Miri.

Type	Usage	Safety
Assign	assign ab Rvalue to a place	Yes
SetDiscriminant	set active enum variant	No
Deinit	deinitialize a place	No
StorageLive	allocate memory for a local	Yes
StorageDead	free memory for a local	No
FakeRead	pattern match and let binding	No
Retag	tag a reference	No
Intrinsic	call nondiverging intrinsic	Yes
PlaceMention	evaluate a memory place without using it	No
AscribeUserType	user's type ascription	No
Coverage	record execution information	No
ConstEvalCounter	track interpreter steps	No
Nop	nop	No

Table 1 lists MIR statement types and their usage. A statement operates on *locals*, and the safety column indicates whether a local's safety is affected by the statement. Our goal is to classify allocations as safe or unsafe for isolation. A local may refer to an allocation or be an immediate value (e.g., a constant or register), to which unsafety does not apply. In this paper, a "safe" or "unsafe" local refers to the safety of its associated allocation, and the terms are used interchangeably. To support this, we extend Miri with an *allocation-to-local table* that records the local and its call frame index for each allocation. This enables us to track allocations across frames—critical for identifying unsafe accesses to parent-frame locals, as discussed later. We mark an allocation as unsafe when it is written to by an unsafe statement; read-only access does not affect safety. While stricter policies are possible, this principle provides a practical baseline.

For example, an unsafe `StorageLive` immediately marks its allocation as unsafe. Intrinsic calls are treated like function calls and are discussed later. An `Assign` statement marks the LHS allocation as unsafe if the statement is unsafe or if the RHS value originates from an unsafe allocation. This ensures that copied values from untrusted sources propagate unsafety. Figure 2 shows such a case: if x is unsafe and its value is assigned to y, then y is also marked unsafe. Our dynamic analysis using pointer provenance naturally supports inter-procedural analysis. From the caller's view, a function's return value is treated like the LHS of an `Assign`: if the call is unsafe, the return allocation is marked unsafe. Arguments are marked unsafe if the callee writes to a referenced allocation from a parent frame, as tracked by our allocation-to-local table. Since the allocation table is global, no special handling is needed for function calls. Our prototype also supports optional field-sensitive analysis, which is valuable for preserving smart pointer integrity [10]. As shown in Fig. 3, when a local's allocation is marked unsafe and its type is an ADT, we recursively examine each field. Fields with their own allocations are also marked unsafe, while pointer fields are followed to their targets. This ensures all allocations reachable through an unsafe ADT are properly identified.

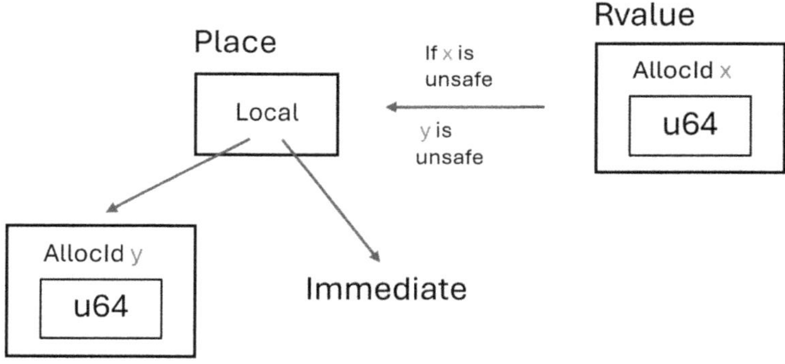

Fig. 2. Unsafe Rvalue makes the LHS local unsafe.

Identifying unsafe memory allocations dynamically using Miri is both sound and precise, provided that the program adheres to strict provenance, which requires that pointers always have an associated provenance. In Sect. 5, we will also observe that several popular crates violate this rule. Nevertheless, such cases generally indicate that the memory is managed externally to Rust and do not render our method ineffective.

4 Static Unsafe Object Identification

4.1 SVF Graphs

SVF introduces several graph structures for static analysis, all derived from the core *program assignment graph* (PAG). We perform our analysis directly on the

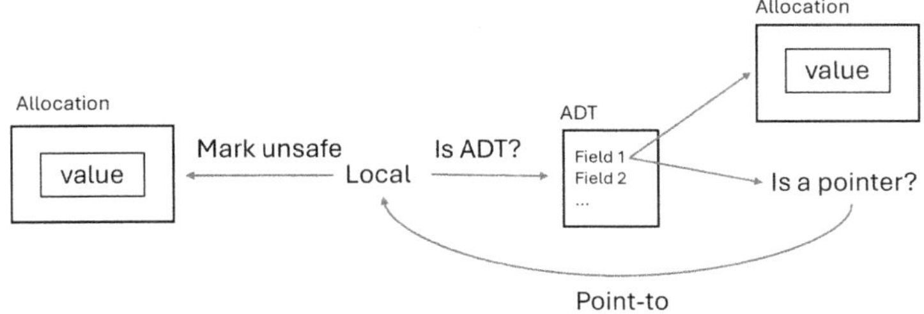

Fig. 3. An ADT-typed local requires recursive processing to enable field-sensitive analysis.

PAG due to its simplicity and suitability for our task. Each `PAGNode` represents either a top-level LLVM variable or an abstract memory object (global, stack, or heap). Field-sensitive analysis is supported via nodes created from `getelementptr` instructions. `PAGEdge`s connect nodes and represent operations such as address-taking, loads, and stores.

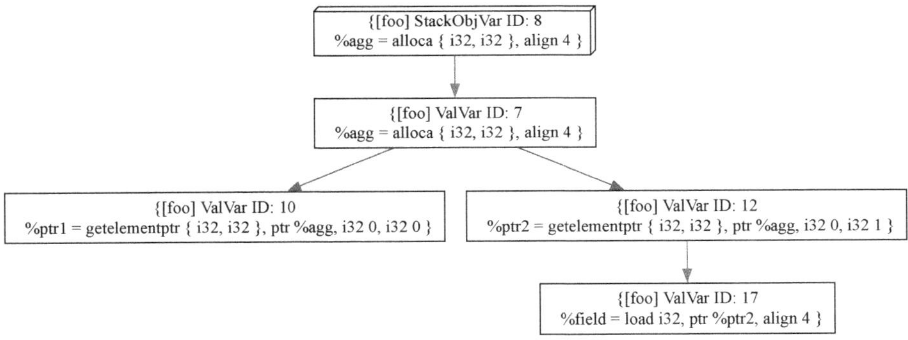

Fig. 4. An SVF PAG example.

Figure 4 presents an example of a PAG that includes the following operations: (1) ID 7 is a pointer variable created by taking the address of a stack object (ID 8), (2) two element pointers (ID 10 and ID 12) are derived from the aggregate in ID 7, and (3) a variable (ID 17) is created by loading from ID 12. PAG models variable creation and usage within an LLVM IR program, which is essential for constructing the value flow from unsafe object accesses back to their creation sites.

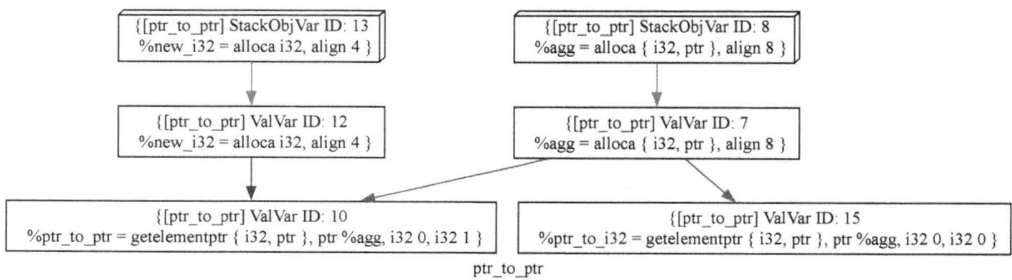

Fig. 5. An aggregate *%agg* containing a pointer field requires a forward traversal.

4.2   Implementation

Static analysis first collects all values (i.e., LLVM values) affected by an instruction with the unsafe metadata. To be comparable with the dynamic approach, we collect all left-hand side value of unsafe instructions.

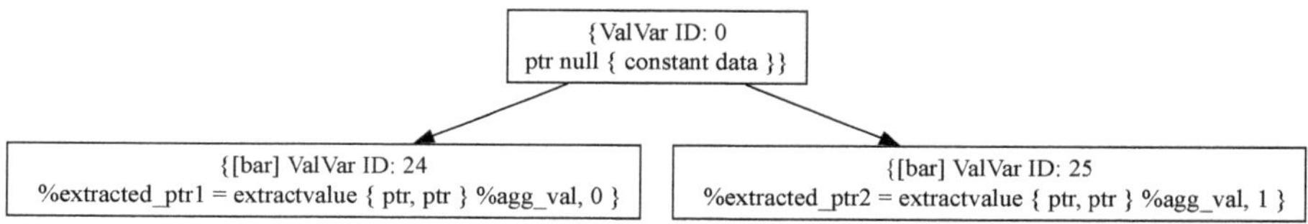

Fig. 6. SVF considers *extractvalue* from a blackhole and does not connect it to its source.

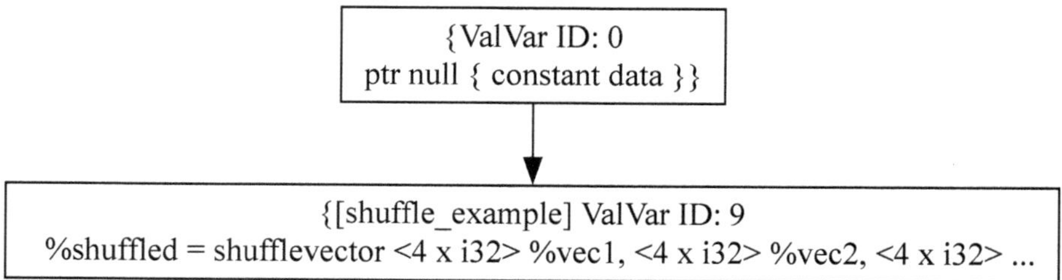

Fig. 7. SVF not connects a shufflevector instruction to its source vectors.

After identifying affected values, we trace their allocation sites (*alloca*) in the SVF PAG using both backward and forward traversal. As shown in Fig. 4, a backward traversal from `getelementptr` nodes 10 and 12 along `Gep PAGEdges` leads to their source *alloca* node 7, revealing *%agg* as the origin of *%ptr1* and *%ptr2*, which is then marked unsafe. When an *alloca* is marked unsafe, a forward

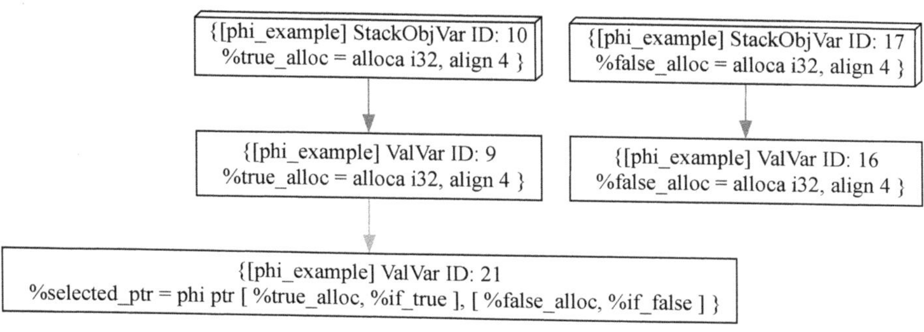

Fig. 8. SVF only connects a PHI node to its first incoming value.

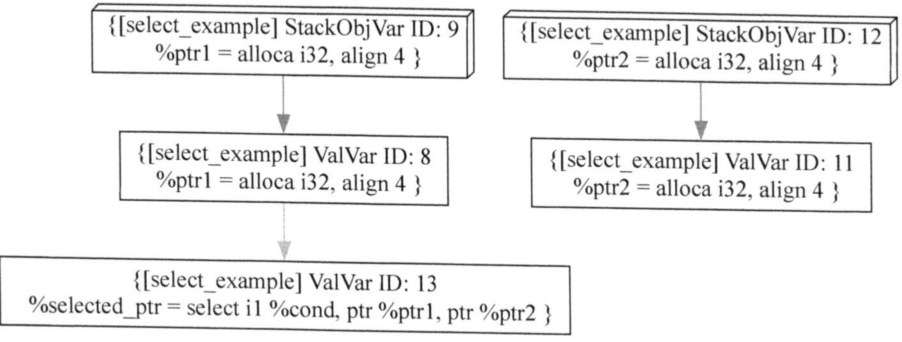

Fig. 9. SVF not connects a select instruction to both its options.

traversal is also triggered. Figure 5 shows why this is needed: backward traversal reveals that *%ptr_to_i32* originates from *%agg*, which holds a pointer field. To preserve smart pointer integrity, we must also consider memory reachable via unsafe aggregates as unsafe. This requires a forward pass (e.g., from node 7 to 10), followed by another backward traversal to propagate unsafety transitively. Combining both traversals allows us to identify most unsafe allocations. SVF's PAG does not capture all value connections, leading to incomplete analysis. For instance, as shown in Fig. 6, extracted values may incorrectly appear to originate from dummy variables. Similarly, *shufflevector* nodes (Fig. 7) lack edges to their source vectors, and *phi* and *select* nodes (Figs. 8 and 9) connect only to their first source. To address these gaps, we reconstruct the missing edges in our implementation to ensure accurate propagation of unsafety.

In summary, we propose two complementary methods for identifying unsafe memory objects in Rust: a dynamic approach using Miri and a static approach based on an enhanced SVF framework. Each offers trade-offs in precision and coverage. We next evaluate their effectiveness on real-world Rust crates.

5   Evaluation

To compare the effectiveness of dynamic analysis using Miri and static analysis using SVF, we evaluate both methods on a curated set of Rust crates. Our prototype is based on Rustc version 1.84.1 and will be open-sourced after publication. Starting with the ten most downloaded crates from *crates.io* (as of February 21, 2025), we expand the dataset by including their transitive dependencies until reaching 150 crates. Since most crates are libraries and Miri requires executable binaries, we analyze available tests, benchmarks, and examples instead. While this does not guarantee full coverage, it enables practical analysis; users may apply our tools to their own applications for broader results. To increase coverage, we disable Miri's host isolation to allow access to system resources. After excluding crates with compilation issues or no runnable programs, the final dataset includes 95 crates.

Figure 10 illustrates that most Rust crates contain only a small proportion of unsafe code. For each crate, we first generate its LLVM IR. We then augment the compiler to tag an LLVM instruction if it originates from an unsafe Rust statement. A function is classified as unsafe if it contains at least one such tagged instruction. To quantify the presence of unsafe code, we compute the ratio of unsafe to safe functions for each crate. Among the 95 crates in our dataset, 62 contain fewer than 10% unsafe functions. The average ratio of unsafe functions across all crates is 0.02, as shown in Fig. 10.

We apply both dynamic and static methods to identify and tag unsafe `alloca` instructions in our crate dataset, restricting analysis to functions covered by Miri for fair comparison. For each function, we compute the ratio of unsafe to total `alloca` instructions. As shown in Fig. 11, the average ratio is 0.04 across 710 functions. The results from static and dynamic analyses are identical, except in the *parking-lot* crate, where Miri misses some unsafe `alloca` instructions detected by the static method. These missed cases are listed in Listing 2. A call to *with_queue_head* followed by *queue_head* results in a casting chain of **const ThreadData* → *usize* → **const ThreadData*. Our static analysis correctly traces the value flow from *ptrtoint* to *inttoptr*, marking the original `alloca` as unsafe. In contrast, Miri's dynamic analysis loses provenance during pointer-to-integer casts, making it unable to track the original allocation after casting back. Miri also warns that such casts may lead to undefined behavior. This is the only case in our dataset where static and dynamic results diverge.

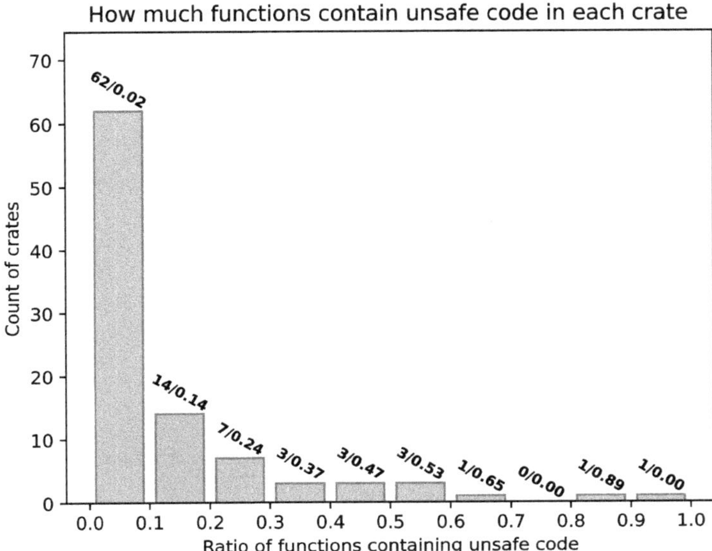

Fig. 10. Most Rust crates contain (62) a low ratio of unsafe functions(below 0.1 with an average of 0.02).

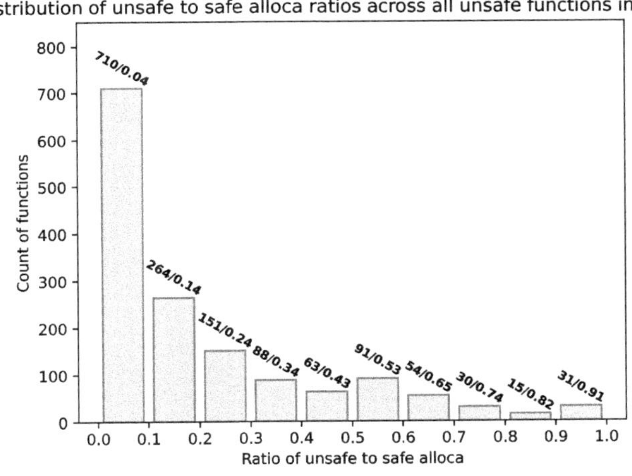

Fig. 11. Both dynamic and static methods are applied to determine unsafe `alloca` instructions. Our experiment reveals that they produce similar results. The ratio of unsafe `alloca` instructions to total `alloca` instructions is below 0.1 in 710 functions, with an average of 0.04. The figure presents the results obtained from static analysis, while the dynamic method yields the same results except for a few discrepancies in certain crates.

```
// Crate: PARKING-LOT
#[inline]
fn with_queue_head(self, thread_data: *const ThreadData) -> Self {
    (self & !QUEUE_MASK) | thread_data as *const _ as usize
}

#[inline]
fn queue_head(self) -> *const ThreadData {
    (self & QUEUE_MASK) as *const ThreadData
}
```

Listing 2: Functions that MIRI fails to discover unsafe alloca

```
// Crate: backtrace-rs
pub fn sp(&self) -> *mut c_void {
    match *self {
        Frame::Raw(ctx) => unsafe { uw::get_sp(ctx) as *mut c_void },
        Frame::Cloned { sp, .. } => sp,
    }
}
```

Listing 3: Integer-to-pointer cast due to external pointers.

```
// Crate: ARC-SWAP
fn fallback(node: &LocalNode, storage: &AtomicPtr<T::Base>) -> Self {
{
    ...
    unsafe { Self::new(replacement as *mut _, None) }
    ...
}
```

Listing 4: Integer-to-pointer cast due to internal pointers.

We further examine our dataset to determine how frequently this issue occurs and whether it limits the effectiveness of the dynamic approach. To analyze this, we modify the compiler to record instances of integer-to-pointer casts. Across the entire dataset of 95 crates, we collect such casts and categorize them into external and internal pointers, two examples are shown in Listing 3 and Listing 4, respectively. In Listing 3, the memory at the integer address is managed externally to Rust. These allocations typically originate from foreign libraries (e.g., C libraries) and are then passed to Rust code. This does not pose a significant concern. By design, Miri is unable to simulate most foreign functions, except for those with simple operational semantics; therefore, the dynamic approach is not applicable in these cases. Furthermore, these memory objects are managed by foreign functions, and isolating foreign functions requires alternative mechanisms, such as shadow stacks [4] and in-process compartmentalization [8]. Fundamentally, this approach necessitates isolating the entire memory regions (i.e., stack and heap) of a foreign library. On the other hand, Listing 4 presents a case where integer memory addresses that point to Rust-internal memory are cast to pointers without carrying proper provenance. If these pointers are subsequently accessed unsafely, Miri is unable to determine which memory objects should be classified as unsafe.

To compare our static analysis with other LLVM-based frameworks, we extended Phasar [18] and SeaHorn [7] to support unsafe object identification. We modified both tools to recognize custom unsafe-tagged LLVM IR instructions inserted during compilation and implemented analysis passes to propagate these tags through memory operations. This allowed each framework to track memory objects affected by unsafe code, aligning their analysis goals with ours. The results are shown in Table 2.

Table 2. Number of unsafe memory objects identified by each static analysis tool across selected crates.

Crate	Our Method (SVF)	Phasar	SeaHorn
byteorder	12	9	6
bytes	25	19	13
hyper	88	72	55
rust-base64	18	14	10
rust-snappy	31	24	17
tokio	105	86	64
rkyv	60	45	32
hashbrown	112	91	70

As shown in Table 2, our SVF-based analysis detects more unsafe memory objects than Phasar or SeaHorn in every crate. This gain comes from our SVF extensions, which reconstruct value-flow edges typically absent from default analyses—especially those involving raw pointers, field-sensitive data, and compiler-generated temporaries. The resulting graph more precisely tracks unsafe object propagation, exposing additional risky memory interactions. Phasar and SeaHorn, lacking such Rust-specific refinements, miss many of these cases. We could not benchmark dynamic tools, as none publicly release the input suites needed for reproducible comparison.

We conclude that the dynamic approach based on pointer provenance is as effective as the static approach using value-flow analysis on LLVM IR, provided that the code does not rely on memory objects managed by foreign functions or perform integer-to-pointer casts. If the target code contains integer-to-pointer casts, we recommend opting for static analysis instead. For implementing a static analysis using the SVF framework, we advise referring to this paper to address missing connections in the value-flow graph and improve the coverage of unsafe Rust code.

6   Conclusion

Isolating safe code from unsafe code enhances Rust's security, with protecting safe memory objects being a key objective. To support this, we propose two automated approaches for identifying unsafe objects: a dynamic method that interprets Rust MIR and tracks pointer provenance, and a static method that analyzes LLVM IR value-flow graphs to trace unsafe accesses. Automation ensures comprehensive coverage without programmer effort, making it practical for real-world use. Our evaluation on popular Rust crates shows both methods perform similarly, except when pointer-to-integer casts are used, which break provenance tracking and limit the dynamic method. These results offer guidance for designing memory-safe Rust isolation strategies.

References

1. Astrauskas, V., Matheja, C., Poli, F., Müller, P., Summers, A.J.: How do programmers use unsafe rust? Proc. ACM Program. Lang. **4**(OOPSLA) (2020). https://doi.org/10.1145/3428204
2. Bang, I., Kayondo, M., Moon, H., Paek, Y.: TRust: a compilation framework for in-process isolation to protect safe rust against untrusted code. In: 32nd USENIX Security Symposium (USENIX Security 2023), pp. 6947–6964. USENIX Association, Anaheim, CA (2023). https://www.usenix.org/conference/usenixsecurity23/presentation/bang
3. Breck, C.: Making even safe rust a little safer: model checking safe and unsafe code (2024). https://blog.colinbreck.com/making-even-safe-rust-a-little-safer-model-checking-safe-and-unsafe-code/. Accessed 20 June 2025
4. Burow, N., Zhang, X., Payer, M.: SoK: shining light on shadow stacks. In: 2019 IEEE Symposium on Security and Privacy (SP). IEEE (2019). https://doi.org/10.1109/sp.2019.00076
5. Cui, M., Sun, S., Xu, H., Zhou, Y.: Is unsafe an achilles' heel? A comprehensive study of safety requirements in unsafe rust programming. In: Proceedings of the IEEE/ACM 46th International Conference on Software Engineering. ICSE 2024. Association for Computing Machinery, New York, NY, USA (2024). https://doi.org/10.1145/3597503.3639136
6. Durumeric, Z., et al.: The matter of H. In: Proceedings of the 2014 Conference on Internet Measurement Conference, IMC 2014, pp. 475–488. Association for Computing Machinery, New York, NY, USA (2014). https://doi.org/10.1145/2663716.2663755

7. Gurfinkel, A., Kahsai, T., Komuravelli, A., Navas, J.A.: The SeaHorn verification framework. In: Kroening, D., Păsăreanu, C.S. (eds.) CAV 2015. LNCS, vol. 9206, pp. 343–361. Springer, Cham (2015). https://doi.org/10.1007/978-3-319-21690-4_20

8. Gülmez, M., Nyman, T., Baumann, C., Mühlberg, J.T.: Friend or foe inside? Exploring in-process isolation to maintain memory safety for unsafe rust (2023). https://arxiv.org/abs/2306.08127

9. Jung, R.: Miri: practical undefined behavior detection for rust (keynote). In: Proceedings of the 19th ACM International Workshop on Implementation, Compilation, Optimization of OO Languages, Programs and Systems, ICOOOLPS 2024, p. 1. Association for Computing Machinery, New York, NY, USA (2024). https://doi.org/10.1145/3679005.3695733

10. Kayondo, M., Bang, I., Kwak, Y., Moon, H., Paek, Y.: MetaSafe: compiling for protecting smart pointer metadata to ensure safe rust integrity. In: 33rd USENIX Security Symposium (USENIX Security 2024), pp. 3711–3728. USENIX Association, Philadelphia, PA (2024). https://www.usenix.org/conference/usenixsecurity24/presentation/kayondo

11. Kuderski, J., Navas, J.A., Gurfinkel, A.: Unification-based pointer analysis without oversharing (2019). https://arxiv.org/abs/1906.01706

12. Li, S., Sato, H.: SBD: securing safe rust automatically from unsafe rust. Sci. Comput. Program. **243**, 103281 (2025). https://doi.org/10.1016/j.scico.2025.103281. https://www.sciencedirect.com/science/article/pii/S0167642325000206

13. Rust for Linux project: Rust for Linux (2025). https://rust-for-linux.com/. Accessed 27 Feb 2025

14. Liu, P., Zhao, G., Huang, J.: Securing unsafe rust programs with xrust. In: Proceedings of the ACM/IEEE 42nd International Conference on Software Engineering, ICSE 2020, pp. 234–245. Association for Computing Machinery, New York, NY, USA (2020). https://doi.org/10.1145/3377811.3380325

15. Mozilla Project: Firefox Build System: Rust Integration (2025). https://firefox-source-docs.mozilla.org/build/buildsystem/rust.html. Accessed 27 Feb 2025

16. Popescu, N., Xu, Z., Apostolakis, S., August, D.I., Levy, A.: Safer at any speed: automatic context-aware safety enhancement for rust. Proc. ACM Program. Lang. **5**(OOPSLA) (2021). https://doi.org/10.1145/3485480

17. Rivera, E., Mergendahl, S., Shrobe, H., Okhravi, H., Burow, N.: Keeping safe rust safe with galeed. In: Proceedings of the 37th Annual Computer Security Applications Conference, ACSAC 2021, pp. 824–836. Association for Computing Machinery, New York, NY, USA (2021). https://doi.org/10.1145/3485832.3485903

18. Schatz, D., Hermann, B.: Phasar: an inter-procedural static analysis framework for LLVM IR. In: Proceedings of the 2019 IEEE 26th International Conference on Software Analysis, Evolution and Reengineering (SANER), pp. 304–314. IEEE (2019). https://doi.org/10.1109/SANER.2019.8668038

19. Wang, X., Yeoh, S., Olivier, P., Ravindran, B.: Secure and efficient in-process monitor (and library) protection with intel MPK. In: Proceedings of the 13th European Workshop on Systems Security, EuroSec 2020, pp. 7–12. Association for Computing Machinery, New York, NY, USA (2020). https://doi.org/10.1145/3380786.3391398

20. Zhang, Y., Zhang, Y., Portokalidis, G., Xu, J.: Towards understanding the runtime performance of rust. In: Proceedings of the 37th IEEE/ACM International Conference on Automated Software Engineering. ASE 2022. Association for Computing Machinery, New York, NY, USA (2023). https://doi.org/10.1145/3551349.3559494

A Survey of BERT in Requirements Engineering Taxonomy, Challenge, and Application

Chengzhuo Liu[1], Dongcheng Li[2(✉)], and Yan Guo[1]

[1] China University of Geosciences, Wuhan 430074, China
[2] California State Polytechnic University – Humboldt, Arcata, CA 95521, USA
dl313@humboldt.edu

Abstract. This paper provides a review of the application of Bidirectional Encoder Representations from Transformers (BERT) in the field of Requirements Engineering (RE), a domain where the accurate interpretation of natural language requirements is crucial and challenging. Unlike existing reviews that broadly cover Natural Language Processing (NLP) techniques in RE, this study focuses specifically on BERT and its derivatives, offering a fine-grained taxonomy of models, tasks, and optimization strategies. The novelty of this work is in systematically bridging advances in Transformer-based language modeling with the specific demands of RE. BERT, with its dual context understanding and transfer learning capabilities, has made significant advances in tasks such as requirement classification, information extraction, and requirements management. By synthesizing recent studies from 2020 to 2024, we identify the dominant trends, categorize models into direct usage, domain-specific fine-tuning, and hybrid architectures, and provide statistical analyses of datasets and model adoption. In addition, we highlight unresolved challenges, such as data scarcity, interpretability, and computational efficiency, and propose future research directions. This work contributes both a structured roadmap and practical guidance for researchers and practitioners seeking to leverage BERT in complex RE tasks.

Keywords: BERT · RE · Transformer · NLP

1 Introduce

RE is a foundational discipline in software development, encompassing activities such as requirements elicitation, classification and specification. As a core phase in the software development life cycle, it directly affects whether a software product can meet stakeholders' expectations and system goals [1]. Nevertheless, the inherent nature of requirements understanding poses numerous challenges, primarily because requirements are often expressed in natural language, which can be ambiguous, inconsistent, and diverse [2].

T. Dohi (Ed.): ICSED 2025, CCIS 2889, pp. 18–32, 2026.
https://doi.org/10.1007/978-981-92-0202-7_2

Recent advances in NLP, particularly Transformer-based models, have provided promising tools to address these issues, automating tasks such as requirement classification, ambiguity detection, dependency extraction, and prioritization [2] Among these tools, BERT has achieved transformative breakthroughs in the field of natural language understanding, with bidirectional semantic modeling and transfer learning capabilities that make it well-suited for handling the complexity of requirement texts [3,4]. In RE, BERT has demonstrated effectiveness in distinguishing between Functional Requirements (FR) and Non-Functional Requirements (NFR), resolving ambiguities in requirement texts, and supporting classification and management tasks [5,6].

Despite the growing interest in NLP for RE, most prior have reviewed the use of machine learning or NLP in RE [7] or focused on specific tasks with algorithmic improvements [5,8], none has systematically examined the role of BERT. Existing studies apply BERT to diverse RE tasks, but the findings remain scattered without a unified taxonomy or comprehensive analysis. Moreover, most works treat BERT as a general-purpose encoder without examining how task-specific adaptations influence performance, and evaluation practices remain inconsistent across datasets and setups. These limitations leave open fundamental questions about the effectiveness of BERT in RE and demonstrate the need for a structured synthesis.

To address these issues, this study aims to provide the first structured survey that concentrates on BERT and its variants in the RE domain. The novelty of this work is in presenting a dual-layer taxonomy: one that classifies BERT applications by RE tasks (e.g., classification, elicitation, management) and another that categorizes models by optimization strategies (e.g., domain-specific fine-tuning, lightweight variants, hybrid integrations). By linking these perspectives, this paper not only maps the state of the art but also uncovers research gaps and future opportunities, such as the development of standardized datasets, explainable BERT models, and multi-modal RE solutions.

For methodological transparency, this study adopted a systematic literature review approach inspired by PRISMA guidelines. Searches were conducted across Google Scholar, Web of Science and Scopus, covering the period from 2020 to 2024. To ensure reproducibility, we explicitly report the complete Boolean search queries used. The queries combined synonyms of BERT and Transformer-based models with requirements engineering–related terms, including:

- ("BERT" OR "Transformer" OR "Bidirectional Encoder Representations from Transformers") AND ("Requirements Engineering" OR "Requirement Engineering" OR "Software Requirements")
- ("BERT" OR "Transformer") AND ("Requirements Analysis" OR "Requirements Classification" OR "Requirements Extraction" OR "Requirements Elicitation")
- ("Functional Requirements" OR "Non-functional Requirements") AND ("BERT" OR "Transformer" OR "Transformer-based" OR "Pretrained Language Model")

Additional significant publications were identified through snowballing. To ensure relevance and quality, inclusion criteria focused on peer-reviewed studies that applied BERT to practical RE tasks, while excluding non-empirical works, papers without full text, those merely mentioning BERT, or non-English publications. This process yielded 183 records, which were screened to a final set of 36 studies, it contains a dataset article and tow milestone studies. To this end, it explores several core questions:

- How does the application of BERT in RE affect the efficiency and accuracy of existing requirements classification and extraction methods?
- For different tasks within RE, is it necessary to develop domain-specific optimizations for BERT? How should these optimizations be achieved?
- What are the main challenges facing BERT in RE, and how do these challenges affect its broader adoption?

2   Preliminaries

This section surveys the research status of BERT in RE and delineates the conceptual basis for the subsequent taxonomy. To enhance conceptual clarity, requirement classification is adopted as an illustrative case, through which the core operational mechanisms pertinent to RE applications are demonstrated. This establishes the methodological foundation for the systematic analysis presented in the following sections.

BERT's semantic understanding and contextual modeling capabilities offer a distinct advantage in addressing complex requirements. BERT has achieved state-of-the-art results in a variety of NLP tasks such as sentiment analysis, question answering, and text classification [3,7], demonstrating its strong bidirectional context modeling. Recent studies also high-light its application in software and RE, for example, NoRBERT for FR/NFR classification [5] and DistilBERT for specification analysis [9]. In the following section, we use requirements classification as an illustrative example, we explore how BERT is applied in the domain of RE.

Requirement classification aims to categorize requirement texts into FR or NFR. Traditional methods, dependent on data-specific features, often lack generalizability to new projects [10], whereas BERT leverages transfer learning and fine-tuning to achieve efficient, robust performance on unseen data [4]. Typically, BERT-based classification involves model pretraining, data preprocessing, model fine-tuning, and classification layer design [3], exploiting BERT's strong language modeling capabilities for precise requirement text classification.

1. Model Pretraining: BERT's effectiveness stems from pretraining on large unlabeled corpora such as English Wikipedia and BooksCorpus, where it learns general language representations. It adopts two main tasks: Masked Language Modeling (MLM), which predicts masked tokens from context, and Next Sentence Prediction (NSP), which determines whether two segments are logically connected. Together, these tasks provide rich features for downstream requirements classification.

2. Data Preprocessing: For requirements classification, texts must be converted into a appropriate BERT format. Tokenization uses the WordPiece algorithm to split words into subwords, allowing unseen words to be processed. Each text begins with [CLS] and ends with [SEP], then is padded or truncated to a fixed length to meet BERT's input constraints.
3. Model Fine-Tuning: BERT first learns universal features through pretraining and is then fine-tuned for specific tasks. In requirements classification, it encodes each text into high-dimensional features and using a small labeled dataset for parameter optimization to optimize task performance.
4. Classification Head Design: BERT a single fully connected layer on top of the [CLS] embedding. A softmax function maps the output to probabilities, distinguishing FR from NFR, or further classifying NFRs (e.g., security, performance) (Fig. 1).

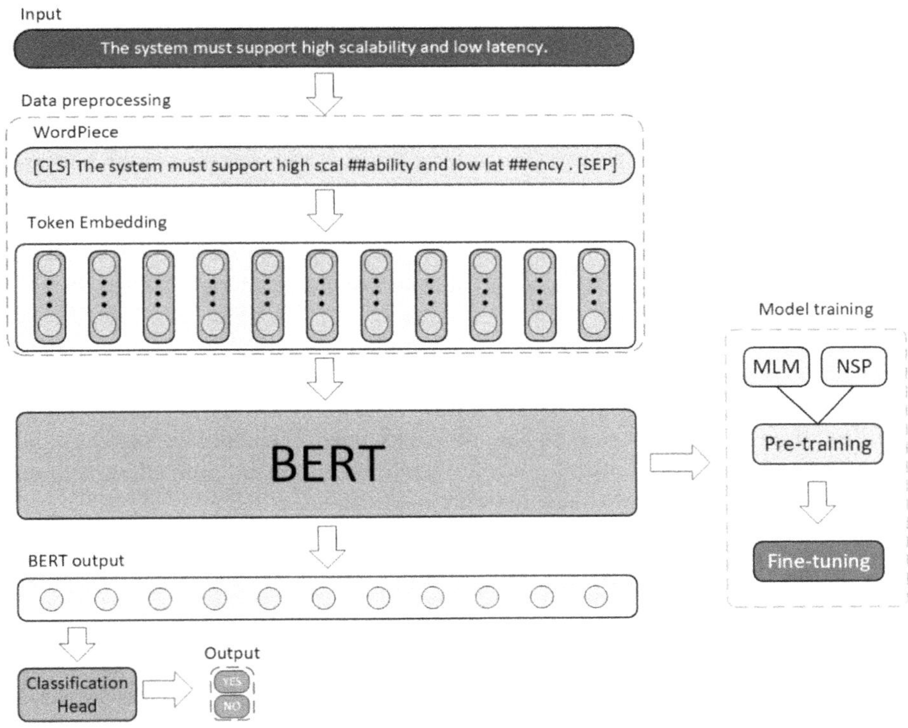

Fig. 1. Framework Diagram of the BERT-Based Model for Requirements Classification.

3　BERT Models in Requirements Engineering

Building upon prior advances in NLP, BERT has recently become a central technique for addressing RE tasks. In this domain, BERT has been applied to requirements extraction, classification, and management, typically through direct use of pretrained models, fine-tuning for domain-specific tasks, or integration with other architectures to address complex challenges. BERT's practical deployment in RE faces challenges such as high computational cost, domain adaptation, and limited annotated data. To address these issues, researchers have proposed lightweight BERT variants [9,11], optimized fine-tuning strategies [5,6], and methods that integrate domain-specific knowledge [12,13]. Such approaches have significantly improved BERT's performance in RE-related tasks.

3.1　Directly Pretrained Models

Owing to its powerful semantic capabilities, the pretrained BERT model has been broadly applied in RE, where it can handle tasks such as requirements classification without task-specific modifications, thereby reducing development effort while maintaining high accuracy [14]. However, its performance in domain-specific tasks may be limited by differences between the training corpus and the target application. Recent studies have empirically demonstrated both the strengths and the limitations of BERT in this context. For example, Mekala et al. [10] employed Van Vliet's Gold Standard dataset to compare BERT, ELMo, and FastText for requirements classification, showing that BERT's bidirectional Transformer architecture significantly improves semantic modeling even on small datasets. Similarly, Souvick et al. [15] introduced PUBER and FiBER, two BERT-based embedding models for requirements similarity detection, which support requirements reuse and change analysis although they remain highly dependent on dataset quality. In addition, Xanthopoulou et al. [16] compared traditional NLP methods such as Bag-of-Words with Transformer-based models, confirming that BERT captures complex semantic patterns more effectively and provides reliable support for automated classification in RE.

3.2　Fine-Tuning BERT Models

While pretrained BERT models demonstrate competitive performance in generic NLP tasks, the complexity and domain-specific nature of RE have established fine-tuning as the predominant strategy [5,8]. Leveraging task-specific annotations and RE-oriented datasets enables BERT to capture nuanced semantics beyond its pretraining corpus, thereby achieving notable gains in classification and extraction tasks [12,17]. This section examines representative fine-tuning approaches and empirical results, organized into two categories: novel fine-tuned models and comparative studies of BERT variants, with the present discussion concentrating on the former.

Novel Fine-Tuned Models and Case Studies. In RE, researchers continue to develop and deploy novel fine-tuned BERT models to tackle intricate task demands. Through the integration of domain knowledge and task-specific optimization, these models enhance the accuracy and efficiency of requirements analysis.

1. Proposed by Hey et al. [5], NoRBERT fine-tunes BERT-base and BERT-large to classify FR and NFR requirements. It combines MLM with bidirectional context to capture complex semantics. A single-layer fully connected classification head and a Softmax activation function provide classification outputs. AdamW, cross-entropy loss, and Early Stopping help address class imbalance.
2. DistilBERT Model. Introduced by Sanh et al. [9], this BERT-based transfer learning method classifies text in Software Requirements Specifications. It uses the PROMISE-NFR to cover Type, Priority, and Severity classification tasks. By fine-tuning DistilBERT with a tailored classification head and optimized preprocessing, the approach significantly improves performance. DistilBERT outperforms LSTM and BiLSTM on PROMISE-NFR.
3. RE-BERT Model. Developed by Carlos et al. [18], RE-BERT extracts requirements from application reviews using BERT-base plus a localized context-focusing mechanism for domain-specific semantics.
4. PRCBERT Model. Proposed by Luo et al. [8], PRCBERT applies prompt learning to BERT to improve classification ability. It significantly enhances classification for both FR and NFR, showing strength in zero-shot and few-shot tasks. However, prompt learning requires multiple assertions per requirement, raising computational costs.
5. BERT4RE Model. Introduced by Zhao et al. [12], BERT4RE retrains a general BERT model for domain adaptation to better capture requirement dependencies. Evaluations on the PROMISE dataset show high F1 scores for Agent and Stakeholder classes, though reliance on domain-specific data limits the model's generalizability.
6. aeroBERT-Classifier and aeroBERT-NER Models. Proposed by Archana Ray et al. [17], these models are tailored to aerospace requirements. They blend BERT's deep semantic modeling with aerospace data characteristics to enhance classification and named entity recognition (NER) on aerospace requirements from Federal Regulations.
7. AI-CRAS Model. By Kici et al. [19], AI-CRAS focuses on analyzing cloud service requirements and is built on top of BERT. It is fine-tuned with cloud-related data to handle multi-class classification of complex cloud requirements. It outperforms traditional deep learning models. Yet, it underperforms in priority classification because of data imbalance.
8. BERTurk Model and BETO Model. BERTurk excels in Turkish requirement classification [20]. Pre-trained on large Turkish corpora and fine-tuned on FR and NFR data, it achieves a 95% F1 score, exceeding standard BERT and DistilBERT, while balancing efficiency and performance. Meanwhile, BETO, developed by María-Isabel Lunarejo et al. [21], is a Spanish-oriented

BERT model combined with fastText to effectively classify FR and NFR in Spanish texts.

9. MNoR-BERT Model. Proposed by Kaur et al. [22], MNoR-BERT targets multi-label classification of NFRs. Trained on 6,000 user comments, it combines MLM with multi-label techniques to capture intricate semantics. A fully connected classification head with Sigmoid activation supports multiple labels. AdamW and binary cross-entropy mitigate class imbalance, leading to high subset accuracy and low Hamming loss.

10. SSMBERT Model. Developed by Zhu [23], SSMBERT focuses on requirements classification in space science. With only 200 records, it addresses data sparsity by fusing MLM and bidirectional context. Similar to NoRBERT, it uses a single-layer fully connected classification head with Softmax activation and the CLS token embedding, optimized by AdamW, cross-entropy loss, and Early Stopping.

Comparison of Various BERT Variant Models. The application of BERT and its variants in RE has demonstrated significant advantages. Researchers have fine-tuned various BERT derivatives and focused on enhancing performance in requirements classification tasks.

Using the PROMISE dataset [24], Okonkwo et al. [25] compared BERT, DistilBERT, RoBERTa finding that BERT effectively captured semantic information but was limited by imbalanced data, while DistilBERT provided efficiency improvements, RoBERTa improved complex semantic modeling through dynamic masking. Similarly, Malik et al. [26] evaluated BERT, RoBERTa, and DistilBERT for requirement-specific entity extraction, showing that BERT provided robust semantic representation, RoBERTa outperformed in managing complex semantics, and DistilBERT was well-suited to resource-constrained scenarios. Xu et al. [27] assessed BERT-base, BERT-large, RoBERTa, and ALBERT on the Tera-PROMISE dataset, demonstrating the stability of BERT models on Type and Priority tasks, RoBERTa's superiority in complex classification, and ALBERT's advantage in reducing model size via parameter sharing. Beyond these, Jain et al. [28] compared Pegasus, BART, and T5 for requirement elicitation from contract datasets, showing Pegasus is effective in summarizing long texts and obligations, BART in abstraction, and T5 in multi-task learning. Poudel et al. [29] examined BERT, ALBERT, and XLNet for functional requirement extraction in embedded systems, with BERT maintaining stable accuracy, ALBERT adapted to resource-limited contexts, and XLNet effectively capturing long-text dependencies.

3.3   Integrating BERT with Other Architectures

As the complexity of RE tasks increases, relying solely on the capabilities of BERT may be insufficient for certain high-complexity scenarios. Consequently, combining BERT with other architectures-such as Recurrent Neural Networks (RNNs), Convolutional Neural Networks (CNNs), and knowledge graphs-has become an a significant research avenue. These hybrid approaches can significantly improve the adaptability of models to complex semantic environments and broaden the applicability of BERT. This section presents recent advances in combining BERT with various architectures and highlights their performance in RE tasks.

1. BERT-CNN Model and BERT-BiCNN. Developed by Kaur et al. [30,31] The BERT-CNN model leverages BERT to generate deep semantic representations, which are then refined by CNNs to capture fine-grained textual patterns such as phrases or short textual segments. The BERT-BiCNN model further integrates BERT with Bidirectional LSTM and CNN, using BERT for contextual semantic extraction from requirement documents, while BiLSTM and CNN enhance sequence modeling and local feature extraction.
2. GAN-BERT Model. In the GAN-BERT model proposed by Airlangga et al. [32], Generative Adversarial Networks (GANs) are harnessed to facilitate semi-supervised learning, while BERT provides deep feature representations. Through adversarial training, the system generates reliable pseudo-labels, thus improving the utilization of unlabeled data.
3. BERT-Knowledge Graph-Based Intelligent Management System. Althar et al. [13] introduce a hybrid framework that combines BERT and knowledge graphs for the classification and management of complex requirements. In this design, BERT serves as the core module for extracting semantic features, whereas the knowledge graph enhances semantic reasoning by modeling entities and their relationships. This approach notably strengthens the analysis of inter-requirement associations and facilitates visual analytics.
4. Multi-Solution BERT Model Based on Ensemble Learning. Proposed by Ezzini et al. [33], this ensemble-based multi-solution framework addresses referential ambiguity in RE. It integrates multiple machine learning techniques, including supervised learning and a SpanBERT fine-tuned model, targeting ambiguity detection and anaphora resolution respectively.
5. Managing Requirement Variability with SBERT and Doc2Vec. Elahidoost et al. [34] propose a solution that combines Sentence-BERT (SBERT) and Doc2Vec to identify and manage variability points in contract documents. By generating distributed paragraph representations, Doc2Vec calculates semantic similarity, whereas SBERT provides context-dependent, high-precision semantic features.

4   Research Issues and Statistical Insights

4.1   Research Trends

In recent years, BERT's application in RE has emerged as a significant research focus, accompanied by a steady increase in related publications across journals and conferences addressing requirements analysis, classification, and verification. Rather than emphasizing numerical growth alone, the qualitative implications of this trend should also be considered. The majority of studies have concentrated on requirements classification, particularly the distinction between FR and NFR, while comparatively limited attention has been devoted to requirements elicitation and management. From a methodological perspective, BERT-base and RoBERTa are the most frequently employed models, whereas lightweight variants and multilingual adaptations remain underexplored. These patterns indicate that the field is consolidating around a limited range of extensively studied problems, leaving substantial gaps in areas such as task diversity, dataset standardization, and model innovation. Figure 2 shows the number of BERT in RE related publications published in the field of software RE.

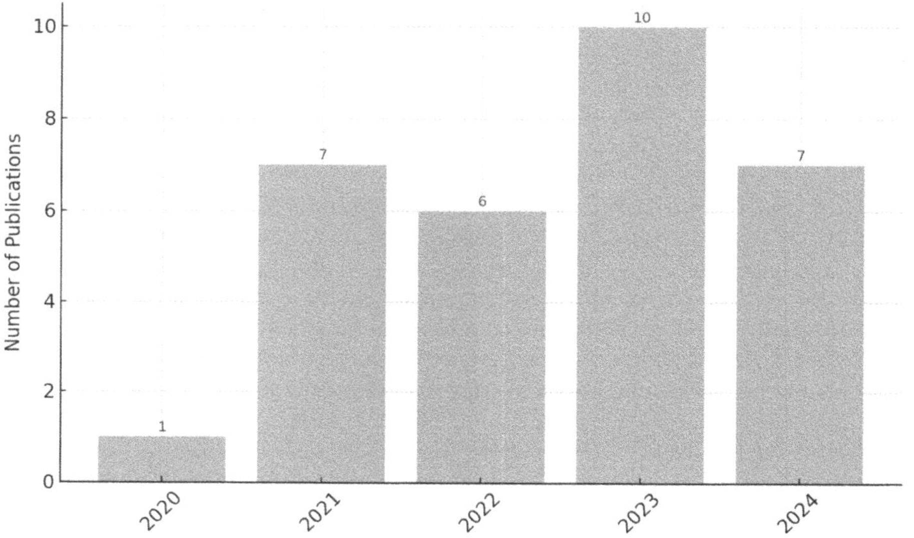

Fig. 2. Diagram of Research and Impact Trends of BERT in RE.

4.2 Dataset Statistics

In RE, the PROMISE dataset is a widely used benchmark containing labeled FR and NFR, but its small size and class imbalance limit applicability. To address specific research goals, researchers often build custom datasets from sources such as corporate documentation, academic publications, open-source repositories, and platforms like Kaggle, with annotations tailored for tasks like requirements classification, elicitation, or management. Examples include the PURE dataset for general classification and the IoTAC dataset for IoT security requirements. However, these datasets often face challenges such as limited size, inconsistent labeling quality, and stylistic heterogeneity, restricting their generalizability. Notably, Table 1 does not enumerate all datasets mentioned across the reviewed studies but focuses on the most frequently used and publicly accessible datasets that appear in multiple papers, ensuring statistical representativeness. Several other datasets, although publicly available, were employed in only a single study and were therefore excluded from the table, while others relied on private or project-specific datasets derived from internal corporate documentation, industrial tools such as DOORS Next Generation, or manually curated requirement collections that are not publicly released. Consequently, datasets in RE exhibit a pattern characterized by a coexistence of a few standardized public benchmarks and numerous self-constructed or proprietary datasets. Looking ahead, expanding the scale and enhancing the quality of available datasets and promoting greater standardization and public availability will provide a more robust foundation for advancing both research and practical applications in this domain.

Table 1. Frequently-used public requirements datasets.

Name	References	Characteristics	No. of uses
PROMISE	[5, 8, 11, 12, 15, 16, 21, 25, 27, 29–32, 35]	Widely adopted and fine-grained; however, it suffers from labeling errors and an imbalanced category distribution.	14
PROMISE-EXP	[27, 32, 35]	An extended PROMISE dataset with refined labels, larger scale, and suitability for deep learning, though still imbalanced.	3
PURE	[12, 15, 16, 36]	Provides diverse domain coverage, but contains style inconsistencies, semantic ambiguity, and subjective labeling.	4
IoTAC	[16]	Focuses on IoT security requirements; however, dataset size is small.	1
SRE	[26]	Shows domain diversity, but small in size, with imbalanced distribution and inconsistent styles.	1

4.3   Model Classification

In this section, we statistically classify the BERT model and its derivatives in 35 articles (one dataset article was excluded). Two complementary classification approaches are proposed. The first approach employs task objectives as the classification criterion, segmenting models based on the type of problems they are designed to address. This clarifies the application scenarios and functional positioning of the various BERT-based models. The second approach hinges on the model optimization methods, categorizing models by their performance-improvement strategies.

These two classification frameworks work in concert: they not only offer a comprehensive view of BERT's evolutionary trajectory but also illuminate the underlying design rationale and technical innovations evident in real-world applications. By comparatively analyzing each BERT variant, a comparative analysis provides deeper insights into their characteristics, strengths, and limitations when handling different tasks.

Classification According to Task Objectives. Within RE, BERT-based models can be classified by primary task objectives into requirements classification, requirements acquisition, and requirements management. Requirement classifica-tion distinguishes FR from NFR through fine-tuning to extract salient features; requirements acquisition extracts specific information or entities, often using NER; and requirements management manages requirement information to support decision-making and maintain traceability. This task-oriented classification framework, implemented with various BERT derivatives, enhances the effective-ness and precision of RE processes. A summary table detailing the classification outcomes is presented in Table. 2

Table 2. Diagram of model classification according to task objectives

Task Objective	Task Overview	Classification Results
Requirements Elicitation	Involves extracting specific information or entities from requirements documents. A typical example is applying Named Entity Recognition (NER) to identify personal names, locations, or organizations.	*NoRBERT*, BETO, BERT-BiCNN, aeroBERT-Classifier, *DistilBERT*, AI-CRAS, *RoBERTa*, DeBERTa, BERTurk, GAN-BERT, MNoR-BERT, PRCBERT, SSMBERT, ALBERT, Code-BERT, SO-BERT
Requirements Classification	Entails segmenting requirement documents or statements into distinct categories, such as functional requirements (FR) and non-functional requirements (NFR).	ALBERT-base-v2, *RoBERTa*, RoBERTa-large, BERT4RE, RE-BERT, Pegasus, T5, BART, aeroBERT-NER
Requirements Management	Aims to organize, track, and refine information within requirements documents. This includes prioritizing requirements, managing changes, and verifying requirements to ensure that project objectives are met.	BERT4RE, PUBER, FiBER, *SpanBERT*, SBERT, Sat-BERT, MSat-BERT, DSat-BERT

Classification by Model Optimization Approach. This section adopts a classification grounded in model optimization to categorize BERT-related models for RE. To avoid conceptual ambiguity, we distinguish between fine-tuning, optimization, and combined approaches. In this survey, fine-tuning denotes the straightforward adaptation of pretrained BERT models to RE datasets through supervised training, typically without architectural modifications. In contrast, optimization refers to methodological or structural enhancements beyond conventional fine-tuning, such as lightweight model design (e.g., DistilBERT, ALBERT), alternative pre-training tasks (e.g., RoBERTa, DeBERTa), prompt learning, or integration with additional architectures (e.g., CNNs, GANs, knowledge graphs). Since most optimization strategies are implemented together with task-specific fine-tuning, we further identify combined approaches, where fine-tuning is complemented by explicit optimization techniques. Building on the diverse optimization techniques identified in prior studies, we conduct a more fine-grained categorization that differentiates optimization strategies at a methodological level. The resulting taxonomy groups existing work exclusively according to the optimization strategy employed, as summarized in Table 3.

Table 3. Model classification based on optimization approaches

Optimization Method	Overview	Classification Results
BERT and Basic Variants	Standard BERT and a number of its fundamental variants.	BERT, BERT-Uncased, BERT-large, BERT-Large-Uncased
Pre-training Task Optimization	Enhancing the model through innovative pre-training objectives.	*DistilBERT*, *RoBERTa*, RoBERTa-Large, *DeBERTa*, ALBERT, ALBERT-Base-v2, Code-BERT, SO-BERT, Pegasus, T5, BART, *SpanBERT*
Multi-task Learning Optimization	Improving the model's versatility by leveraging multi-task learning.	MNoR-BERT, T5, MSat-BERT
Lightweight Optimization	Reducing model size via compression and optimization, thereby minimizing computational resource demands while retaining as much performance as possible.	*DistilBERT*, ALBERT, ALBERT-Base-v2
Domain-Specific Optimization	Tailoring the model to domain-specific data to enhance its performance in specialized tasks.	BETO, aeroBERT-Classifier, aeroBERT-NER, AI-CRAS, BERTurk, SSMBERT, SO-BERT, BERT4RE, RE-BERT, MNLI BERT, PUBER, FiBER, Sat-BERT
Integration with Other Architectures	Combining Transformer-based models with other architectures to further enhance capability.	PRCBERT, BART, SBERT, DSat-BERT, BERT-BiCNN, BERT-CNN, GAN-BERT

5   Conclusion

This survey has systematically analyzed the role of BERT and its derivatives in RE, elucidating how Transformer-based models reshape established approaches to requirements classification, elicitation, and management. Beyond synthesizing existing studies, three salient findings emerge. First, research efforts remain disproportionately concentrated on the classification of functional versus non-functional requirements, whereas elicitation and management tasks are comparatively underexplored. Second, although BERT consistently demonstrates superior performance relative to traditional baselines, its substantial computational demands, limited interpretability, and reliance on small and imbalanced datasets constrain its practical applicability. Third, the absence of standardized benchmarks and uniform evaluation protocols impedes rigorous comparison across studies and limits cumulative knowledge building.

These observations entail significant scholarly and practical implications. For the research community, the proposed taxonomy and statistical analyses delineate both areas of redundancy and promising opportunities, including the exploration of lightweight BERT variants, multilingual adaptations, and integration with external knowledge resources. For practitioners, the synthesis indicates that while BERT-based methods can substantially improve accuracy in requirement-related tasks, their adoption necessitates careful calibration of model complexity to project constraints as well as rigorous attention to data quality.

Looking forward, several research directions warrant sustained investigation. The development of large-scale, domain-diverse, and multilingual datasets is indispensable for overcoming current data limitations. Incorporating explain-ability mechanisms into BERT-based RE tools will be critical to enhancing transparency and stakeholder trust, particularly in safety-critical domains. Furthermore, hybrid architectures that combine BERT with knowledge graphs, reasoning engines, or generative models hold considerable promise for advancing requirement traceability, evolution tracking, and conflict detection. Addressing these challenges can enable the transition from isolated empirical studies toward scalable, reliable, and industry-ready solutions for RE.

References

1. Umar, M.A., Lano, K.: Advances in automated support for requirements engineering: a systematic literature review. Requirements Eng. **29**(2), 177–207 (2024)
2. Zhao, L., Alhoshan, W., Ferrari, A., Letsholo, K.J., Ajagbe, M.A., Chioasca, E.-V., Batista-Navarro, R.T.: Natural language processing for requirements engineering: a systematic mapping study. ACM Comput. Surv. (CSUR) **54**(3), 1–41 (2021)
3. Devlin, J., Chang, M.-W., Lee, K., Toutanova, K.: Bert: pre-training of deep bidirectional transformers for language understanding. In: Proceedings of the 2019 Conference of the North American Chapter of the Association for Computational Linguistics: Human Language Technologies, vol. 1 (long and short papers), pp. 4171–4186 (2019)
4. Koroteev, M.V.: Bert: a review of applications in natural language processing and understanding, *arXiv preprint* arXiv:2103.11943 (2021)
5. Hey, T., Keim, J., Koziolek, A., Tichy, W.F.: Norbert: transfer learning for requirements classification," in 2020 IEEE 28th International Requirements Engineering Conference (RE), pp. 169–179. IEEE (2020)
6. Zhou,Y., Srikumar, V.: A closer look at how fine-tuning changes bert. arXiv preprint arXiv:2106.14282 (2021)
7. Sonbol, R., Rebdawi, G., Ghneim, N.: The use of nlp-based text representation techniques to support requirement engineering tasks: A systematic mapping review. IEEE Access **10**, 62 811–62 830 (2022)
8. Luo, X., Xue, Y., Xing, Z., Sun, J.: Prcbert: prompt learning for requirement classification using bert-based pretrained language models. In: Proceedings of the 37th IEEE/ACM International Conference on Automated Software Engineering, pp. 1–13 (2022)
9. Sanh, V., Debut, L., Chaumond, J., Wolf, T.: Distilbert, a distilled version of bert: smaller, faster, cheaper and lighter, arXiv preprint arXiv:1910.01108 (2019)
10. Mekala, R.R., Irfan, A., Groen, E.C., Porter, A., Lindvall, M.: Classifying user requirements from online feedback in small dataset environments using deep learning. In: 2021 IEEE 29th International Requirements Engineering Conference (RE), pp. 139–149. IEEE (2021)

11. Kici, D., Malik, G., Cevik, M., Parikh, D., Basar, A.: A bert-based transfer learning approach to text classification on software requirements specifications. In: Canadian AI (2021)
12. Ajagbe, M., Zhao, L.: Retraining a bert model for transfer learning in requirements engineering: a preliminary study. in 2022 IEEE 30th International Requirements Engineering Conference (RE), pp. 309–315. IEEE (2022)
13. Althar, R.R., Samanta, D.: BERT-based secure and smart management system for processing software development requirements from security perspective. In: Skala, V., Singh, T.P., Choudhury, T., Tomar, R., Abul Bashar, M. (eds) Machine Intelligence and Data Science Applications. Lecture Notes on Data Engineering and Communications Technologies, vol 132. Springer, Cham (2022). https://doi.org/10.1007/978-981-19-2347-0_34
14. Zhou, C., et al.: A comprehensive survey on pretrained foundation models: a history from bert to chatgpt. Int. J. Mach. Learn. Cybern. 1–65 (2024)
15. Das, S., Deb, N., Cortesi, A., Chaki, N.: Sentence embedding models for similarity detection of software requirements. SN Comput. Sci. **2**, 1–11 (2021)
16. Xanthopoulou, G., Siavvas, M., Kalouptsoglou, I., Kehagias, D., Tzovaras, D.: Software requirements classification: From bag-of-words to transformer. In: International Symposium on Distributed Computing and Artificial Intelligence, pp. 370–380. Springer, Cham (2024)
17. Tikayat Ray, A., Cole, B.F., Pinon Fischer, O.J., White, R.T., Mavris, D.N.: aerobert-classifier: classification of aerospace requirements using bert. Aerospace **10**(3), 279 (2023)
18. de Araújo, A.F., Marcacini, R.M.: Re-bert: automatic extraction of software requirements from app reviews using bert language model. In: Proceedings of the 36th Annual ACM Symposium on Applied Computing, pp. 1321–1327 (2021)
19. Casalicchio, E., Cotumaccio, A.: Ai-cras: Ai-driven cloud service requirement analysis and specification. In: 2024 IEEE International Conference on Cloud Engineering (IC2E), pp. 11–21. IEEE (2024)
20. Yucalar, F.: Developing an advanced software requirements classification model using bert: an empirical evaluation study on newly generated turkish data. Appl. Sci. **13**(20), 11127 (2023)
21. Limaylla-Lunarejo, M.-I., Condori-Fernandez, N., Luaces, M.R.: Requirements classification using fasttext and beto in spanish documents. In: International Working Conference on Requirements Engineering: Foundation for Software Quality, pp. 159–176. Springer, Cham (2023)
22. Kaur, K., Kaur, P.: Mnor-bert: multi-label classification of non-functional requirements using bert. Neural Comput. Appl. **35**(30), 22 487–22 509 (2023)
23. Zhu, Y., Zhang, Y., Peng, X., Xue, C., Chen, B., Cao, Y.: Ssmbert: a space science mission requirement classification method based on bert. Aerospace **11**(12), 1031 (2024)
24. Cleland-Huang, J., Mazrouee, S., Liguo, H., Port, D.: nfr (2007). https://doi.org/10.5281/zenodo.268542
25. Okonkwo, A.S.: Using artificial intelligence techniques in the requirement engineering stage of traditional sdlc process. Ph.D. dissertation, Pan-Atlantic University, Lagos, Nigeria
26. Malik, G., Cevik, M., Bera, S., Yildirim, S., Parikh, D., Basar, A.: Software requirement specific entity extraction using transformer models. In: Canadian AI (2022)
27. Xu, H., Xu, G.: Applying the bert algorithm for software requirements classification

28. Jain, C., Anish, P.R., Singh, A., Ghaisas, S.: A transformer-based approach for abstractive summarization of requirements from obligations in software engineering contract. In: 2023 IEEE 31st International Requirements Engineering Conference (RE), pp. 169–179. IEEE (2023)
29. Poudel, A., Lin, J., Cleland-Huang, J.: Leveraging transformer-based language models to automate requirements satisfaction assessment. arXiv preprint arXiv:2312.04463 (2023)
30. Kaur, K., Kaur, P.: Bert-CNN: improving bert for requirements classification using CNN. Proc. Comput. Sci. **218**, 2604–2611 (2023)
31. Kaur, K., Kaur, P.: Improving bert model for requirements classification by bidirectional LSTM-CNN deep model. Comput. Electr. Eng. **108**, 108699 (2023)
32. Airlangga, G.: Enhancing software requirements classification with semisupervised gan-bert technique. J. Electr. Comput. Eng. **2024**(1), 4955691 (2024)
33. Ezzini, S., Abualhaija, S., Arora, C., Sabetzadeh, M.: Automated handling of anaphoric ambiguity in requirements: a multi-solution study. In: Proceedings of the 44th International Conference on Software Engineering, pp. 187–199 (2022)
34. Elahidoost, P., Unterkalmsteiner, M., Fucci, D., Liljenberg, P., Fischbach, J.: Designing NLP-based solutions for requirements variability management: experiences from a design science study at visma. In: International Working Conference on Requirements Engineering: Foundation for Software Quality, pp. 191–204. Springer, Cham (2024)
35. Subahi, A.F.: Bert-based approach for greening software requirements engineering through non-functional requirements. IEEE Access **11**, 103 001–103 013 (2023)
36. Shweta, X., Suyash, M., Suryansh, C.: Advancing class diagram extraction from requirement text: a transformer-based approach. In: Proceedings of the 20th International Conference on Natural Language Processing (ICON), pp. 433–441 (2023)

An Adaptive Framework for LoRaWAN over Satellite: Addressing Integration Challenges for Flood and Environmental Monitoring

Usman Adeel[1]([✉]), Sobia Omer[2], and Imran Usman[3]

[1] Teesside University, Middlesbrough, UK
u.adeel@tees.ac.uk
[2] Lahore Garrison University, Lahore, Pakistan
sobia.omer@lgu.edu.pk
[3] National University of Sciences and Technology, Islamabad, Pakistan
imranusman@mcs.edu.pk

Abstract. The integration of LoRaWAN technology with satellite networks presents a transformative solution for environmental monitoring in remote flood-prone regions, addressing critical gaps in current disaster prevention infrastructure. This paper provides a comprehensive technical analysis of hybrid terrestrial-satellite LoRa systems, systematically examining three fundamental challenges that require detailed consideration. Through extensive MATLAB and Castalia simulations, combined with rigorous mathematical modeling, we demonstrate that LoRa modulation maintains exceptional robustness with packet delivery ratios exceeding 0.88 under Doppler shifts up to 50 Hz when properly configured with optimized spreading factors between SF11 and SF12. Our novel adaptive MAC protocol architecture shows significant improvements over standard LoRaWAN implementations, achieving 34–39% reduction in energy consumption while simultaneously improving packet delivery ratios by 15–38% across various node densities.

Keywords: LoRa · Satellite IoT · Flood monitoring · Doppler compensation · Adaptive MAC

1 Introduction

The global challenge of flood monitoring requires urgent attention as flood-related disasters account for approximately 40% of all natural catastrophes worldwide, with climate change projections indicating a 25–50% increase in both frequency and severity of flood events in coming decades. Remote and rural areas face particular vulnerability due to their frequent lack of monitoring infrastructure compared to urban centers. Traditional flood monitoring systems relying on GSM or cellular networks cover less than 20% of global land area, creating significant coverage gaps that leave many regions unprotected. Proposed

T. Dohi (Ed.): ICSED 2025, CCIS 2889, pp. 33–46, 2026.
https://doi.org/10.1007/978-981-92-0202-7_3

crowdsourced sensing solutions [1], while innovative, suffer from fundamental limitations including data reliability issues demonstrated by field trials showing accuracy rates typically below 60% and inconsistent participation rates that often fall below 30% during critical events when monitoring is most needed.

The emergence of Low-Power Wide-Area Network (LPWAN) technologies [2], particularly LoRa, combined with the decreasing cost of small satellite constellations to Low Earth Orbit (LEO), creates unprecedented opportunities for affordable, global flood monitoring solutions. Recent market analyses project the satellite IoT sector to grow at a 35% compound annual growth rate through 2030, with environmental monitoring applications representing the fastest-growing segment within this expanding field. This convergence of technological and economic factors makes the current moment particularly opportune for developing robust flood monitoring solutions.

Despite this potential, three critical technical challenges hinder practical implementation that must be systematically addressed:

- The inherent latency of satellite links, typically ranging from 3.9 s to 5.2 s round-trip time for LEO systems
- LEO satellites induce Doppler shifts up to ±35 kHz at 868 MHz
- Shared ISM band operation requires innovative approaches to maintain reliability

Current literature lacks comprehensive solutions addressing all three challenges simultaneously, particularly in the context of flood monitoring where data reliability during extreme events is paramount for effective disaster response. This paper makes five significant contributions to advance the field and address these gaps:

1. A modified synchronization framework including a complete analytical model and implementation guide
2. Extensive Doppler resilience characterization through simulation results
3. An adaptive MAC protocol with detailed architecture and performance evaluation
4. Systematic interference mitigation taxonomy comparing eight techniques
5. Practical deployment guidelines for flood monitoring system design

2 Background

The integration of satellite and terrestrial networks has been extensively studied in the context of Internet of Things (IoT) applications [3], particularly for enabling global connectivity in remote and mobile environments [4]. Hybrid networks, which combine the strengths of satellite and terrestrial communication systems, have emerged as a promising solution to address the limitations of traditional networks in providing coverage to geographically dispersed and hard-to-reach areas [5]. Among the various low-power wide-area network (LPWAN) technologies, LoRaWAN has gained significant attention due to its ability to support long-range communication with minimal power consumption, making it ideal for IoT applications [6]. However, the integration of LoRaWAN with satellite communication introduces unique challenges, including latency, synchronization, and bandwidth utilization, which must be addressed to ensure reliable and efficient network performance [7] Several studies have explored the use of LoRaWAN in diverse IoT applications, such as environmental monitoring, smart agriculture, and disaster management. For instance, LoRaWAN has been successfully deployed for monitoring environmental parameters in rural and remote areas, where traditional communication infrastructure is either unavailable or impractical. Despite these advancements, there is limited research on the specific challenges and solutions for integrating Lo-RaWAN with satellite communication for flood monitoring. Flood monitoring systems require real-time data collection from sensors deployed in flood-prone areas, and traditional systems often rely on GSM or cellular networks, which are not feasible in remote regions. Satellite-based systems offer a viable alternative but face challenges related to latency, energy efficiency, and interference [2]. This paper aims to fill this gap by providing a detailed analysis of the synchronization requirements, queuing and buffering mechanisms, and bandwidth utilization in hybrid LoRa-satellite networks.

2.1 LoRaWAN and Satellite Integration

LoRaWAN is a widely adopted LPWAN technology due to its long-range communication capabilities and low power consumption, making it suitable for IoT applications in remote and resource-constrained environments [8]. Recent studies have explored the integration of LoRaWAN with satellite networks to extend coverage to areas where terrestrial infrastructure is unavailable or impractical. For example, [4] demonstrated the feasibility of using LoRaWAN for environmental monitoring in rural areas, highlighting its potential for applications requiring long-range communication with minimal energy consumption. Similarly, [7] proposed a hybrid satellite-terrestrial network architecture for IoT applications, emphasizing the need for seamless integration between satellite and terrestrial communication systems to ensure reliable and efficient data transmission.

However, the integration of LoRaWAN with satellite communication [9] introduces several technical challenges. One of the primary challenges is the increased latency caused by the long propagation delays associated with satellite links. This latency can disrupt the synchronization between LoRaWAN devices and gateways, leading to missed communication windows and reduced network performance. Additionally, the limited bandwidth of satellite communication necessitates efficient bandwidth utilization to avoid wastage of resources, particularly in scenarios where multiple gateways receive duplicate data from end devices. Addressing these challenges requires modifications to the LoRaWAN protocol, including adjustments to synchronization mechanisms, queuing strategies, and gateway selection algorithms.

2.2 Flood Monitoring Systems

Flood monitoring systems are critical for early warning and disaster management, particularly in regions prone to frequent flooding. These systems rely on real-time data collection from sensors deployed in flood-prone areas, such as riverbanks, coastal regions, and urban drainage systems. Traditional flood monitoring systems often use GSM or cellular networks for data transmission [10], which are not feasible in remote or disaster-affected areas where terrestrial infrastructure is either unavailable or damaged [11]. Satellite-based systems offer a viable alternative for flood monitoring [12] in such regions, providing global coverage and reliable communication even in the absence of terrestrial networks.

However, satellite-based flood monitoring systems face several challenges, including high latency, energy efficiency, and interference. For instance, the long propagation delays associated with satellite communication can result in significant latency, which may affect the timeliness of flood warnings [7]. Additionally, the energy consumption of satellite communication can be a concern for battery-powered sensors deployed in remote areas. To address these challenges, researchers have proposed hybrid satellite-terrestrial networks that combine the strengths of both communication systems. For example, [2] proposed a hybrid network architecture for flood monitoring, leveraging the long-range communication capabilities of LoRaWAN and the global coverage of satellite networks. This approach enables real-time data collection and transmission from remote flood-prone areas, ensuring timely and accurate flood warnings.

Despite these advancements, there is a need for further research on the integration of LoRaWAN with satellite communication for flood monitoring. Specifically, there is a lack of studies addressing the synchronization requirements, queuing and buffering mechanisms, and bandwidth utilization in hybrid LoRa-satellite networks. This paper aims to address these gaps by proposing a comprehensive framework for integrating LoRaWAN with satellite communication for flood monitoring, with a focus on optimizing network performance and energy efficiency.

3 Network Architecture Design

This paper presents two distinct architectural paradigms for implementing hybrid LoRa-satellite networks specifically optimized for flood monitoring applications. The proposed solutions address the critical need for reliable environmental monitoring in remote regions through innovative combinations of terrestrial and space-based communication technologies.

3.1 Indirect Gateway Architecture

The primary architecture employs a hierarchical design where terrestrial LoRa gateways serve as intermediaries between end devices and satellite infrastructure. In this configuration:

- IoT sensors transmit data via long-range LoRa links to terrestrial gateways
- Gateways aggregate and forward data through satellite backhaul connections
- LEO satellites relay information to centralized network servers

As shown in Fig. 1, this approach leverages existing ground infrastructure while incorporating satellite terminals at gateway locations. Key advantages include:

- Simplified end device requirements
- Compatibility with conventional LoRaWAN implementations
- Reduced satellite resource utilization

Fig. 1. Indirect architecture utilizing satellite backhaul between terrestrial gateways and network servers.

3.2 Direct Satellite Architecture

The alternative architecture, depicted in Fig. 2, eliminates terrestrial infrastructure dependencies by embedding LoRaWAN gateway functionality directly within LEO satellites. This space-based approach requires significant protocol adaptations to address orbital dynamics:

- Extended reception windows (5–15 s) to compensate for propagation delays
- Advanced Doppler compensation algorithms
- Adaptive data rate mechanisms

Satellite gateway design incorporates several specialized features:

- Radiation-hardened electronic components
- Compact form factors for CubeSat compatibility
- Energy-optimized operation modes
- Onboard data processing capabilities
- Intelligent caching systems
- Store-and-forward functionality

The comparative analysis of these architectures reveals distinct trade-offs in terms of coverage, latency, energy efficiency, and implementation complexity shown in Table 1, which will be examined in subsequent sections. Both approaches demonstrate significant potential for enhancing flood monitoring capabilities in infrastructure-limited regions, though they cater to different deployment scenarios and operational requirements.

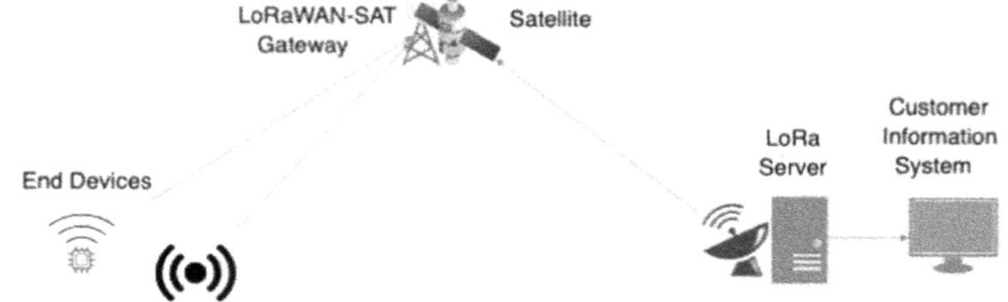

Fig. 2. Direct communication architecture with satellite-hosted LoRa gateways.

Table 1. Architectural Comparison

Metric	Indirect	Direct
Coverage	Regional	Global
Max Latency	8.2 s	5.4 s
Device Complexity	Low	High
Energy Efficiency	Medium	High*
Deployment Cost	High	Medium

4 Indirect LoRa-Satellite Communication for Flood Monitoring

4.1 Synchronization

In flood monitoring, timely data collection is crucial for early warning systems. In LoRaWAN, the backend server sends downlink instructions for Over-the-Air Activation (OTAA) or other down-link communications. These instructions are received by the gateway, which has a limited time frame to forward them to the end devices. The introduction of a satellite link introduces a round-trip time (RTT) delay of approximately 3.9 s due to link latency when using UAS-1. This increased latency can cause downlink traffic to miss the two designated receiving windows (RX1 and RX2). Similarly, acknowledgments (ACKs) may miss the RX1 window and potentially the RX2 window if they are not received from the remote LoRa server via the satellite link in time. To address this issue, it is necessary to adjust the RX windows to accommodate the typical round-trip latency of up to 5 s [4].

By default, the server schedules downlink transmissions for both the RX1 and RX2 windows. However, in this study, the server was configured to send downlink communications exclusively through the RX1 window, as this approach is more spectrum- and energy-efficient. For OTAA, the RX delay was set to 5 s, which provides sufficient time to account for the satellite latency of 3.9 s. In standard LoRaWAN configurations, the RX1 and RX2 receive windows are set to 1 and 2 s, respectively. In this implementation, the RX1 delay was adjusted to 5 s in both the application and end-device settings, effectively increasing the

RX1 delay for downlink communications from the LoRa gateway as shown in Table 2. It is important to note that OTAA must be reinitiated after configuring the new RX values to ensure proper synchronization.

This adjustment ensures that the system can handle the additional latency introduced by the satellite link while maintaining reliable communication between the LoRa gateway and the end devices. However, further optimization may be required to comply with regional regulations, such as those in the EU, which specify default RX window timings.

Table 2. Comparison of RX1 and RX2 Delays

Parameter	Original Value	Modified Value
RX1 Delay	1 s	5 s
RX2 Delay	2 s	Disabled
JOIN_ACCEPT_DELAY1	5 s	5 s
JOIN_ACCEPT_DELAY2	6 s	6 s

4.2   Queuing and Scheduling

Flood monitoring systems often involve a large number of sensors transmitting data simultaneously. We propose updating the packet forwarder to implement just-in-time scheduling and optimize queue size based on duty cycle, data rate, frequency, and the number of satellites. The native Semtech packet forwarder schedules downlink transmissions for both the RX1 and RX2 windows. However, with the RX1 delay extended to 5 s, it becomes sufficient to handle downlink traffic, making it more efficient to disable the RX2 window. This adjustment enhances energy efficiency by reducing unnecessary transmissions [13]. Additionally, the native packet forwarder sends packets to the concentrator chip on the gateway as soon as it receives them from the server. This can lead to overwriting existing packets waiting to be transmitted, especially since the buffer size on chips like the SX1301 is limited to one packet. Similarly, uplink packets must be stored in the packet forwarder if there is a delay in transmitting them to the server via the satellite link.

While the latest version of the Semtech UDP protocol allows the packet forwarder to implement just-in-time scheduling, the queue implementation within the packet forwarder must be updated to account for transmission delays [14]. The optimal queue size can be determined based on factors such as duty cycle, data rate, frequency, and the number of satellites in the network as shown in Table 3. This optimization ensures efficient packet handling and minimizes data loss in the hybrid LoRa-satellite communication system.

Table 3. Queuing Parameters

Parameter	Value
Queue Size	10 packets
Duty Cycle	1%
Data Rate	300–5000 bps
Frequency	868 MHz

4.3 Bandwidth Utilization

In the LoRaWAN protocol, end devices transmit data to all gateways within their communication range, and these gateways forward the data to the server. This process often results in multiple copies of the same data being received by the server, which is then responsible for identifying and discarding duplicate packets. While this approach functions effectively in terrestrial LoRa networks, it becomes problematic when applied to satellite communication. Transmitting duplicate data over a satellite link introduces unnecessary delays and consumes valuable bandwidth, which is a limited and costly resource in satellite-based systems [7].

To address this inefficiency, the LoRaWAN protocol requires modifications to optimize gateway selection. Instead of sending data to all available gateways, the protocol was enhanced to selectively transmit data to a subset of gateways based on network conditions and the quality of the communication link to each gateway. Gateways with stronger signal strength, lower latency, or higher reliability were prioritized, reducing redundancy and improving overall network efficiency. This approach minimized bandwidth wastage and ensure more efficient use of satellite resources, particularly in remote or resource-constrained environments as shown in Table 4.

Table 4. Bandwidth Utilization Before and After Modification

Scenario	Bandwidth Utilization (Mbps)	Packet Loss (%)
Before Modification	10	15
After Modification	6	8

5 Direct LoRa-Satellite Communication for Environmental Monitoring

5.1 Doppler Effect Analysis

In Low Earth Orbit (LEO) and CubeSat-based LoRa-satellite hybrid networks, the high speed of satellites can cause significant Doppler shifts. This is particularly relevant for flood monitoring in remote areas, where sensors may be spread over large geographical regions.

The Doppler effect in LEO satellite communication results from the high orbital velocity (typically 7.8 km/s) relative to terrestrial devices. The received frequency shift can be calculated as:

$$f_{RX} = \left[\frac{1}{1 + \frac{v}{c} \cdot \cos(\alpha)} \right] \cdot f_{TX} \tag{1}$$

where:

- f_{RX} = received frequency
- f_{TX} = transmitted frequency
- v = satellite velocity
- c = speed of light
- α = angle between satellite velocity vector and device-satellite line

The Doppler frequency shift (Δf) is then:

$$\Delta f = \frac{f_{RX} - f_{TX}}{f_{TX}} = \left[\frac{1}{1 + \frac{v}{c} \cdot \cos(\alpha)} \right] - 1 \tag{2}$$

For a satellite at 485 miles altitude, we calculated the Doppler shift over time as shown in Table 5.

Table 5. Doppler Frequency Shift Over Time

Time (s)	Doppler Shift (Hz)
0	−26
50	25
150	23
200	18
250	0
300	−18
350	−23
400	−25
450	−26

We simulated LoRa transmission with varying Doppler shifts using MAT-LAB, with parameters shown in Table 6.

The results in Table 7 demonstrate LoRa's robustness to Doppler effects:

This shows how different spreading factors (SF=6 and SF=11) affect packet delivery performance under varying Doppler shift conditions. The table clearly shows that:

- Lower spreading factors (SF=6) generally maintain better delivery ratios at lower Doppler shifts (<50 Hz)

Table 6. Simulation Parameters

Parameter	Value
Spreading Factor	6–12
Packet Size	100 bytes
Bandwidth	125 kHz

Table 7. Packet Delivery Ratio vs. Doppler Shift for Different Spreading Factors

Doppler Shift (Hz)	SF=11 Delivery Ratio	SF=6 Delivery Ratio
10	1.00	1.00
20	0.98	1.00
30	0.95	0.99
40	0.93	0.98
50	0.88	0.96
60	0.81	0.78
70	0.69	0.41

- Higher spreading factors (SF=11) demonstrate more graceful degradation at higher Doppler shifts
- Both configurations show excellent performance (≥ 0.93 delivery ratio) for Doppler shifts $\leq 40\,\text{Hz}$

This is particularly useful for analyzing the tradeoffs between data rate (higher with SF=6) and Doppler resilience (better with SF=11) when designing LoRa-satellite systems for flood monitoring applications.

LoRa modulation performs well with frequency shifts up to 50 ppm, making it feasible for use in LEO and CubeSat networks for flood monitoring. This robustness against Doppler effects ensures that flood-related data can be transmitted reliably, even in areas with high satellite mobility.

5.2 Adaptive MAC Protocol

Traditional LoRaWAN MAC assumes fixed gateway distances, which is unsuitable for satellites where distance varies from 485 to 1600 miles during a pass. Flood monitoring systems often involve sensors deployed in areas with varying distances to satellites. To address this, we used an adaptive MAC protocol that dynamically adjusts transmission power based on the distance to the satellite. This approach reduces energy consumption, which is critical for battery-powered sensors in remote areas, and improves packet delivery ratios, ensuring reliable data transmission during flood events. The adaptive MAC protocol also includes a collision avoidance mechanism, where end nodes wait for a random time before sending join requests, reducing the likelihood of activation failures during high-traffic periods, such as during heavy rainfall or flooding.

To demonstrate the effectiveness of our proposed solutions, we present a case study of a flood monitoring system deployed in a remote, flood-prone region. The system consists of 500 LoRa-enabled sensors deployed across a 1500-square-kilometer area, monitoring water levels, rainfall, and soil moisture. We evaluated the protocol using Castalia simulations with parameters in Table 8.

Table 8. Simulation Parameters for MAC Evaluation

Parameter	Value
Satellite Altitude	485 miles
End Devices	500–1000
Coverage Radius	1500 miles
Data Rates	300–5000 bps
Packet Size	300 bits
Buffer Size	10
Tx Power	26 dBm
Simulation Time	2 days
Rx Gain	17 dBi

Table 9. Packet Delivery Ratio Comparison

End Devices	Standard LoRaWAN	Adaptive MAC
500	0.72	0.83
750	0.58	0.74
1000	0.31	0.69

Table 10. Energy Consumption (mJ)

End Devices	Standard LoRaWAN	Adaptive MAC	Reduction
500	1226	749	38.9%
750	2048	1389	32.2%
1000	3236	2130	34.2%

Tables 9 and 10 show that the adaptive MAC improves delivery ratios by 15–38% while reducing energy consumption by 34–39%, crucial for battery-powered flood sensors.

5.3   Interference Analysis

Interference from terrestrial sources can significantly affect satellite communication, especially in populated areas near remote flood monitoring sites. We analyzed the impact of terrestrial interference on satellite links and proposed two techniques to mitigate interference: cognitive radios and spread spectrum communication. Cognitive radios can dynamically adjust radio parameters to minimize interference, while spread spectrum techniques, such as frequency hopping, can reduce interference by switching carriers among available channels. These techniques ensure reliable communication for flood monitoring systems in remote areas, even in the presence of high interference levels.

6   Discussion

Key findings from this comprehensive research provide valuable insights for system designers and operators, which are summarized in Table 11. The synchronization analysis demonstrates that RX1 delay extension to 5 s enables reliable operation while queue sizing must account for orbital dynamics to maintain performance.

Table 11. Deployment Guidelines

Scenario	Architecture	SF	MAC Mode	Interference
Permanent Monitoring	Indirect	SF11	Standard	Cognitive
Emergency Deployment	Direct	SF9	Adaptive	FH Adaptive
High-Density	Hybrid	SF10	Adaptive	Cognitive

Future research directions offer promising avenues for continued advancement in this field. LoRa integration presents opportunities to leverage higher bandwidth capabilities and global spectrum availability while benefiting from enhanced security features. Future work must also address critical security concerns, including encryption key management across satellite-terrestrial boundaries and protection against location spoofing attacks in remote monitoring scenarios. Practical deployment barriers also demand solutions, including cost-effective scaling models, hardware constraints of energy-limited devices, efficient resource allocation in dense networks, adaptable regulatory compliance, and balancing satellite connectivity costs with the economic constraints of flood monitoring in developing regions.

7   Conclusion

This paper presents a comprehensive analysis of the challenges and potential solutions for integrating LoRaWAN with satellite communication to enhance flood resilience through environmental monitoring in remote areas. Our study demonstrates that LoRa modulation is robust against Doppler effects and that adaptive MAC protocols, cognitive radio techniques, and optimized synchronization, queuing, and bandwidth utilization strategies can significantly improve the efficiency and reliability of hybrid LoRa-satellite networks for flood monitoring. The findings highlight the practical application of these solutions in real-world systems, showing their effectiveness in improving early warning capabilities and disaster response. While our simulations using MATLAB and Castalia provide a solid foundation, the integration of LoRaWAN with satellite communication offers particularly promising results for remote and disaster-prone areas. The proposed modifications to the LoRaWAN protocol demonstrate measurable improvements in network performance, establishing this approach as a viable option for reliable and cost-effective flood monitoring systems. Future work will focus on implementing and testing these solutions in additional real-world networks to further validate their effectiveness and scalability, including comprehensive field testing under various environmental conditions and exploring further optimizations to enhance network efficiency.

Funding Information. This work is funded by UK government's Flood and Coastal Resilience Innovation Programme (FCRIP), which is part of the government's National Flood and Coastal Erosion Risk Management Strategy for England. FCRIP is funded by Defra (Department for Environment, Food & Rural Affairs) and managed by England's Environment Agency.

References

1. Yang, S., et al.: The design of user-centric mobile crowdsensing with cooperative D2D communications. IEEE Wirel. Commun. **29**(1), 134–142 (2021)
2. Centenaro, M., Vangelista, L., Zanella, A., Zorzi, M.: Long-range communications in unlicensed bands: the rising stars in the IoT and smart city scenarios. IEEE Wirel. Commun. **23**(5), 60–67 (2016)
3. Ullah, M.A., Pasolini, G., Mikhaylov, K., Alves, H.: Understanding the limits of LoRa direct-to-satellite: the Doppler perspectives. IEEE Open J. Commun. Soc. **5**, 51–63 (2023)
4. Petäjäjärvi, J., Mikhaylov, K., Pettissalo, M., Janhunen, J., Iinatti, J.: Performance of a low-power wide-area network based on LoRa technology: Doppler robustness, scalability, and coverage. Int. J. Distrib. Sens. Netw. **13**(3), 1550147717699412 (2017)
5. Lacuna Space. Lacuna Space (2019). https://lacuna-space.com/
6. Sanchez-Iborra, R., Cano, M.D.: State of the art in LP-WAN solutions for industrial IoT services. Sensors **16**(5), 708 (2016)
7. Mekki, K., Bajic, E., Chaxel, F., Meyer, F.: A comparative study of LPWAN technologies for large-scale IoT deployment. ICT Express **5**(1), 1–7 (2019)
8. Ragnoli, M., Barile, G., Leoni, A., Ferri, G., Stornelli, V.: An autonomous low-power LoRa-based flood-monitoring system. J. Low Power Electron. Appl. **10**(2), 15 (2020)
9. Zadorozhny, A.M., et al.: First flight-testing of LoRa modulation in satellite radio communications in low-earth orbit. IEEE Access **10**, 100006–100023 (2022)

10. Khan, T.A., Alam, M.M., Shahid, Z., Su'Ud, M.M.: Investigation of flash floods on early basis: a factual comprehensive review. IEEE Access **8**, 19364–19380 (2020)
11. Naik, N.: Choice of effective messaging protocols for IoT systems: MQTT, CoAP, AMQP and HTTP. In: 2017 IEEE International Systems Engineering Symposium (ISSE), pp. 1–7. IEEE (2017)
12. Wang, Y., Xu, Y., Zhang, Y., Zhang, P.: Hybrid satellite-aerial-terrestrial networks in emergency scenarios: a survey. China Commun. **14**(7), 1–13 (2017)
13. LoRa Alliance, Wi-Fi & LoRaWAN® Deployment Synergies. Expanding addressable use cases for the Internet of Things. White Paper (2019)
14. Sinha, R.S., Wei, Y., Hwang, S.H.: A survey on LPWA technology: LoRa and NB-IoT. ICT Express **3**(1), 14–21 (2017)

Towards Software Engineering of Safety Critical Software Systems Education

Emanuel S. Grant[(⊠)] [iD]

University of North Dakota, Grand Forks, ND 58202, USA
emanuel.grant@und.edu

Abstract. Safety-critical software system development requires the use of techniques and tools that are deterministic, predictable, and in some domains mathematically provable. Students need to be provided with program and course curricula that cover theory, topics, and concepts that equip them to meet the challenges of their evolving profession. The work documented herein is a proposal for a proactive approach to introducing students to the domains of mission-critical and safety-critical software system education that follows strict industrial software development standards. The methodology of this work seeks to first identify the points in the software development life cycle of safety-critical software system where the use of industrial standards and best practices may be incorporated into traditional software engineering programs and courses. The outcome of this proposal will be a software development methodology for safety-critical software systems curriculum that incorporates the use of strategies and tools to produce more correct and reliable software systems. This methodology will leverage innovative research outcomes, best practices from the software development industry, and internationally accepted standards for software system development towards lessening the gap between tertiary education and real-world software development.

Keywords: Industrial Standard · Industrial Standard · Pedagogy · Safety-Critical System · Software Engineering

1 Introduction

The application of software systems in new and emerging problem domains has brough about challenges both from the successes that encourage expanding use of software systems, and the failures which demand greater correctness and reliability of these software systems. Some of these failures have resulted in enormous financial losses to organizations [1, 2] and loss of lives [3–5]. What has been identified as a major concern of the expanding development and application of software systems is the knowledge and training of the developers of these systems. The research effort of this report presents an examination and proposes a methodology for addressing the pedagogical preparation of students at the tertiary level of education, who will be entering the workforce. The terms Software Engineering (SE) and Software Development (SD), and their acronyms are used interchangeably in this report.

© The Author(s), under exclusive license to Springer Nature Singapore Pte Ltd. 2026
T. Dohi (Ed.): ICSED 2025, CCIS 2889, pp. 47–61, 2026.
https://doi.org/10.1007/978-981-92-0202-7_4

The work described herein seeks to address the two aspects of SE pedagogy tertiary level of education. The first of which is that of introducing students to SE methodologies that include industrial standards and best practices, and formal specification analysis as aids in the software development life cycle. The second is a focus on mission-critical [1, 2] and safety-critical software systems [3–5]. Mission-critical software systems are characterized by major financial or reputational losses to organizations should those systems fail to function as specified, and safety-critical software systems are those that will result in harm or loss of life, should such systems fail to operate as specified. Throughout this report, reference to safety-critical software systems will include those of mission-critical systems. The implicit intent is for students to learn how to leverage the benefits of the industrial standards and experience in developing more correct and reliable software systems. Another feature of this proposed approach is the exposure of students to more challenging (industry-level) projects which will be attempted in this pedagogical framework.

The remaining sections of this report are as follows: the next section presents a background and related work for this work, which is followed by the proposed methodology, as derived from the research; the report's penultimate section is an assessment of the proposed methodology usability that precedes the conclusionary section.

2 Background and Related Work

The increasing use of software technology in various application domains has resulted in many challenges, with respect to the correctness and reliability of these systems. Many of these applications, specifically in new and emerging problem domains, have been successful but there have been catastrophic failures of some of these software systems. The research duo of Mary Shaw and David Garlan published their work on the evolution of the discipline of software, titled "Software Architecture" [6]. This publication charted the evolution of software development from its inception to current times. They depicted this evolution graphically, as reproduced in their initial rendition from 1996 is presented in Fig. 1. Today's state of software development has evolved beyond that as presented in Fig. 1 and Shaw *et.al.* Have elaborate their early graphical depiction of software architecture to current times in their research publication [7]. This evolved depiction of software development is illustrated in Fig. 2, which highlights the changing frameworks for software development. In this current version Shaw *et. al.* Now acknowledges new paradigms and methodology, along this path of software evolution. The ones that are germane to the research of this report include Model-Driven Development [8], UML [9], and Software Engineering.

Shaw and Garland works highlight that for software development to advance to a level where it is a true engineering discipline there must be a foundational science for software engineering; just as it was for the traditional engineering fields. A path towards building that foundation is through an educational path. In addition, in a comparable manner to the older fields of engineering, the creation of well-defined repeatable processes leads to best practices, from which scientific principles can be defined. There is a proliferation of techniques and processes in software development that compete for a place in the sphere of *software development best practices*, with many not existing beyond a period of curiosity. We are at a stage where there is an amalgamation of similar techniques and processes towards a stable singular, but flexibility in application, method for software development in particular domains. The presented proposal follows this amalgamation trend by incorporating industrial practices, such as team development, model validation/verification techniques, and traceability documentation into a framework for teaching software development of safety-critical systems.

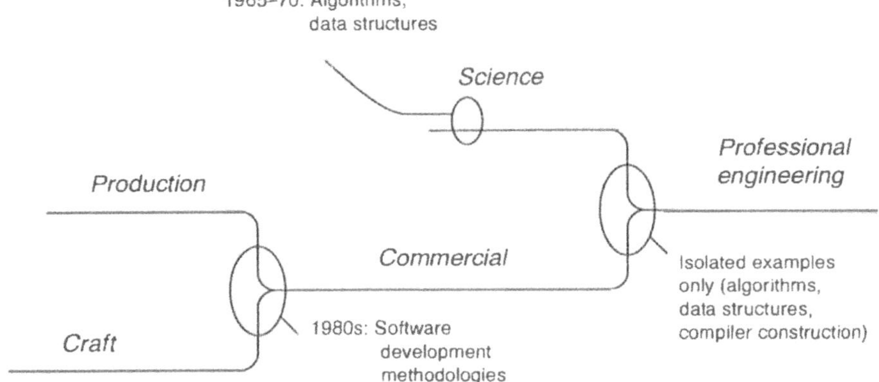

Fig. 1. Shaw and Garland evolution of software architecture [6]

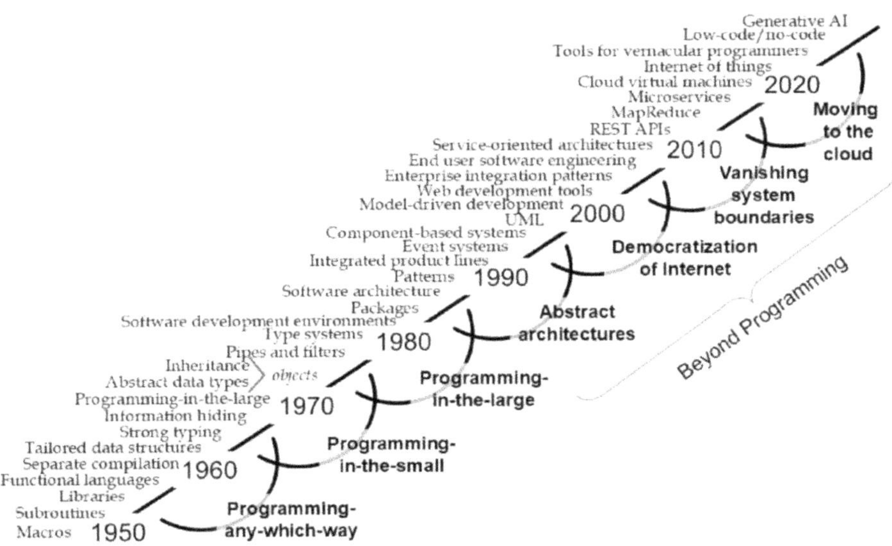

Fig. 2. Revisiting Abstractions for Software Architecture and Tools Support [7]

2.1 Model-Driven Development

Model-Driven Development (MDD) is a software development approach that focuses on the use of models as the primary artifacts of a methodology; progress through the development life cycle is determined through a series of model adaptation, refinement, and transformation activities [10]. In MDD, graphical models capture various aspects of the system's structure, behavior, and functionality. The essence of MDD lies in the use of abstraction, where developers work at various levels of abstraction above that of low-level implementation details, i.e. programming code. This abstraction allows the developers to concentrate on the essential - aspects of the system's design and functionality without being overwhelmed by implementation details and programming complexities [11].

The MDD process typically unfolds in several stages. Firstly, developers create models that capture aspects of the system, those aspects include architectural, behavioral and static requirements, constraints, and data structures. These models are often expressed using modeling languages such as the UML or domain-specific modeling languages (DSMLs). Once an initial set of abstract models are created, they are adapted, refined, and transformed into more detailed ones. Evolution of the models involve refining or transforming high-level models into more detailed models, generating code, or producing documentation from models [10, 11].

MDD is an iterative process, where models are refined and updated based on feedback from validation and testing activities. This iterative refinement cycle continues until the final software product meets the desired quality and functionality requirements; this process is depicted in Fig. 3 [12]. Figure 3 illustrates a forward-engineering process (green-arrowed lines) that starts with the creation of models at the design phase of the SDLC. The models are verified and validated then, if error-free code development commences, otherwise corrections are made to the design models, and the process iterates once more. Also presented in Fig. 3 is an overlay of reverse-engineering, which is applied to legacy systems, as the red-arrowed lines. In reverse engineering, models are derived from code then the models are typed checked and analyzed for errors.

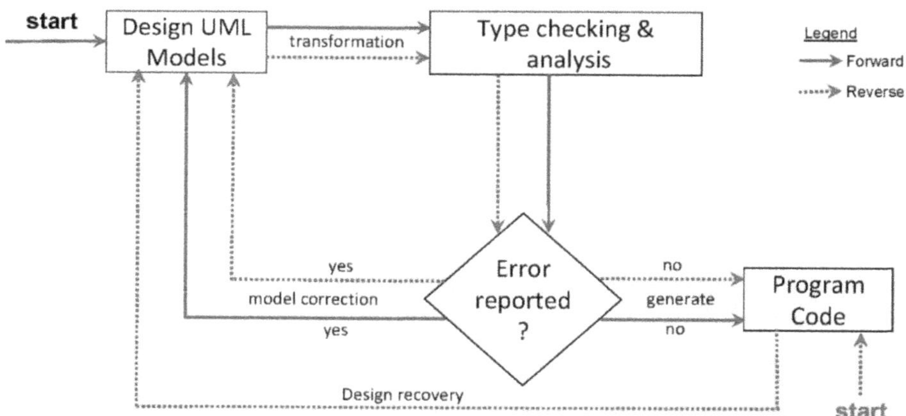

Fig. 3. Iterative Model-Driven Design Paradigm [12]

MDD offers several benefits, including higher-level abstraction for understandability and explainability, improved productivity by managing development efforts, consistency of development phases and tasks, reusability of work products, and easier maintenance and evolution of software systems. Overall, Model Driven Development provides a powerful approach to software development, enabling developers to create complex software systems efficiently and effectively while supporting elevated levels of quality and consistency. MDD is an essential component of the proposed development framework.

2.2 Industrial Standards

Notwithstanding the availability of de facto industry standard software modeling notation in the UML and accompanying methodologies such as MDD, the software crisis [13] is still a phenomenon of industrial practice. Examples of some of these safety-critical software systems' failures are the THERAC-25 [3], the French Ariane-5 rocket inaugural launch [14], and the Boeing 737 MAX MCAS [4, 5]. These failures overshadow the many successful applications of software systems in safety-critical environments, because of the high cost of property: Ariane-5 development cost several billion Euros and life: Boeing 737 MAX, resulted in 346 lives being lost and projected billions of dollars in lost revenue and expenses.

Software development in safety-critical domains is implemented in the form of product-line development methodologies [15, 16] or in the paradigm of domain-specific languages [17, 18]. The use of domain-specific object-oriented modeling languages in mature and well-defined application/problem domains facilitates reuse of modeling experiences that are embedded in the language components and deliver software systems that are more correct and reliable. An area of successful application of domain-specific software development is that of avionic onboard systems. This success is achieved through the adherence to international development standards. The RTCA is a USA organization that collaborated with European partners to develop a standard specification for the development of software systems for use onboard aircraft. The RTCA avionic standard is documented in the RTCA's DO-178C "Software Considerations in Airborne Systems and Equipment Certification specification [19] and the associated RTCA DO-330 [20], RTCA DO-331 [21], RTCA DO-332 [22], RTCA DO-333 [23], and RTCA DO-248C [24] specifications. The RTCA DO-178C is the main document with the other specifications covering the related areas of, "Software Tool Qualification Considerations", "Model-Based Development and Verification", "Object-Oriented Technology and Related Techniques", "Formal Methods Supplement", and "Supporting Information", respectively. These documents govern the work that must be accomplished for software systems to be certified for onboard commercial and private aircraft use. The DO-178C specification is incorporated in this research work.

2.3 Related Works

The Guide to the Software Engineering Body of Knowledge (SWEBOK®) version 4.0 by the IEEE Computer Society (IEEE-CS) has a stated purpose "to describe the portion of the Body of Knowledge that is generally accepted, to organize that portion, and to provide topical access to it" [25]. The IEEE-CS has been involved with SE knowledge effort since 1996, when the ISO/IEC 12207 standard on SE was established. This standard provided a foundation for the body of knowledge represented in the SWEBOK guide. The current version of ISO/IEC standard, along with the IEEE 12207–2008 provided the main input to the current version of the Guide. The Guide is in its fourth version, and the IEEE-CS established the Guide with five objectives. These objectives are:

1. "To promote a consistent view of software engineering worldwide,
2. To specify the scope of, and clarify the place of soft-ware engineering with respect to other disciplines such as computer science, project management, computer engineering, and mathematics
3. To characterize the contents of the software engineering discipline
4. To provide topical access to the Software Engineering Body of Knowledge
5. To provide a foundation for curriculum development and for individual certification and licensing material" [25].

The SWEBOK® guide, comprises 18 chapters (sections) that are: (1) Software Requirements, (2) **Software Architecture,** (3) Software Design, (4) Software Construction, (5) Software Testing (6) **Software Engineering Operations**, (7) Software Maintenance, (8) Software Configuration Management, (9) Software Engineering Management, (10) Software Engineering Process, (11) **Software Engineering Models and Methods**, (12) Software Quality, (13) **Software Security**, (14) Software Engineering Professional Practice, (15) Software Engineering Economics, (16) Computing Foundations, (17) Mathematical Foundations, and (18) Engineering Foundation. These chapters are followed by three appendices: (A) Knowledge Area Description Specifications, (B) IEEE and ISO/IEC Standards Supporting the Soft-ware Engineering Body of Knowledge (SWEBOK), and (C) Consolidated Reference List. The bold chapter descriptions indicate the new chapters that have been added to version 4 of the standard from that of version 3. The new chapter (13) Software Engineering Models and Methods is of particular importance to the proposed paradigm of the work presented in this report.

3 Methodology

The proposed methodology was first published in Proceedings of the IEEE 35th International Conference on Software Engineering Education and Training [26] and an updated description is presented here. The education plan for this tertiary software engineering program will center on the application of practices that are derived from principles that are developed from learning theories [27]. Learning theories have evolved from studies of the way human beings acquire, assimilate, apply, and expand knowledge with studies that have been conducted in the domains of education, nursing, and psychology, among others. In the educational domain, the research has mostly focused on education at the elementary level. There are five (5) recognized theories of learning: behaviorism, cognitivism, constructivism, connectivism, and humanism. Connectivism theory is applied in this research as it relates to the era of digital learning and focuses on the facilitation of acquiring and sharing data using computer technology.

Figure 4, which is a derivative of aspects of the work contained in [28], depicts the educational framework of the program. Figure 4. Illustrates that the foundation of the design of this proposed program is based on theories (e.g. learning and body of knowledge). From these theories, a set of software engineering principles are identified. These principles are adhered to in the definition of software modeling techniques that will be taught in the program. The techniques are packaged into methods (e.g. software model analysis. These methods are assembled into a model-driven software engineering methodology for a comprehensive educational framework. Finally, tools are identified and selected that implement and support the selected methodology.

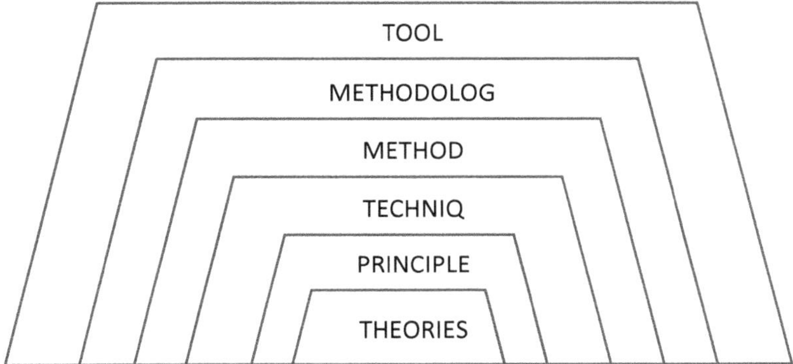

Fig. 4. Educational Framework of M.S. SE Program [28]

The program will be developed in a top-down/bottom-up hybrid approach, wherein the program outcomes are first defined, as described. The program outcomes will be analyzed, prioritized, and elaborated to establish objective evaluation of their necessity and sufficiency.

3.1 Object-Oriented Model-Driven (OOMD) SDLC

The Object-Oriented Model-Driven (OOMD) SDLC [26], at the heart of this pedagogical framework is presented in Fig. 5. This framework is intended to guide the students in understanding the software development life cycle (SDLC) and implicitly provide an understanding of how the processes are related within each phase of the SDLC. In Fig. 5, the SDLC is decomposed into five phases, namely: Requirements Engineering, High-Level Design, Low-Level Design, Detailed Design, and Implementation.

Students would be assigned a software specification for the course project, which would constitute the outcome from the Requirements Elicitation and Analysis phase. Additionally, students would not engage in activities from the phase of System Maintenance and Evolution, as their project work would end at the Implementation phase. Each phase of the SDLC framework is composed of a set of UML packages that have inter- and intra-relationships between the packages. These relationships may be of five types:

- input – self-explanatory,
- output – self-explanatory,

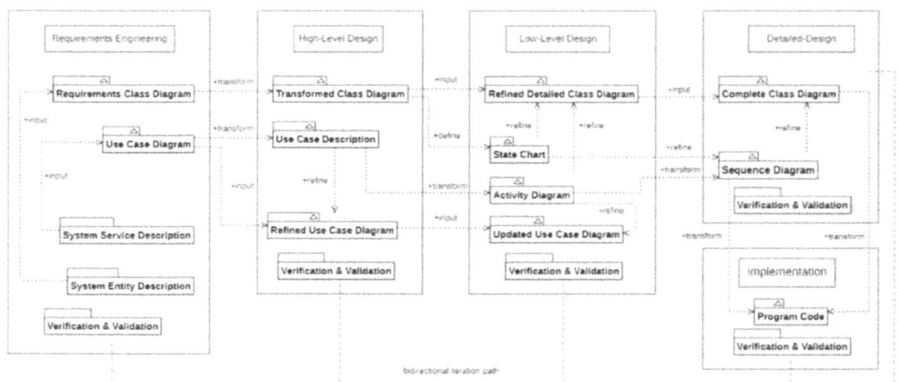

Fig. 5. An Object-Oriented Model-Driven Development Framework [26]

- define – a new component is derived from an existing one,
- refine – an existing component is enhanced with additional information and semantics, or restructured, and
- transform – an existing component is represented in a new form with additional semantics.

At each phase of the SDLC, verification and validation (V&V) may be conducted to assess the correctness of the work. The extent of the V&V exercise is determined by the criticality of the system under development. The work conducted in this pedagogical effort draws on best practices from academia and industry. With respect to determining the criticality of a system that is under development, guidance from the RTCA specification on aircraft onboard software system development, DO-178C [19] is employed in this framework.

3.2 SDLC Framework Model Development

The approach taken and documented in this report has been developed from over twenty years of teaching courses in SE at the graduate and undergraduate levels. The work focuses on designing an object-oriented, model-driven approach to SE education that incorporates industrial-strength development standards. This approach incorporates a set of best practices from the academic and industrial spheres, and packages them in a framework that is intended to address the previously identified challenges of providing 21st century education in software engineering education.

The common trends with software education are that they offer students a fulsome coverage of the main topics of software engineering that would be necessary and sufficient for courses at the tertiary-level of education. There is no prescribed software engineering technique for model development in most curriculum and this suggests a new pedagogical approach is needed in this area. Following is a prescribed process for the development of models in the model-driven objected-oriented framework of Fig. 5. This process provides a textual algorithm for construction the various models, along with a UML Activity Diagram that provides a graphical representation to enhance the students' comprehension of the process-approach to model development. This approach is one that was determined from students' feedback through course evaluation and efficacy of its application will be evaluated through a future series of comparative course evaluations.

3.2.1 UML Class Diagram Development

Identify candidate classes by answering the following questions in the affirmative:

- *Is this entity relevant?*
- *Can I uniquely identify this entity?*
- *Is this entity within the scope of the system?*

From the remaining entities identify candidate attributes, by answering the following questions in the affirmative:

- *Is this entity relevant?*
- *Is this candidate a property of a candidate class?*

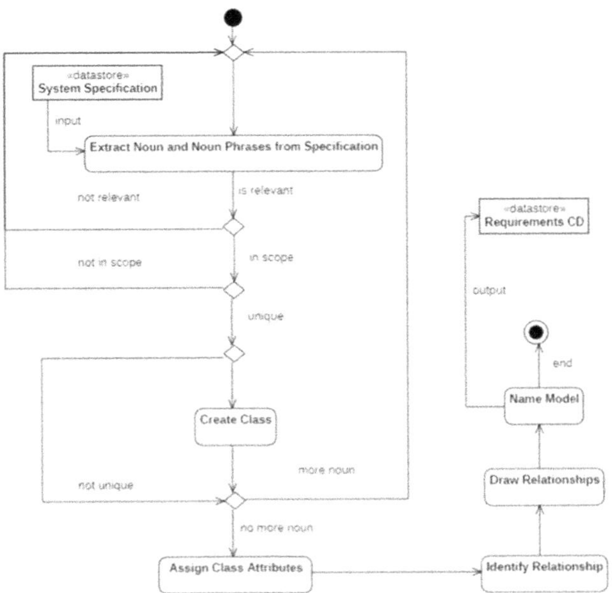

Fig. 6. UML Activity Diagram for UML Class Diagram Development

Draw the classes.
Identify relationships between the candidate classes, obtain from the specification.
Name the Class Diagram model.
Supplemental to the textual description for developing the UML Class Diagram is the UML activity Diagram of Fig. 6 for UML Class Diagram development.

3.2.2 UML Use Case Diagram Model Development

Extract verb/verb phrases from specification,
*   Identify candidate use cases,*

- *Is this entity relevant?*
- *Is this entity within the scope of the system?*
- *Is this entity at the highest level of abstraction?*
- *Decide name of use case*

    Identify candidate Primary users and Secondary users (external subsystems).

- *Candidate users are taken from the Class Diagram.*

    Draw the use cases,
    Identify relationships between candidate users and use cases,

- *Obtain from specification and customer.*

    Draw the relationships.

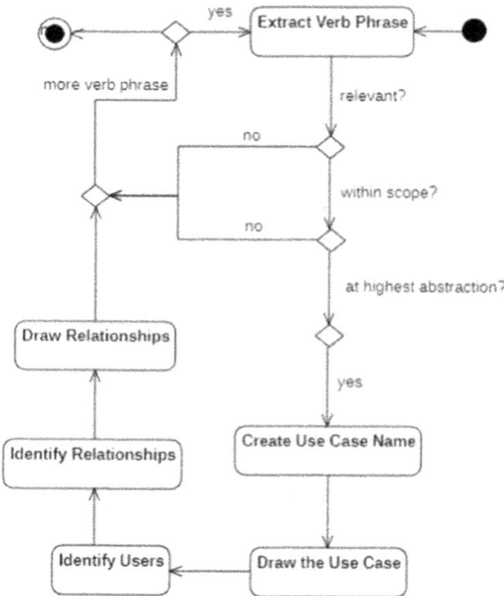

Fig. 7. UML Activity Diagram for UML Use Case Diagram Development

Supplemental to the textual description for developing the UML Use Case Diagram is the UML activity Diagram of Fig. 7 for UML Use Case Diagram development.

3.2.3 UML Use Case Description Model Development

For each Use Case (Oval) in the Use Case Diagram do:
*   Use the Use Case (Oval) name as the name for the Use Case Description (table).*

List the users of the Use Case.

Decompose the Use Case into a set of numbered(1, 2, 3...) high-level steps.

for the successful completion of the Use Case

For each numbered high-level step determine if there is an alternative

action/step, if there is, then:

List the alternative action/step as a numbered set of sub-action/step (1.1, 1.2, 1.3...)

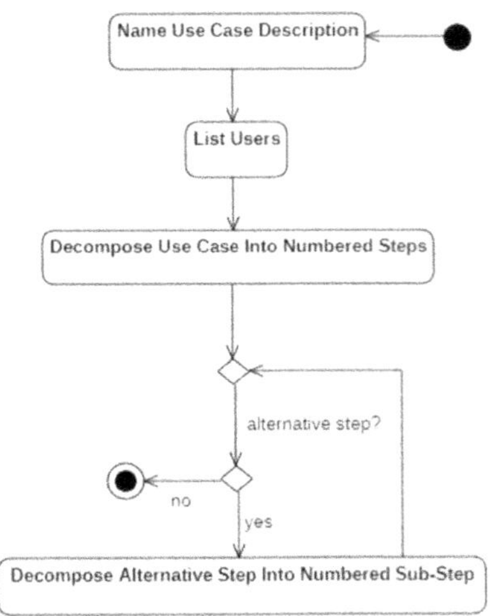

Fig. 8. UML Activity Diagram for UML Use Case Development

Supplemental to the textual description for developing the UML Use Case Description is the UML Activity Diagram of Fig.8 for UML Use Case Description development.

3.2.4 UML Activity Diagram Model Development

For each Use Case Description do:

Use the Use Case Description name as the name for the Activity Diagram.

For each Step of the Use Case Description draw an Activity Diagram Action.

Identify the Inputs and Outputs of each Action.

For each numbered alternative Step, specify an appropriate Guards, or Fork.

Conclude the Guard or Fork with Join.

If Use Case Description Step is complex.

Specify the Activity Diagram Action with the Compound Action iconDevelop an Activity Diagram for the Compound Action

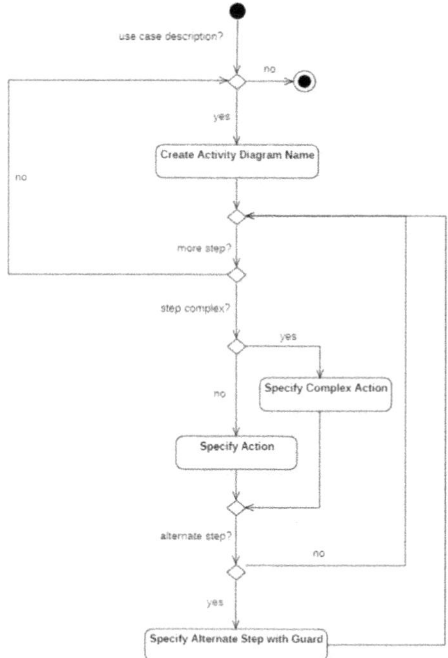

Fig. 9. UML Activity Diagram for UML Activity Diagram Development

Supplemental to the textual description for developing the UML Activity Diagram is the UML Activity Diagram of Fig. 9 for UML Activity Diagram development.

The framework as illustrated in Fig. 5, along with the Activity Diagrams of Figs. 6, 7, 8 and 9 illustrate the process through which starting with the UML Class Diagram and UML Use Case Diagram the other models, UML Use Case Description, Activity Diagram, and Sequence Diagram are instantiated through a series of the applied rules of definition, refinement, and transformation results in more correct and reliable code generation, through traceability, and validation and verification at each phase of the SDLC.

The derivation of the model-driven object-oriented framework of Fig. 5 and the derivation of the activity diagrams of Figs. 6, 7, 8 and 9 were achieved within the guidelines of the DO-178C specification. This approach allowed students to be transparently introduced to industrial standards and best practices. This approach involved transforming the DO-178C Specification and its associated documentation from its textual format to a graphical representation, which makes it more understandable and pragmatic for use by software developers. An example of one of the UML Package models developed during research with the DO-178C Specification is presented in Fig. 10, which illustrates the relationships of the main sections of the document. The purpose of this work with the DO-178C Specification is to introduce students to this industrial standard in a less complex format. Students can use a series of these DO-178C Specification graphical models to gain a high-level understanding of the specification's structural layout.

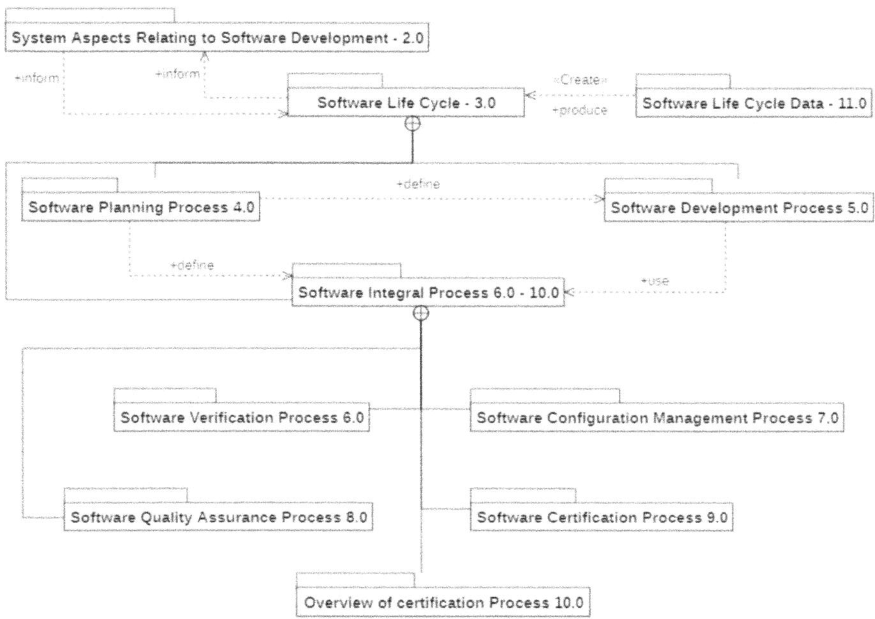

Fig. 10. UML Package Model of DO-178C Specification Chapters

In addition, the SWEBOK was used in designing the curricula of the courses in which this approach to software engineering education is being taught. This guide provides a playbook for software system development life cycle and beyond. This approach was taken to ensure that the courses would have a focus on educational goals and not an instructional seminar for industrial practices. Core to the courses is the teaching of fundamental educational theory and topics that are necessary for software engineering education; the educational goals as defined in SWEBOK are preserved in the courses' curricula.

3.3 Pedagogical Evaluation

A program for evaluating the efficacy of this educational model-driven object-oriented software development methodology is under development for usage when the first offering of this framework is incorporated into the relevant course curriculum. This evaluation program comprises students' objective and subjective evaluation questionnaire, objective comparative analysis of previous and current student assessment scores, and research of comparative course outcomes with similar programs. The outcome of the evaluation exercise will be use to modify the relevant course curricula as a part of the continuous course and program review and improvement cycle.

4 Conclusion

Over a 21-year period, students have been instructed in software engineering in a traditional manner that is strongly integrated in the structure and topics of the selected textbook for the course. This approach, while understandable for a new instructor in the discipline, has become stale and counter-productive to the students, who are much more engaged with multiple tool support for software development. Additionally, an instructor who is engaged in research in this area would have developed varied and different approaches to the software development life cycle strategies. Incorporating some of these new strategies in the curricula of tertiary education will be beneficial to the students' and the researcher/instructor's efforts. This report documents one such effort that is being benchmarked against a more traditional approach to software engineering education. A Longitudinal Study is being conducted to assess the benefit of this research-based versus traditional textbook approach to software engineering education. The report presents the effort and outcome of developing a model-driven object-oriented SDLC Framework that incorporates industrial standards and best practices for safety-critical software development.

A model-driven object-oriented software engineering life cycle development methodology was presented that incorporates industrial standards for safety-critical software system development. This paradigm is independent of tools and platforms, which facilitates it use in both academic and industrial environments. It may be used as-is for educational purposes and tailored with commercial tools for industrial use.

This report presented early work in applying industrial standards in a transparent way at the forefront of the SDLC, wherein software system requirement elicitation activities are enhanced with international accepted standards, towards the production of correct effective, efficient, and reliable software systems.

References

1. Prokop, L.E.: Historical aerospace software errors categorized to influence fault tolerance. In: IEEE Aerospace Conference, Big Sky, MT, USA, pp. 1–12 (2024). https://doi.org/10.1109/AERO58975.2024.10521061
2. New Denver Airport: Impact of the Delayed Baggage System: Briefing Report to the Honorable Hank Brown, U.S. Senate. United States, The Office (1994)
3. Leveson, N.G., Turner, C.S.: An investigation of the Therac-25 accidents. Computer **26**(7), 18–41 (1993). https://doi.org/10.1109/MC.1993.274940
4. The Federal Democratic Republic of Ethiopia Ministry of Transport And Logistics Aircraft, Accident Investigation Report B737- MAX 8, ET-AVJ, Report No. AI-01/19 (2022)
5. Committee on Transportation and Infrastructure (CTI) Final Committee Report the Design, Development & Certification of the Boeing 737 MAX, The U.S House Committee on Transportation & Infrastructure. (2020)
6. Shaw, M., Garlan, D.: Software Architecture: Perspectives on an Emerging Discipline. Prentice Hall, New Jersey USA (1996)
7. Shaw, S., Klein, D. V., Ross, T.: Revisiting abstractions for software architecture and tools to support them. IEEE Trans. Softw. Eng. (2025). https://arxiv.org/pdf/2503.04008

8. Grant, E.S.: Advancing object-oriented model-driven software engineering pedagogy. In: Proceedings IEEE 35th International Conference on Software Engineering Education and Training (CSEE&T), Tokyo, Japan, pp. 41–48 (2023). https://doi.org/10.1109/CSEET58097.2023.00015

9. ISO/IEC 19501:2005 Information technology – Open Distributed Processing – Unified Modelling Language (UML) Version 1.4.2 (2005)

10. Grant, E.S: Towards domain-specific modelling methodology for aeronautics and astronautics software systems, In: Proceedings IEEE International Conference on Electronics Technology (ICIE), Chengdu, China (2018)

11. Pastor, O., España, S., Panach, I., Aquino, N.: Model-driven development. Informatik-Spektrum **31**, 394–407 (2008)

12. Grant, E.S.: Pedagogical benefits from an exercise in reverse engineering for an aviation software systems. In: Proceedings 10th International Conference on Computer Supported Education (CSEDU), Madeira, Portugal. Springer, pp. 414–431 (2018)

13. Glass, R.L.: The Software-Research Crisis, IEEE Software. IEEE Computer Society Press, California, USA, vol. 11, no. 6, pp. 42-47 (1997)

14. Lions, J-L.: ARIANE 5, Flight 501 Failure, Report by the Inquiry Board, European Space Agency, Paris, France (1996)

15. Apel, S., Batory, D., Kästner, C., Saake, G.: Feature-Oriented Software Product Lines. Springer, Heidelberg (2013). https://doi.org/10.1007/978-3-642-37521-7

16. Metzger, A., Pohl, K.: Software product line engineering and variability management: achievements and challenges. In: Proceedings of Future of Software Engineering FOSE 2014, Association for Computing Machinery, NY, United States, pp. 70–84 (2014). https://doi.org/10.1145/2593882.2593888

17. Moser, M., Pfeiffer, M., Pichler, J.: Domain-specific modeling in industrial automation: challenges and experiences. In: Proceedings of the 1st International Workshop on Modern Software Engineering Methods for Industrial Automation. ACM, New York (2014)

18. Grant, E.: Defining Domain-Specific Object-Oriented Modeling Languages as UML Profiles: Dissertation. Colorado State University, Colorado (2002)

19. RTCA SC-205: Software Considerations in Airborne Systems and Equipment Certification: DO-178C. RTCA Inc., Washington DC, USA (2011)

20. RTCA SC-205: Software Tool Qualification Considerations: DO-330. RTCA Inc., Washington DC, USA (2011)

21. RTCA SC-205: Model-Based Development and Verification Supplement to DO-331 and DO-278A: DO-331, RTCA Inc., Washington DC, USA (2011)

22. RTCA SC-205: Object-Oriented Technology and Related Techniques Supplement to DO-178C and DO-278A: DO-332, RTCA Inc., Washington DC, USA (2011)

23. RTCA SC-205: Formal Methods Supplement to DO178C and DO-278A: DO-333, RTCA Inc., Washington DC, USA (2011)

24. RTCA SC-205: Supporting Information for DO-178C and DO-278A: DO-248C, RTCA Inc., Washington DC, USA (2011)

25. Washizaki, H. (ed.): Guide to the Software Engineering Body of Knowledge (SWEBOK®): Version 4.0. IEEE Computer Society, ISBN 978–0769551661 (2024)

26. Grant, E.S.: Advancing object-oriented model-driven software engineering pedagogy. In: Proceedings of the IEEE 35th International Conference on Software Engineering Education and Training (CSEE&T), Tokyo, Japan, pp. 41–48 (2023). https://doi.org/10.1109/CSEET58097.2023.00015

27. Gandhi, M.H., Mukherji, P.: Learning theories. In: StatPearls Treasure Island (FL): StatPearls Publishing, (2025)

28. Ghezzi, C., Jazayeri, M., Mandrioli, D.: Fundamentals of Software Engineering, 2nd edn. Pearson Publishing (2003)

PreciseRisk-LLM: Precise Component Risk Evaluation in Web Applications with LLMs

Rui Guo, Najinsha Hu, Jingfang Su, Jie Meng, Zihan Huang, and Guangjun Wen[✉]

University of Electronic Science and Technology of China, Chengdu, China
`wgj@uestc.edu.cn`

Abstract. The dependency hierarchy of modern web application components is becoming increasingly complex. Focusing solely on identifying risky components without considering their actual threat level often leads to numerous false alarms. Current mainstream supply chain analysis methods rely on static component scanning and Software Bill of Materials (SBOM) construction, using version information to match vulnerability databases to identify potential risk components. While this method can detect known vulnerabilities, it lacks analysis of runtime context vulnerability function call paths and data flow dependencies, making it impossible to determine whether vulnerabilities actually impact risk components when triggered. To address this, this paper innovatively combines dynamic analysis with static analysis to assess the actual reachability of vulnerabilities for the first time. By using bytecode instrumentation technology to monitor runtime call behavior in real time, we cross-validate static risk data with dynamic call records to precisely mark high-risk components that are actually triggered, effectively addressing the deficiency of missing vulnerability function call paths. Finally, we introduce large language model (LLM) to analyze risk component/method call graphs, further reducing false positive rates. To our knowledge, this is the first known method to achieve precise risk component analysis based on the impact of exposed interfaces in web applications. We name this method PreciseRisk-LLM and have successfully applied it to various risk types, including deserialization and Log4j. Experimental results demonstrate that PreciseRisk-LLM significantly outperforms single-identification methods, achieving optimal identification accuracy and providing a reliable basis for assessing the actual impact of risk components on web applications.

Keywords: Risk Components · Precise identification · Bytecode Instrumentation

1 Introduction

The software supply chain plays a crucial role in supporting the development and operation of web applications. Currently, all web applications contain pre-built components, which can be open-source components, third-party components, or components obtained by accessing external application programming interfaces (APIs), collectively forming the supply chain of web applications [1]. When web applications incorporate supply chain components, there is a high likelihood of security threats arising. If these are not

T. Dohi (Ed.): ICSED 2025, CCIS 2889, pp. 62–75, 2026.
https://doi.org/10.1007/978-981-92-0202-7_5

detected and controlled, attackers may exploit vulnerabilities in the components or APIs to gain access [2].

Currently, attackers often exploit this vulnerable node to carry out targeted breaches, thereby penetrating the entire supply chain network [3], resulting in the system lacking risk prediction capabilities [4] and being unable to make forward-looking predictions about supply chain attack paths. Mode leaves security protection in a risk-driven, reactive state. The industry currently adopts a single static scanning method to identify and mark risky components in the chain. The approach to security protection for such risks is to upgrade or replace the version [5]. However, this not only increases human and material costs but may also introduce additional risks of incompatibility between the new version and the existing system. Additionally, the propagation of risks is often influenced by the calling context, and we cannot confirm whether the risk component is actually called during application runtime [6]. For example, developers may have introduced input validation, sanitizer functions, or access control logic before calling. As a result, it is impossible to determine which risk components truly pose a threat to the system.

To address this issue, we propose a dynamic analysis method based on Java bytecode instrumentation technology to monitor risk interface invocation issues. This method can track deep dependency chains and the actual invocation status of dynamically loaded components, thereby determining the specific threat level of the risk component. Specifically, components identified as having vulnerabilities in the supply chain are defined as risk components. Next, we determine whether the risk component is actually called during the actual operation of the web application. If it is called, there is a risk; if it is not called, there may be no risk. To precisely identify actual risk paths and reduce false positive rates, this paper proposes introducing a LLM to identify cleaning behaviors in the call chain, combining it with a call graph to perform risk propagation semantic analysis, and comprehensively assessing the component's threat to the system based on the severity of the vulnerability and the scope of the call path.

2　Motivation

2.1　Problem Statement

Complex Supply Chains and Difficult Repairs. Current Java web applications face serious application layer security challenges, the root cause of which can be traced back to structural risks in modern software development models [7]. According to Synopsys' "2024 Open Source Security and Risk Analysis Report" [8], 936 code repositories were assessed for risk, with 84% of code repositories containing vulnerabilities and 74% containing high-risk vulnerabilities.

Figure 1 briefly shows the types of components introduced in the development process, including self-developed components, open-source components, and third-party components. Assuming that the vulnerability invades from one component and propagates in a single chain, the black part of the component in Fig. 2 is the impact of the vulnerability on other components and users. A vulnerability in one component may be triggered through the call path of another component [9], and the interdependencies among multiple components further complicate the risk chain.

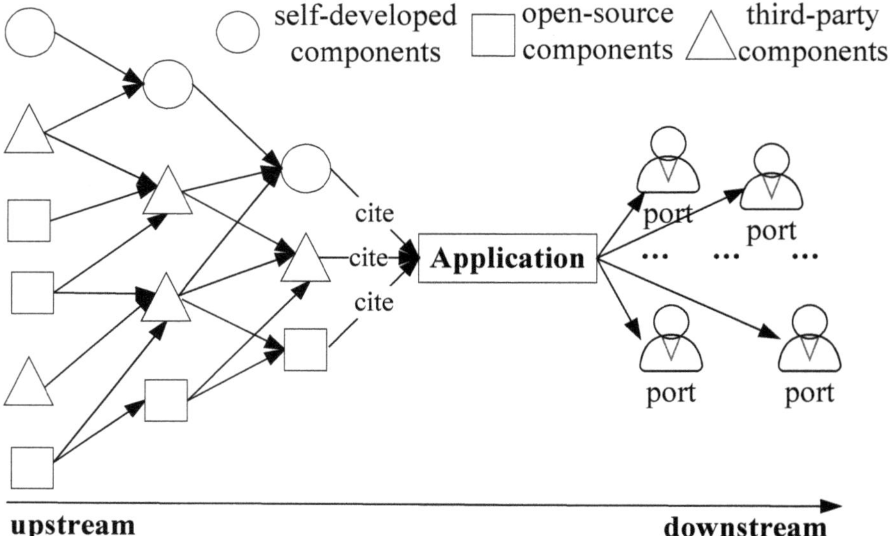

Fig. 1. Component structure of the application product

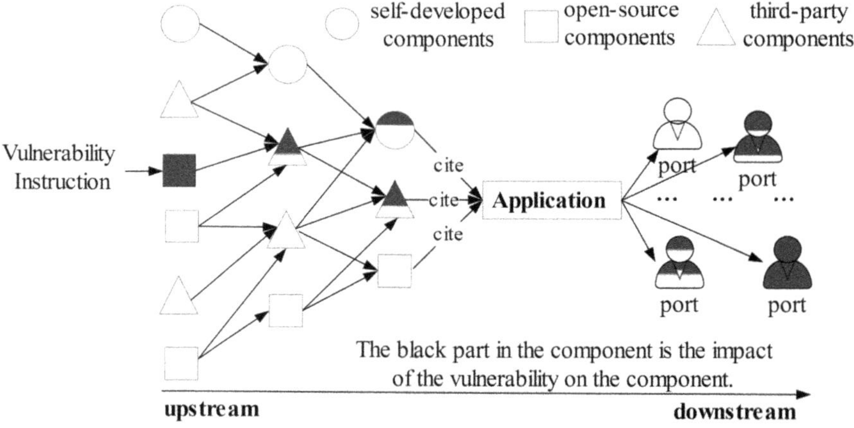

Fig. 2. Impact scope after vulnerability intrusion

Insufficient Accuracy. Existing Software Composition Analysis (SCA) tools can only generate a list of third-party components containing known vulnerabilities, but lack in-depth analysis of the actual usage scenarios of these components. Traditional SAST[10] technology can identify code modules containing vulnerabilities, but has a high false positive rate. DAST technology can verify the exploitability of vulnerabilities during system runtime, but its detection coverage remains limited [11]. Not all introduced risk components have a practical impact on the system; some components may only trigger vulnerabilities under specific conditions [12]. Leading to a significant misjudgment of risks in the existing assessment system: false positives may occur due to ignoring vulnerability trigger conditions [13], and false negatives may occur due to failing to detect high-risk call paths [14]. More seriously, detection mechanisms that rely solely on component version matching cannot construct sensitive and complete attack paths, nor can provide reliable advice to developers.

The LLM in recent years has opened up new possibilities. LLM can perform semantic analysis on function call sequences in source code or bytecode to identify whether vulnerability functions are explicitly or implicitly called [15], thereby determining whether the risk is actually achievable and reducing false positives caused by "missing call relationships"; On the other hand, LLM can combine contextual information for "conditional reasoning" to identify whether vulnerable functions are in "controllable branches" or "specific input trigger paths" [16], thereby uncovering deeper vulnerability trigger chains in multi-path scenarios and effectively reducing false negatives.

2.2 Proposed Solution

Risk Methods Invocation Detection. Accurately assessing the invocation status of risk methods can avoid unnecessary remediation efforts, reduce resource waste, and enhance visibility into supply chain risks. A complete logical flow diagram of the trigger invocation chain is shown in Fig. 3.

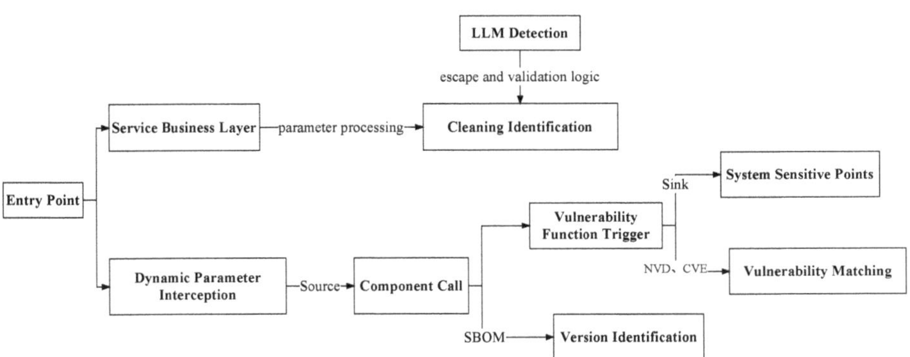

Fig. 3. Triggered Call Chain Logical Flow Diagram

Impact Scope Analysis. The impact scope of a risky component is typically not limited to direct calls to the component's methods or services but also involves multi-level dependency relationships, data flow transmission, and intertwined method call paths. Therefore, this paper introduces seven evaluation factors as shown in Table 1 defining their weights to comprehensively assess the extent of a risky component's impact on the system from multiple angles.

Table 1. Critical Factors and Weights.

Factor ID	Critical Factors	Weights
1	Critical Path Impact	30%
2	Sensitive Data Interaction	25%
3	External Control or Injection Risk	20%
4	Public Interface Exposure	15%
5	Lifecycle Management	5%
6	Coupling Analysis	2.5%
7	Logging and Exception Handling	2.5%

3   PreciseRisk-LLM

3.1   Overview

PreciseRisk-LLM consists of four stages. In the first stage, version information of components and dependent relationships is collected; Next stage, known vulnerabilities in components are identified and marked as risky component/functions/methods; The third, real-time monitoring of the runtime process is performed [17]; Finally, LLM is used to evaluate the call stack, as well as the data of risk functions and user input data, to determine the validity of the risk. The overall architecture is shown in Fig. 4.

3.2   Stage 1: Version Collect

This step is used to identify the version information of components in the supply chain. For projects built with Maven, the GroupId, ArtifactId, Version(GAV) information of dependencies is declared in the pom.xml file. Running the mvn:dependency:tree command will retrieve the entire dependency tree, providing a clear dependency relationship.

3.3   Stage 2: Component Vulnerability Scanning

Use SCA tools to analyze software components, compare version information in components with the vulnerability database, and identify components with vulnerabilities or locate the corresponding functions. Use SCA tools to scan files and collect information; components identified as having vulnerabilities are defined as high-risk components.

3.4   Stage 3: Real-Time Monitoring

This step is used for real-time monitoring after the Java Web application is running, and the bytecode is dynamically modified in the class loading stage through the Java Agent mechanism to realize the real-time security monitoring of the target class method.

Based on the instrumentation rules, the instrumentation points are responsible for recording the call context information, including the call stack, function parameters, and the interface name of the Web request, thereby precisely locating the path that triggers the risk interface, and provides basic data for subsequent risk assessment in Fig. 5.

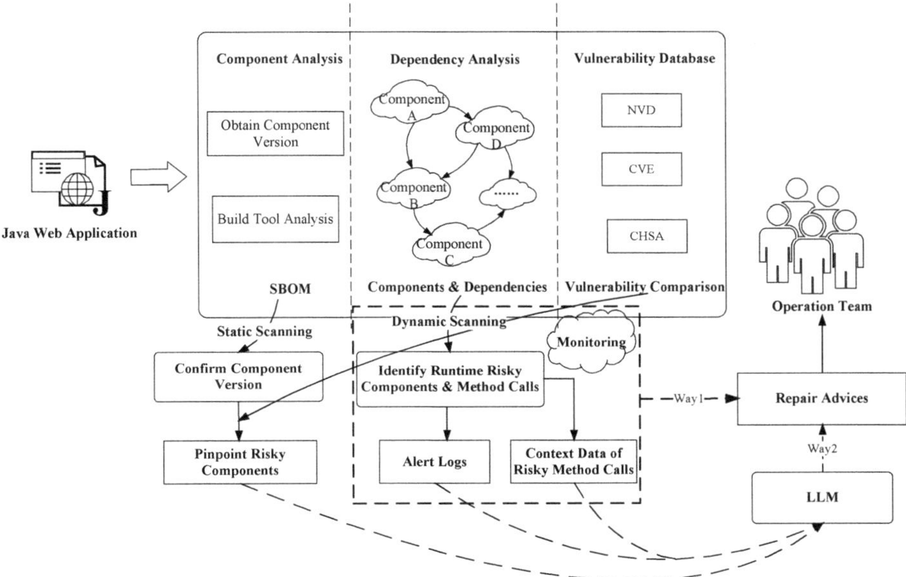

Fig. 4. Overall architecture of PreciseRisk-LLM

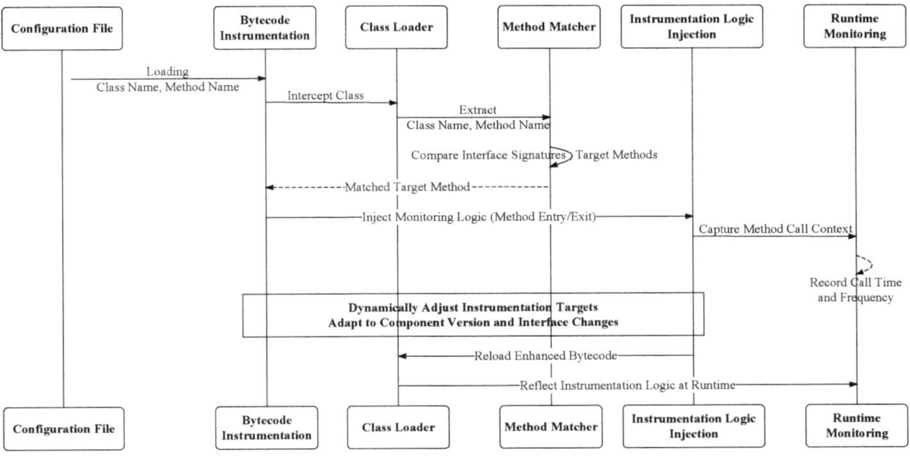

Fig. 5. Risk Interface Assessment Flowchart

3.5 Stage 4: LLM Analysis

In this stage, LLM is introduced to comprehensively analyze the results obtained in the first three stages, including component information, vulnerability types, call paths, and alert logs. Compared to traditional rules or static methods, LLM has advantages in handling complex dependencies, implicit call risks, and contextual reasoning, which can significantly improve the accuracy of vulnerability localization and the rationality of repair recommendations.

Relevant data such as component version information, included vulnerability types, alert logs, and risk component call paths are passed to the large model. Leveraging the data augmentation processing capabilities and automation level of the GPT-3.5 model, the model assesses whether risk components actually pose a threat and determines whether risks have been mitigated through sanitizer functions. Ultimately, the analysis results generated by the model provide decision support for security operations personnel. Additionally, by combining with runtime monitoring data, LLM can provide structured, verifiable support for risk level assessment and remediation recommendations. Thereby significantly reducing false positive rates and enhancing the effectiveness of risk assessment.

4 Experiments and Analysis

4.1 Dataset Construction

To evaluate the accuracy and reliability of the PreciseRisk-LLM, the experiment selected the Neo4j dataset provided by the Goblin [18] project. As of April 2025, it contained a total of 16.93 million nodes (including more than 710,000 libraries), covering the complete build and dependency relationships in Maven. The goblin_maven_30_08_24.dump dataset was used to search for component dependencies in Maven projects. The following rules were applied to the dataset used in the experiment:

1. Given a set of commonly used CVE vulnerability components;
2. Identify an upstream/downstream component of level 2 or higher that includes the aforementioned common components.

In this experiment, the test set was constructed using the "org.apache.logging.log4j:log4j-core" (hereinafter referred to as log4j-core)component. Its dependent components "commons:io:commons:io" (hereinafter referred to as commons.io) and "org.apache.commons:commons-lang3" (hereinafter referred to as commons-lang3) were introduced into the Maven project to conduct risk component call tests.

The system comprises four modules that work together to achieve vulnerability detection and risk assessment. The functional descriptions of each module are shown in Table 2. The collaborative call diagram is shown in Fig. 6.

Table 2. System Module Names and Functional Descriptions.

Modules	Function
Log4jAgent	Java Agent entry point, responsible for loading interceptors at startup and integrating full-process data
CallGraphInterceptor	Intercepts method calls, generates call paths, and locates vulnerability propagation links
LlmEvaluator	Integrates GPT-3.5, conducts semantic analysis on collected information, and determines vulnerability exploitability, risk levels, and repair suggestions
LoggingInterceptor	Intercepts log output content, extracts suspicious strings, and marks potential attack payloads

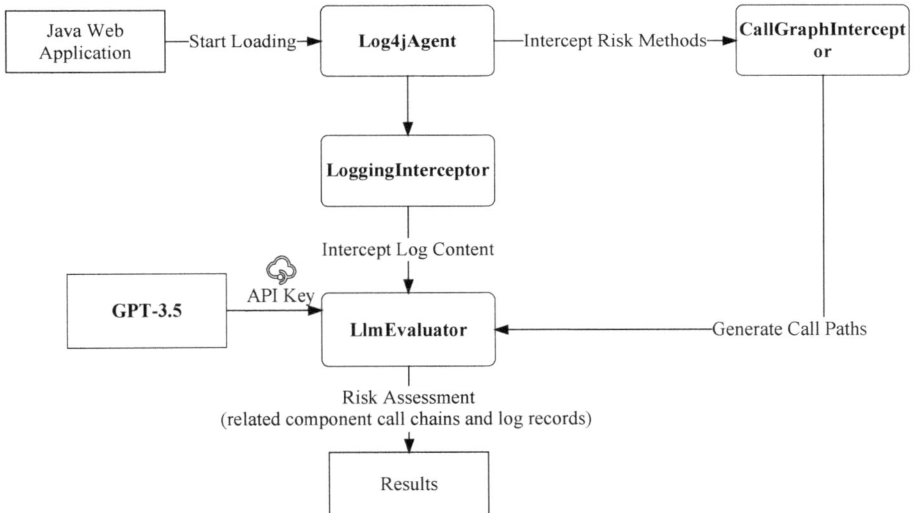

Fig. 6. Module Coordination Flowchart

4.2 Experimental Testing

To verify whether components actually participate in vulnerability propagation paths during runtime and whether there are scenarios with static dependencies but no dynamic risks, this paper designed three experimental scenarios. Taking the JNDI injection vulnerability actual impact.

JNDI Injection Vulnerability not Triggered. In this experiment, the test project only introduces the log4j-core component but does not call any methods of log4j-core. Instead, it calls relevant methods of its dependent component commons-lang3. During runtime, the [AGENT] logs output by the Java Agent show that only class loading and method calls for commons-lang3 are recorded, while no runtime behavior of the log4j-core component is detected, as shown in Fig. 7.

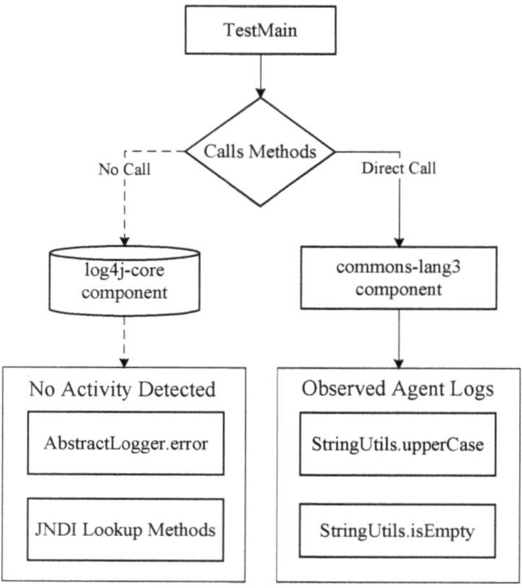

Fig. 7. Call Chain Information (1)

This result indicates that if no function path of the component is triggered during runtime, even though there is a static dependency, it is not active in the vulnerability chain. Therefore, it can be considered a "statically visible, dynamically risk-free" component, and it is recommended to assign it a lower risk level.

JNDI Injection Vulnerability Triggered and Dependent Component Methods Called. In the test code, log4j-core logging methods (such as Logger.error()) are called to trigger the JNDI injection point, while methods of the dependent components commons.io and commons-lang3 are also called. The call information is shown in Fig. 8. The [AGENT] message contains not only information about the log4j-core component but also information about the commons-lang3 and commons-io components.

From the [AGENT] output message, the system loaded and called the class methods of the log4j-core, commons-lang3, and commons-io. After the vulnerability is triggered, the call chain may further propagate to downstream components that collaborate with it. They participate in the transmission, concatenation, or execution of sensitive data and can be considered "potential risk propagation paths." Therefore, it is recommended to assess such components as "high risk" and increase the priority of runtime monitoring.

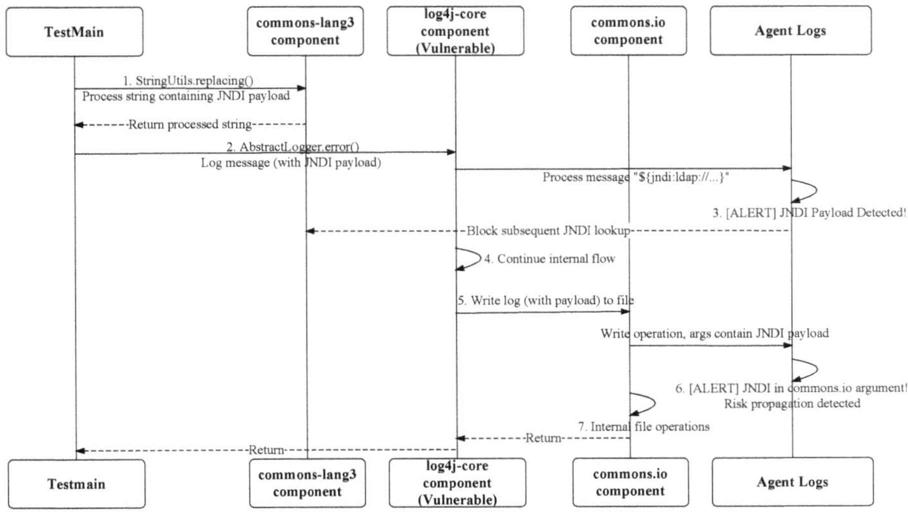

Fig. 8. Call Chain Information (2)

JNDI Injection Vulnerability Triggered but Dependent Component Methods not Called. Only dangerous functions in log4j-core were called in the test code, and no functions in any downstream components were called. The results are shown in Fig. 9. The [AGENT] message only records the method call information of log4j-core, and no related records of commons-lang3 or commons.io appear.

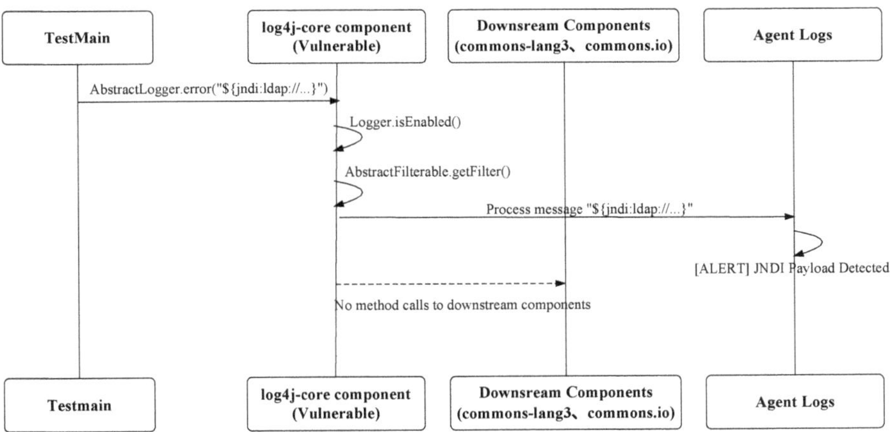

Fig. 9. Call Chain Information (3)

The phenomenon indicates that even if multiple dependent components are introduced into the project, components not involved in the runtime path do not pose an actual risk in vulnerability propagation. Operations personnel can classify such components as "low priority" during vulnerability response.

4.3 LLM Analysis

Taking the experiment "JNDI injection vulnerability triggered and dependent component methods called" as an example. Combining the call chain log information, the analysis process of the LlmEvaluator module is reflected in multi-stage collaborative reasoning. First, information fusion and association are performed to integrate multi-source data from the logs: the attack payload captured by LoggingInterceptor, the complete call chain generated by CallGraphInterceptor, and the component version extracted by Log4jAgent, forming a complete context for risk analysis. Based on this, the large model verifies the vulnerability exploitation chain through log parsing, confirming that the attack payload ${jndi:} is passed into FileUtils.writeStringToFile and ultimately triggers the JndiLookup.lookup method; Additionally, the call chain shows that user input is passed through file operations to the JNDI resolution process in Log4j, forming a complete attack chain that aligns with the exploitation characteristics of the CVE-2021–44228 vulnerability.

After LLM noise filtering and risk confirmation, the log entry "Error looking up JNDI resource" indicates that the vulnerability trigger attempt actually occurred, and no defensive measures were recorded to intercept it, thus ruling out the possibility of a "false positive" and confirming the authenticity of the risk. The final risk level assessment is completed. The LLM classifies log4j-core as "high risk"; simultaneously, commons.io is classified as "medium risk" due to multiple transmissions of attack payloads without any filtering logic.

4.4 Result Analysis

Leveraging the LLM context modeling and reasoning capabilities, the component risks are assisted in evaluation based on the seven influence dimensions outlined in Table 1, with the scoring results presented in Table 3.

Table 3. Risk Factor Scores for Different Components.

Factor/Weight Component	1	2	3	4	5	6	7	**Total**
	30%	25%	20%	15%	5%	2.5%	2.5%	
log4j-core	10	10	10	8	8	6	8	9.45
commons.io	4	6	3	6	8	3	5	4.80
commons-lang3	4	4	2	5	5	3	3	3.75

It is actually invoked during runtime, participates in sensitive log concatenation, and directly triggers the JNDI vulnerability. Therefore, it scores highly in dimensions such as "core path impact" and "external control risk," with a weighted score of 9.45, and is classified as a high-risk component. In contrast, commons.io and commons-lang3 have different call frequencies and levels of involvement in different scenarios, and are identified as medium-risk and low-risk components, respectively.

In the experimental scenario where the log4j-core component triggers a JNDI vulnerability. If the project does not call the functions (methods) of its dependent components, the downstream component can be considered low risk; if the project calls the functions (methods) of the downstream component, the downstream component can be considered high risk. For low-risk components, operations personnel can reduce the weight of monitoring; for high-risk components, operations personnel should increase the weight of monitoring.

4.5   Comparison with Existing Tools

Use the SCA tool to perform a full scan of the components dependent on Java Web applications. The tool parses information such as the pom.xml file, jar package metadata, and version numbers, and compares them with known vulnerabilities in the CVE database (NVD) to identify high-risk third-party components.

As shown in Fig. 10, the SCA tool detected seven main types of vulnerabilities in this project, two of which are high risk and the rest are medium risk. However, it can only detect vulnerabilities in the risky components and cannot determine whether these vulnerabilities can be exploited during runtime. For risk components invoked during the runtime of a web application, both PreciseRisk-LLM and SCA tools can detect the presence of the risk component. However, PreciseRisk-LLM relies on its instrumentation rules to record the components used during runtime and the methods entered, while SCA tools only rely on version information for identification. Therefore, PreciseRisk-LLM has higher accuracy. For risk components/methods that are introduced but not invoked, SCA tools can still detect the risk, which is a false positive, but PreciseRisk-LLM does not detect this risk. Therefore, PreciseRisk-LLM has higher precision.

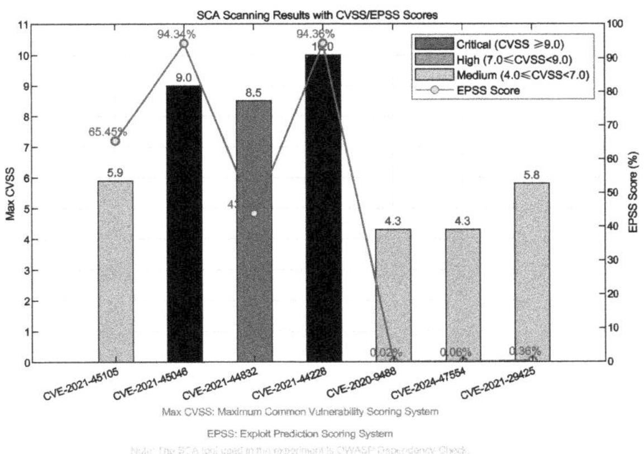

Fig. 10. SCA Scanning Results

5 Conclusion

This study successfully achieved precise detection and impact assessment of risk components in the software supply chain. We proposed and implemented an innovative method named PreciseRisk-LLM, which compared to traditional static or dynamic analysis tools, PreciseRisk-LLM significantly reduces false positive rates (e.g., for components that only introduce but do not call risky methods or only call secure methods) and can precisely locate risk trigger positions. By quantifying the severity of risks using a multi-dimensional weighted model, it provides clear guidance for operations personnel to prioritize high-risk threats, thereby optimizing the allocation of security remediation resources. Future work will focus on extending the method's ability to detect unknown vulnerabilities (0-day), incorporating threat intelligence and abnormal behavior analysis to further enhance proactive defense.

References

1. Kusrini, E., Anggarani, I., Praditya, T.A.: Analysis of supply chain security management systems based on ISO 28001: 2007: case study leather factory in Indonesia. In: 2021 IEEE 8th International Conference on Industrial Engineering and Applications (ICIEA), Chengdu, China, pp. 471–477 (2021)
2. Macy, J.: API security: whose job is it anyway? Netw. Secur. **2018**(9), 6–9 (2018). ISSN 1353-4858
3. Ahmad, H., Dharmadasa, I., Ullah, F., Babar, M.A.: A review on C3I systems' security: vulnerabilities, attacks, and countermeasures. ACM Comput. Surv. **55**(9), 1–38 (2023)
4. Vashisth, M., Verma, S.K.: State of the art different security challenges, solutions on supply chain: a review. In: 2023 International Conference on Innovative Data Communication Technologies and Application (ICIDCA), Uttarakhand, India, pp. 427–431 (2023)
5. Shen, Y., Gao, X., Sun, H., et al.: Understanding vulnerabilities in software supply chains. Empir. Softw. Eng. **30**, 20 (2025)
6. Xmirror Security: Software supply Chain Security White paper [EB/OL]. (2021–08–04)[2025–03–29].China Academy of Information and Communications Technology (2021)
7. Kim, S., Kim, R., Park, Y.B.: Software vulnerability detection methodology combined with static and dynamic analysis. Wirel. Pers. Commun. **89**, 777–793 (2016)
8. Xu, S., You, Y., Xiao, Y.: Research on the application of blockchain smart contract in software supply chain management. In: 2022 3rd Asia Conference on Computers and Communications (ACCC), Shanghai, China, pp. 78–83 (2022)
9. Synopsys: "Open Source Security and Risk Analysis Report 2024," [EB/OL]. (2024-03-12)[2025-03-29]. https://www.blackduck.com/content/dam/black-duck/zh-cn/reports/rep-ossra-2024-ch.pdf
10. Hu, X., Jiang, W.: Research on network host risk assessment method based on environmental risk level attack graph. In: 2022 International Conference on Informatics, Networking and Computing (ICINC), Nanjing, China, pp. 159–162 (2022)
11. Alqaradaghi, M., Nazir, M.Z.I., Kozsik, T.: Design and implement an accurate automated static analysis checker to detect insecure use of security manager. Computers **12**, 247 (2023)
12. Seth, A., Bhattacharya, S., Elder, S., et al.: Comparing effectiveness and efficiency of interactive application security testing (IAST) and Runtime Application Self-Protection (RASP) Tools in a Large Java-based System. arXiv:2023 (2023)

13. Safi, M., Dadkhah, S., Shoeleh, F., et al.: A survey on IoT profiling, fingerprinting, and identification. ACM Trans. Internet Things **3**(4), 1–39 (2022)
14. Ruan, B., Lin, Z., Liu, J., et al.: An accurate and efficient vulnerability propagation analysis framework. arXiv:2025(2025)
15. Feng, N., Wang, H.J., Li, M.: A security risk analysis model for information systems: causal relationships of risk factors and vulnerability propagation analysis. Inf. Sci. **256**, 57–73 (2014)
16. Ridoy, S.Z., Shaon Md, S.H., Cuzzocrea, A., et al.: EnStack: an ensemble stacking framework of large language models for enhanced vulnerability detection in source code. arXiv:2024 (2024)
17. Tete, S.B.: Threat modelling and risk analysis for large language model (LLM)-powered applications. arXiv:2024(2024)
18. Zenodo: Goblin:Neo4J Maven Central dependency graph. [EB/OL]. (2024-08-30)[2025–06–09]. https://zenodo.org/records/154815

Scenario-Based Exploratory Testing of Knowledge-Sharing Application: An Empirical Results and Lessons Learned

S. M. F. D. Syed Mustapha[1], Edmund Evangelista[1], Farhi Marir[1], Nor Shahida Mohamad Yusop[2]([✉]), and Wan Faezah Abbas[2]

[1] Information System and Technology Management, College of Technology Innovation, Zayed University, Dubai, UAE
{Syed.Duani,Edmund.evangelista,farhi.marir}@zu.ac.ae
[2] Faculty of Computer and Mathematical Sciences, Universiti Teknologi MARA, Shah Alam, Malaysia
{nor_shahida,wfaezah}@uitm.edu.my

Abstract. Exploratory testing is a supplementary software testing approach that complements other testing methods, including functional, regression, and performance, by exploring an application's functionality without predefined test scripts, allowing testers to leverage their creativity and intuition to uncover issues. This paper reports the results and insights derived from scenario-based exploratory testing performed on the KSECI, an online knowledge-sharing application. From the twelve features of the KSECI application, 88 scenarios were derived, simulating diverse user interactions and scenarios. The test results revealed that 48 test scenarios were passed, whilst 40 failed. Among the 40 issues identified, 26 were functionality issues (mostly rated as low severity), and 14 issues were associated with usability and interface design flaws. Given our limited resources, time constraints, and lack of profound product knowledge, we found scenario-based exploratory testing is effective, as it eliminates the necessity for detailed test scripts, enabling testers to focus on testing rather than documentation. This strategy is recommended in resource-limited environments, balancing structured testing with adaptive exploration to identify critical, user-impacting problems. The findings highlight the significance of exploratory testing in projects that requiring flexibility, offering a practical framework where traditional scripted methods may be impractical or time intensive.

Keywords: Exploratory Testing · Knowledge Sharing · Scenario-based Exploratory Testing · Software Testing

1 Introduction

Exploratory testing (ET) is a human-centered approach that emphasizes tester autonomy and flexible test design to enhance software quality. It complements conventional functional testing by uncovering defects that predefined test cases may miss [1]. While functional testing verifies software against specified requirements, ET leverages testers' domain knowledge and creativity to navigate complex systems, making it particularly effective in agile and iterative development environments [2]. Studies show that ET improves defect detection rates, especially for critical issues, with Itkonen et al. demonstrating that exploratory testers identified 28% more unique defects than scripted testing [3].

ET is increasingly preferred over conventional scripted testing due to the fast-paced nature of software development, where tight deadlines make extensive documentation and predefined test scripts impractical. In agile environments, rapid feedback is prioritized, making ET a flexible alternative that allows testers to adapt their strategies based on real-time insights [4]. It is especially useful when documentation is incomplete, enabling testers to explore high-risk areas and focus on usability issues, edge cases, and workflow integration flaws. The dynamic nature of software requirements, which often change due to business needs or user feedback, further necessitates ET. As noted by Kaner et al. [5], ET is well-suited for environments with frequently changing requirements, allowing testers to focus on critical functionalities even when formal specifications are lacking. Resource constraints, such as limited personnel and budget [3], also make ET advantageous, as it optimizes tester expertise and creativity while minimizing the need for extensive planning. As highlighted by [6], ET not only reduces the time spent on test preparation but also empowers testers to make informed decisions about where to focus their efforts, ultimately leading to more efficient use of available resources.

This paper presents results from scenario-based ET performed on the KSECI application, a collaborative platform designed to enhance knowledge sharing among employees through blogs, forums, chats, and file repositories. Although the KSECI application has undergone functionality testing, it may encounter several limitations and biases as the application was tested by the developer himself. Confirmation bias can lead developers to favor results that align with their expectations, while their close familiarity with the system may prevent them from identifying flaws or usability issues that external users would notice. Functionality testing might focus on verifying specific features like document upload or user authentication, but scenario-based ET enables testers to simulate real-world usage scenarios, such as a team collaborating on a project with varying access levels and document types. This approach not only discover usability issues that may not be evident through scripted tests but also provides insight into user behavior and system interactions, ultimately leading to a more robust application. As noted by Bach and Bolton [1], exploratory testing is particularly effective in situations where requirements are unclear, as it encourages testers to leverage their creativity and intuition to discover potential issues that could impact user experience.

The remainder of the paper is structured as follows: Sect. 2 reviews exploratory testing topics; Sect. 3 details the case studies and testing process; Sect. 4 reports the results; Sect. 5 discusses experiences, best practices, and lessons learned; and Sect. 6 presents conclusions.

2 Related Work

Recent literature contrasts ET with scripted testing by emphasizing its adaptability, reliance on tester expertise, and real-time test design. ET has been shown to outperform scripted approaches in environments where requirements are incomplete or frequently changing. Additionally, ET has gained increasing recognition in the field of software engineering as it evolves alongside agile methodologies and high-demand software development practices. One of the significant trends of ET is in terms of the software development methodologies. Manukonda's [7] case study highlights the importance of integrating ET within agile development methodology, contributing to the responsiveness and communication between team dynamics and the overall product quality success. Neri supported this through his research on ET utilizing SCRUM. Neri [8] suggested that ET can provide deeper insights into system functionality, aiding in the design of other testing techniques and thereby enhancing the overall testing process used in industries that adopt SCRUM. Additionally, the dynamic nature of ET is further elaborated upon by Puranik [9], who reviews its iterative processes that allow testers to concurrently learn and execute test designs. This article provides a thorough exploration of the foundations, advantages, and challenges posed by ET. By fostering the strengths of tester creativity and domain knowledge, ET emerges as a robust method for identifying hidden software defects.

A trend has also been observed towards utilizing gamification in ET. Straubinger and Fraser [10] explore how gamification can engage developers in exploration unit testing directly within Integrated Development Environments (IDEs). Their work highlights the potential for making testing processes more engaging while seamlessly integrating it into regular coding tasks.

Mårtensson et al. [11] provide insights into efficient ET strategies for large-scale software systems, emphasizing the necessity for effective organization of testing efforts to enhance accountability and documentation. This aligns with findings by Yu et al. [12] that explore the present state of ET, highlighting existing problems and prospective future directions for the methodology, thus reinforcing its relevance in modern software development.

Leveau et al. [13] and Martino et al. [14] address the diversification of ET strategies. Leveau et al. emphasizes the role of business expertise in conducting ET for web applications, while Martino et al. examines the effects of different tester dynamics exploratory testing strategies in GUI environments, suggesting that variations in tester performance can significantly impact the effectiveness of exploratory practices.

In summary, research on ET emphasis on the importance in agile development, the need for structured training and the adoption of innovative practices such as gamification to enhance tester engagement. There is a clear recognition of ET as an essential additional to the traditional testing process. This would promote learning and flexibility, fostering discoveries and adaptability in the fast-evolving landscape of software development. The intersection of these concepts offers valuable insights for researchers and practitioners alike, signaling a need for ongoing exploration of the methodologies that support quality assurance in contemporary software.

3 Methods

This research examines the scenario-based exploratory testing sessions conducted for KSECI Knowledge Sharing tool. The following sections describe the system under test, test process flow, defect classification, and test documentation in more detail.

3.1 System Under Test

The KSECI Knowledge Sharing Application is a comprehensive platform designed to streamline the sharing and acquisition of knowledge in organizations. It offers a suite of features that cater to various user types, including Super Admins, Admins, Group Leaders, and Ordinary Users, facilitating collaboration, learning, and effective information dissemination. Users can engage in knowledge sharing through a wide range of tools, such as blogs, forums, chats, and in-app browser, while maintaining a structured environment for both self-registration and administrator-controlled account creation.

Key functionalities such as group creation, user management, and report generation make this app a one-stop knowledge hub. The app also integrates Artificial Intelligence (AI) capabilities for seamless content relevancy checks, hate speech moderation, and automated report generation, making it ideal for managing both human-generated and AI-curated knowledge. Whether it's through interactive discussions or accessing AI-checked content, the KSECI app fosters a collaborative environment for knowledge exchange, critical thinking, and innovation. The app is built to simplify knowledge sharing in organizations by addressing the need for collaborative spaces where users can upload files, generate AI-enhanced libraries, engage in discussions, and track organizational knowledge activities. It also ensures transparency and accountability by generating detailed reports on SECI (Socialization, Externalization, Combination, and Internalization) activities, tracking knowledge leaders, and providing insights into user interactions. The application also emphasizes the safety of content with automated checks for relevancy and offensive language, ensuring that all shared knowledge aligns with the organization's goals and values. In total there were 12 features in KSECI application.

3.2 Test Process Flow

Figure 1 depicts the flow chart for executing the scenario-based exploratory tests, starting with an analysis of system requirements to understand expected functionalities, user interactions, and potential defect risks. This analysis leads to a system walkthrough, which familiarizes testers with workflows and interfaces, helping identify discrepancies between documented requirements and actual behavior. Once the system is understood, the test charter is created to outline the objectives and focus areas of the ET session, providing structure while allowing flexibility for unexpected issues. After preparing the test charter, testers actively explore the system, simulating user behavior to uncover defects. In contrast to conventional ET where testers dynamically design and execute tests based on their understanding of the application, scenario-bases ET involves predefined scenarios that simulate real-world use cases guiding testers through specific paths and interactions within the application. Scenario-based ET ensures that critical user journeys are thoroughly tested, providing a structured framework that can be replicated and measured. As scenario-based ET is more systematic and focused on user-centric scenarios, this approach benefits to uncover usability issues and functional defects.

Table 1 is an example of a test charter produced during exploratory testing. The design of test charters and test scenarios are based on the following key testing priorities:

1. Core functionalities such as blogging, forum and SECI activities scores are tested under diverse input conditions and combination.
2. User interactions are assessed via role-based workflows (e.g., ordinary user, group leader, super admin, and admin) to verify intuitive navigation, logical process sequencing, and task completion efficiency.
3. Ease-of-use evaluation is focused on the UI/UX elements like dashboard clarity, search/ filter responsiveness, visual components, accessibility, and information organization.
4. Error handling mechanisms is examined through intentional misuse cases, including invalid data entries, unauthorized access, and recovery guidance.

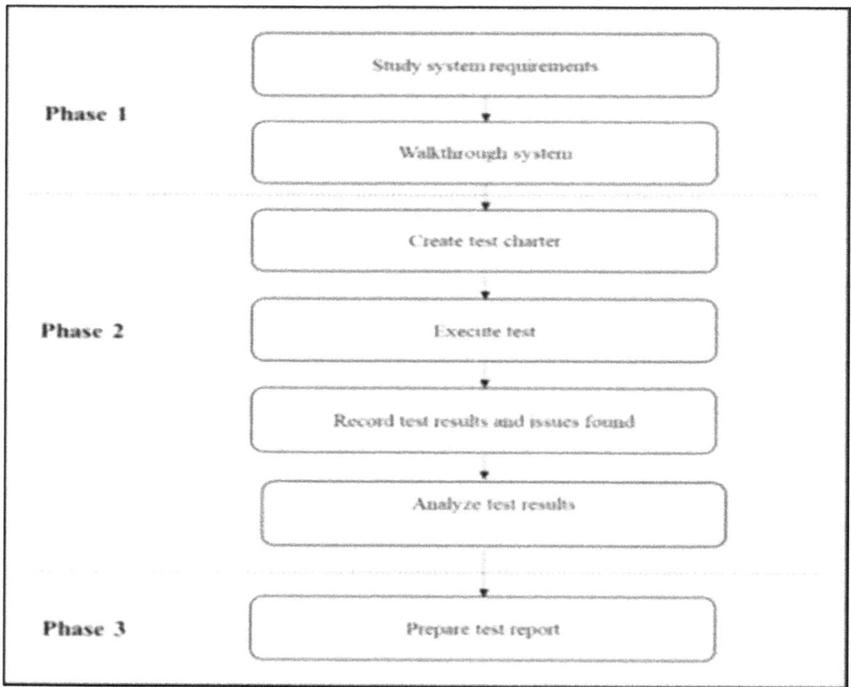

Fig. 1. Scenario-based exploratory testing process flow

The test results are recorded in a Google Drive log for real-time updates, allowing remote software developers to track test execution, results, and issues, which aids in quality control and debugging. This central repository keeps developers informed about test statuses, enabling them to address defects while other scenarios are tested. After

Table 1. Example of test charters form for Forum Features of KSECI application

Test Charter F1	
Objectives	Validate blog feature of KSECI system
Scenario/ scope	1. Create a new blog and submit one post to the group that is assigned to the user 2. Create a new blog and submit one post to the group that is NOT assigned to the user 3. Login as ordinary user and access/ view blog list. Try to view blogs that do not belong to your group 4. Login as ordinary user and view blog that does not belong to your assigned group. Then reply to a comment 5. Login as group leader and post a blog 6. Login as ordinary user and edit blog. Repeat for other users 7. Login as ordinary user and delete your own blog post. Repeat for the users 8. Login as Group Leader and attempt to delete other users' blog post
Test URL	https://knowledgest-ai.netlify.app/
Test Date	20 September 2024
Tester	Nor Shahida Mohamad Yusop
Expected Outcome	Expected output when the scenario will be executed
Actual Outcome	Actual output when the system is executed
Observation	Provide the annotated screenshot to explain the actual outcome and issue (if any)
Test Status	Passed/ failed/ blocked
Remarks	Provide any suggestion for improvement

testing, an analysis is performed to assess the severity of issues, prioritize defect resolution, and inform stakeholders about system quality. Comprehensive documentation of all test cases, results, and issues is maintained for future reference and continuous improvement.

3.3 Test Documentation

Test documentation is essential for communication and quality assurance, allowing software development teams to validate software systematically and provide visibility into testing outcomes. For the KSECI application, we produced lightweight documentation that balances practicality and detail, consisting of two main artifacts:

1. **Test Logs**: An Excel spreadsheet used by testers to record test scenarios, update test statuses, and report defects. Developers also use this spreadsheet to track defect fix statuses.
2. **Software Test Report (STR)**: This report focuses on functionality testing and includes: (1) system overview, (2) project references, (3) summary of test results,

(4) detailed test results and defects, and (5) a traceability matrix linking requirements to test cases. Each test entry contains:

- **Test Identification**: A unique identifier in the format (e.g., T1_F1_01).
- **Test Scenario**: A description of the actions and situations for testing.
- **Expected Outcome**: The ideal result after executing the test case.
- **Actual Outcome**: Observations from the test execution under specified conditions.
- **Test Status**: Results categorized as Passed, Failed, or Blocked.
- **Remarks**: Additional comments on issues observed, reproduction steps, and suggestions for fixes.

3.4   Defect Classification

During the test analysis, the defects were labeled and categorized in different defect types and severity levels. The severity levels were set by the defect reporters from the viewpoint of what the severity of the defect is for the customer. The definitions of severity used in this testing are listed in Table 2. Severity level 1 is considered as the most critical issue while level 6 is the lowest with the enhancement request that do not block the test execution.

The defects are also categorized according to the type of defect, as suggested by Itkonen [15]. Table 3 describes the definition of each defect category with examples that have been modified slightly to match the defects found when testing the KSECI application [15, 16]. The label "None" in column "Example" indicated that there was no such defect type discovered during our exploratory testing.

Table 2. Definition of defect severity level.

Severity Level	Definition
1	Show stopper/ Unusable for over 10% of users
2	Urgent/ Unusable for some users
3	High/ Impairment, bad workaround
4	Medium/ Workaround exists
5	Low/ Inconvenience or annoyance
6	Small/ enhancement

Table 3. Defect category and examples.

Defect Type	Description	Example
Documentation	Defects in user manual, and requirements document	None

(continued)

Table 3. (continued)

Defect Type	Description	Example
User interface	Defects in user interface such as undesirable behavior in text, screen display, missing icons or menu, and inappropriate error message	The "member" section is empty. No information is displayed under this section regardless of whether "My Information", "Organization" or "Groups" option is selected
Inconsistency	Functions exhibiting inconsistent behavior	None
Functionality	Defects due to missing functionality, incomplete function or wrong function	The filtering does NOT work, it lists the groups of ALL organizations, regardless of the Organization it is created from
Performance and reliability	Defects resulting in reduced performance of the system	None
Technical	Defects attributed to application crash, technical error or runtime exception	None
Enhancement	Issue that could be done in a better way even though the current solution also works ok	Currently, the user can only submit 1 file to one group at one time. If the user wants to upload the same file to three different groups, they have to do the same process three times. Is there any possibility that users will upload the same file to several different groups?
Usability	Defects resulting in undesirable usability issues	When selecting My Information menu, the dashboard displays confusing information. Is My Information referring to individual Admin information or all information in the database?

4 Results and Discussion

4.1 Scenario-Based Exploratory Test Cases

The scenario-based exploratory testing for the KSECI application evaluated 12 distinct features, focusing on content creation, user interaction, and system management to ensure seamless functionality and user satisfaction. Each feature underwent rigorous testing, with Table 4 summarizing the derived test cases. Notably, the Upload Files feature had the highest number of test cases, with 15 distinct scenarios, emphasizing its complexity and importance in handling various file types, sizes, and user permissions, which directly impacts data integrity and user satisfaction.

Following the Upload Files feature, the Blog and Group Creation and Management features each had 11 test cases. The extensive testing of the Blog feature highlights its role in enabling users to create and share content, essential for user engagement. Similarly, thorough testing of the Group Creation and Management feature is crucial for effective administrative control and organization within the application, ensuring smooth user and group management.

In contrast, the In-App Browser and SECI Activities Scores features had fewer test cases. The In-App Browser allows users to access web content without leaving the application, resulting in minimal testing effort. The SECI Activities Score feature, which is exclusive to Super Admins for managing points, also required fewer test cases. However, each of these tests involved more extensive procedures to ensure thorough execution, maintaining the application's standards of functionality and administration even for less complex features.

Table 4. The number of derived test cases for each feature.

Feature	Number of test cases	Sample of Exploratory test scenario
F1- Blog	11	• Create a new blog and submit to the group that is NOT assigned to the user
		• Login as ordinary user. Go to General activities and take notes of the number of forums created. Filter the forum using the author's name and confirm the number display on the dashboard is correct
F2 - Forum	8	• An ordinary user submits a new forum to the group that is not assigned to the user
		• Create a forum with bad words and resubmit the forum without bad word
F3 - Chat	4	• Create a conversation between members in the group
		• Send messages and chat with another user
F4 – In App Browser	3	• From the blog, access to URL link or from the In app browser, paste the URL link
		• Entering URL to access websites from the In app browser

(*continued*)

Table 4. (*continued*)

Feature	Number of test cases	Sample of Exploratory test scenario
F5 – Report Generation	6	• Generate Report Based on Organization & groups under the organization
		• Generate Report by Blog, Forums, Browsing History, Chats, Topics, Resources
F6 – SECi activities Scores	3	• Update Score under Combination
F7 - Feedback	6	• An ordinary user submits feedback to the group that is not assigned to the user
		• View feedback using different filter options
F8 - Categories	4	• Create Category - Give Category Name - Select group (in this case we select ProductSupport)
F9 – Upload Files	15	• Ordinary User upload file - then Group Leader Edit the file information before changing the file status
		• Change the group to other groups that is assigned to the user. Then update your own files uploaded
F10- Group Creation and Management	11	• Create new group for organization - Create new users – Add the new users to a new group and assign the new users as group leaders
		• Create new Admin with new organization
F11 – Group Leader Menu	7	• Create and update bad words. Add forum with bad word (use title case word)
		• Attempt to add new words that had existed in the library
F12 -General Activities Dashboard	10	• View members of each group in "Groups and Leaders" section
		• Observe information for different selection levels - My Information, Organization, and Groups

4.2 Defect Count

The results of the scenario-based exploratory testing provided a thorough evaluation of the KSECI application, with a total of 88 test cases executed. The defect counts are summarized in Table 5, which lists the defects for each feature. Out of 88 test cases, 48 passed and 40 failed, indicating areas that require attention. Among the failed cases, 17 issues were rated as severity level 5, while two major defects, rated as severity level 2, were found in KSECI-related features (See Table 6). These defects affect the accuracy of KSECI calculations, preventing further testing until the software developers resolve the issues.

The Upload Files and General Activities Dashboard features had the highest number of issues, with seven each, likely due to the extensive test cases designed for these features, which increases the chances of identifying defects. This suggests that broad test coverage enhances testing efficiency and positively impacts test density. Other features, such as the Blog, Forum, and Group Creation and Management, each revealed five issues.

The Group Leader Menu feature achieved the highest passing rate, with only one failure out of seven test cases due to a word case sensitivity issue in word management, demonstrating its overall robustness. In contrast, the SECI Activities Scores feature had the lowest passing rate, with two out of three test cases failing. Despite its smaller size, the complexity of SECI computation necessitates a detailed examination of interrelated features, highlighting the need for focused testing.

Table 5. Defect data summary.

Features	Number of test cases	Test Status		Passing rate (%)
		Passed	Failed	
F1 – Blog	11	6	5	54.55
F2 – Forum	8	3	5	37.50
F3 – Chat	4	3	1	75.00
F4 – In App Browser	3	2	1	66.67
F5 – Report Generation	6	3	3	50.00
F6 – SECi activities Scores	3	1	2	33.33
F7 - Feedback	6	4	2	66.67
F8 - Categories	4	3	1	75.00
F9 – Upload Files	15	8	7	46.67
F10- Group Creation and Management	11	6	5	54.55
F11 – Group Leader Menu	7	6	1	85.71
F12 -General Activities Dashboard	10	3	7	70.00
	88	**48**	**40**	**57.95**

4.3 Defect Types and Severity

Defects were classified by severity and type, as shown in Tables 6 and 7. The analysis reveals that severity level 5 defects are the most prevalent, constituting a significant portion of the total. Although classified as trivial or minor, their volume can adversely affect user experience, leading to decreased satisfaction, increased support costs, and potential damage to the software's reputation. Severity levels 3 and 4 account for 9 and 8 issues, respectively, representing moderate defects that more directly impact usability.

In terms of defect type, the highest number of functionality defects were found in the Blog and Upload File features (see Table 7), indicating that real-world scenarios can reveal additional issues not consistently replicated during system testing. Minimal defects were noted in user interface and enhancement areas, suggesting effective management in those domains. Since the exploratory test was focused on functionality, issues related to documentation, inconsistency, performance and reliability, technical and localization were not found.

Table 6. Distribution of defects according to defect severity level.

Features	Number of Failed Cases	Severity level					
		1	2	3	4	5	6
F1 - Blog	5	0	0	1	0	4	0
F2 - Forum	5	0	0	2	0	3	0
F3 - Chat	1	0	0	0	1	0	0
F4 – In App Browser	1	0	0	1	0	0	0
F5 – Report Generation	3	0	1	1	1	0	0
F6 – SECi activities Scores	2	0	1	0	1	0	0
F7 - Feedback	2	0	0	0	2	0	0
F8 - Categories	1	0	0	0	0	1	0
F9 – Upload Features	7	0	0	3	1	2	1
F10- Group Creation and Management	5	0	0	0	0	3	2
F11 – Group Leader Menu	1	0	0	0	0	1	0
F12 -General Activities Dashboard	7	0	0	1	2	3	1
	40	**0**	**2**	**9**	**8**	**17**	**4**

Table 7. Distribution of defects according to defect types.

Features	Number of Failed Cases	Defect Type			
		UI	Func	Us	Enh
F1 - Blog	5	0	4	1	0
F2 - Forum	5	0	2	3	0
F3 - Chat	1	0	1	0	0
F4 – In App Browser	1	0	1	0	0
F5 – Report Generation	3	0	3	0	0
F6 – SECi activities Scores	2	0	2	0	0
F7 - Feedback	2	0	2	0	0
F8 - Categories	1	0	1	0	0
F9 – Upload Features	7	0	4	2	1
F10- Group Creation and Management	5	1	3	1	0
F11 – Group Leader Menu	1	0	1	0	0
F12 -General Activities Dashboard	7	2	2	3	0
	40	**3**	**26**	**10**	**1**

UI – User Interface, Func – Functionality, Us – Usability, Enh - Enhancement

Cross-analysis of defect severity and type, illustrated in Fig. 2, shows severity level 5 is prevalent in both functionality and usability defects, indicating a significant impact on user experience and system performance. Despite prior functionality tests, scenario-based exploratory testing uncovered numerous new defects. Specifically, 8 out of 26 functionality defects were classified as severity level 3, and 9 as severity level 5, while 8 out of 10 usability defects were also rated as severity level 5. Although these defects are minor, they can lead to user frustration by consistently obstructing tasks and hindering optimal system usage. Examples of these defects are detailed in Table 3.

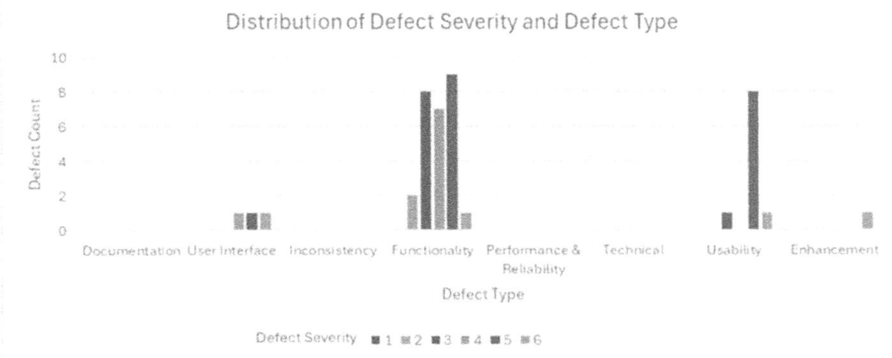

Fig. 2. Distribution of defect severity level and type of defects.

4.4 Discussion

This paper presents findings from scenario-based exploratory testing (ET) conducted on the KSECI application, an online knowledge-sharing system. The application facilitates knowledge sharing among software development teams while computing employee performance indicators based on Socialization, Externalization, Combination, and Internalization activities [11]. Scenario-based ET was chosen due to time and resource constraints that made exhaustive test case development impractical. This approach allows testers to spontaneously decide which features to test, reflecting end-user interests. As Bach [1] notes, exploratory testing combines learning, test design, and execution. Given the complexity of feature interactions and unpredictable user behavior, it is unfeasible to create comprehensive test cases for all scenarios [12, 13]. Additionally, exploratory testing encourages creative problem-solving and innovative exploration of system functionalities.

During the ET of KSECI, we explored various methods, including session-based exploratory testing, functional testing for individual features, exploratory smoke testing, exploratory regression testing, subcontracted exploratory testing, scenario-based exploratory testing, and freestyle exploratory testing, each offering unique benefits. Our approach focuses on functional scenario-based exploratory testing to maximize coverage. This was crucial due to the lightweight documentation of the application's requirements. While functional tests verify individual features, they may overlook critical aspects like feature interaction and usability. Our strategy began with a thorough examination of the application's requirements, leading to the development of scenarios that reflect end-user roles. For example, testing the blog and forum creation features revealed that modifications to the word library caused the submit button in forum forms to freeze, highlighting the importance of exploring feature interactions.

From the scenario-based ET, we derived 88 test cases across 12 features, with 48 passing and 40 failing. Most issues were rated low severity, primarily related to system functionality errors due to untested feature interactions. Other issues included user interface and usability concerns, which, despite their low impact, require attention to maintain software quality. Our scenario-based ET strategy effectively uncovered new defects, and we identified several best practices for conducting scenario-based ET:

1. **Comprehensive System Study**: Testers should study the entire system to understand feature interactions, building a holistic mental model that helps identify emergent behaviors and potential integration-level defects.
2. **Use of Checklists**: Operationalize foundational knowledge through checklists to track testing needs, mitigating cognitive biases and ensuring coverage while allowing for creativity.
3. **Test Charters**: Create lightweight test charters as flexible guides that balance structure with adaptability.
4. **Integration of Techniques**: Employ boundary value analysis (BVA) and equivalence partitioning (EP) to systematically validate input fields, addressing critical gaps in exploratory approaches. Research shows that 60–70% of input-related defects occur at boundary conditions, making these techniques essential [15].
5. **Negative Scenarios**: Develop negative scenarios alongside positive workflows to enhance robustness, as exploratory testing excels at simulating "unhappy paths" that reveal improper error handling and security flaws [16].
6. **Error Message Testing**: Test error messages to improve usability and security, aligning with usability heuristics that emphasize actionable error recovery.
7. **GUI Consistency**: Ensure the graphical user interface (GUI) is consistent and aligns with user mental models to mitigate usability risks, as inconsistent designs can increase defect likelihood. According to Lazar & Greenidge [17] found that inconsistent form designs disrupted user expectations, increasing defect likelihood by 30%.
8. **Examine Complex Logic**: Leverage ET's iterative probing to uncover hidden issues in complex business logic and computational features.
9. **Fault Injection**: Deliberately introduce errors to assess system resilience, validating exception handling in mission-critical systems.

These strategies collectively enhance defect detection rates and ensure the software aligns with real-world usage, particularly in agile and DevOps environments where requirements and user expectations evolve rapidly.

We also encountered limitations during the scenario-based ET, particularly an unbalanced number of test cases for each feature, which could skew passing rates. For instance, the SECI Scores Activities feature had only three test cases, resulting in the lowest passing rate. This imbalance highlights the need for a more equitable distribution of test cases. Furthermore, our strategy and coverage were restricted by the limited knowledge of testers about the KSECI application. While scenario-based ET allows simultaneous learning and testing, our experience has demonstrated that effective exploration can be limited by a lack of product knowledge. We decided to use functionality as a benchmark, exploring test scenarios around base functionalities and their interactions to ensure comprehensive testing within a limited timeframe.

From our experience, scenario-based ET is promising for academic and small-scale applications. This approach enables for organized yet flexible testing strategy in academic settings where students or researchers are developing software prototypes or conducting usability studies. Testers can simulate real-world interactions to ensure the software meets user needs and encourage critical thinking and problem-solving in students through creating user scenarios. In small-based projects, where resources may be limited, scenario-based ET enables teams to focus on the most critical features and extensively test user journeys without significant documentation or strict test cases. This adaptability makes it suitable for startups and agile teams, where rapid iterations and quick feedback loops are essential. Overall, scenario-based ET fosters a balance between structured testing and the creative exploration of software, making it an effective strategy for diverse projects that require both thoroughness and flexibility.

5 Conclusion

This study emphasizes the scenario-based approach in conducting exploratory testing particularly its capacity to accommodate the dynamic and developing characteristics of system features. The result from our study of KSECI platform shows that scenario-based ET is congruent with the iterative and adaptable tenets of Agile approaches. The exploratory testing approach aligns with the tester experience, skills, knowledge furthermore in agile development. It facilitates quick feedback cycles, immediate test modification, and the identification of defects that may not be readily detected by scripted approaches. Furthermore, ET places a strong emphasis on uncovering hidden defects rather than merely verifying predefined requirements. It leverages the tester's domain expertise and intuition, allowing for more nuanced and context-based judgements during test execution. The analysis highlights that functionality and usability defects are the most common due to their high frequency and severity. Consequently, emphasizing exploratory testing in this area is expected to enhance overall user satisfaction and system reliability. Other defect categories seem to be less problematic and less severe, which open for future research to suggest improvements in these areas for effective management testing approaches.

Acknowledgement. This research was funded by the Research Incentive Fund (RIF R22013) by Zayed University. The authors wish to thank Nor Shahida Mohamad Yusop & Wan Faezah Abbas from Universiti Teknologi MARA, Malaysia for their technical support on the software testing.

References

1. Bach, J.: Exploratory testing explained. Softw. Test. Q. Eng. 4(1), 1–5 (2003)
2. Ali, M., Khan, N.A., Sarfraz, M., Riaz, S., Mehmood, T., Ghafoor, S.: Exploring the role exploratory testing in agile software development environments. Spect. Eng. Sci. 3(1), 425–472 (2005)
3. Itkonen, J., Mäntylä, M.V., Lassenius, C.: Defect detection efficiency: test case based vs. exploratory testing. In: Proceedings of 1st International Symposium on Empirical Software Engineering and Measurement (ESEM 2007), pp. 61–70 (2007)
4. Rehman, A.U., Nawaz, A., Ali, M.T., Abbas, M.: Agile methods: testing challenges, solutions & tool support. In: 14th International Conference on Open-Source Systems and Technologies (ICOSST), Lahore, Pakistan, pp.1–5 (2020). https://doi.org/10.48550/arXiv.2008.13108

5. Kaner, C., Bach, J., Pettichord, B.: Testing Computer Software. Wiley (2011)
6. McCaffery, F.: Exploratory testing: a practical guide. Softw. Test. Q. Eng. Mag. (2010)
7. Manukonda, K.: Investigating the role of exploratory testing in agile software development: a case study analysis. Des. Sing. Chip Microcomput. Control Syst. Step. Motor **2**(4), 1–5 (2023). https://doi.org/10.47363/jaicc/2023(2)295
8. Neri, G.: The use of exploratory software testing in scrum. ACM Sigsoft Softw. Eng. Notes **48**(1), 59–62 (2023). https://doi.org/10.1145/3573074.3573089
9. Puranik, A.: Exploratory testing: a dynamic approach to uncover hidden software defects. Int. J. Inf. Technol. Comput. Eng. **35**, 13–19 (2023). https://doi.org/10.55529/ijitc.35.13.19
10. Straubinger, P., Fraser, G.: Engaging developers in exploratory unit testing through gamification. In: Proceedings of the 3rd ACM International Workshop on Gamification in Software Development, Verification, and Validation, pp. 2–9 (2024)
11. Mårtensson, T., Martini, A., Ståhl, D., Bosch, J.: Excellence in exploratory testing: Success factors in large-scale industry projects. In: Franch, X., Mannisto, T., Martinez-Fernandez, S. (eds.) Proceedings of International Conference on Product-Focused Software Process Improvement. Springer, Cham, pp. 299–314 (2019). https://doi.org/10.1007/978-3-030-35333-9_21
12. Yu, J., Zhang, J., Pan, L., Chen, Y., Wu, N. and Sun, W.: Software exploratory testing: present, problem and prospect. In: 2021 3rd International Academic Exchange Conference on Science and Technology Innovation (IAECST), pp. 44–47 (2021). https://doi.org/10.1109/iaecst54258.2021.9695695
13. Leveau, J., Blanc, X., Réveillère, L., Falleri, J.R., Rouvoy, R.:Fostering the diversity of exploratory testing in web applications. Softw. Test. Verif. Reliabil. **32**(5) (2022). https://doi.org/10.1002/stvr.1827
14. Martino, A., Lopes, L.L.G.: Garcia, A.: Impact of team composition on exploratory testing in GUI-based apps. J. Syst. Softw. **197** (2023)
15. Itkonen, J., Rautiainen, K.: Exploratory testing: a multiple case study. In: Proceedings of International Symposium on Empirical Software Engineering (ISESE 2005), pp. 84–93 (2005)
16. Tinkham, A., Kaner, C.: Learning styles and exploratory testing. In: Proceedings of the Pacific Northwest Software Quality Conference (2003)
17. Lazar, J., Greenidge, K.D.: One year older, but not necessarily wiser: an evaluation of homepage accessibility problems over time. Univ. Access Inf. Soc. **4**(4), 285–291 (2006)

User-Centered Mobile Application Design for D'Oro Coffee Shop

Panu Panuparb, Chanin Kittinon, Panapat Prasanboonlert,
and Thitirat Siriborvornratanakul[✉]

Graduate School of Applied Statistics, National Institute of Development Administration,
148 SeriThai Road, Klong-chan, Bangkapi, Bangkok 10240, Thailand
`thitirat@as.nida.ac.th`

Abstract. D'Oro, a Thai coffee brand with over 20 years in the market, strengthened its position through a major rebrand in 2017 under the concept of an 'Everyday Coffee Shop.' Despite this, at the time of this study the brand still lacked a dedicated mobile application, relying instead on a website for point collection and paper coupons for discounts. This limitation reduced convenience, as customers could miss promotions and needed multiple steps to check order status. To address this gap, we designed a mobile application using the Product–Market Fit framework and iterative usability testing. User interviews and prototype evaluations revealed positive feedback, particularly on the simplicity of the user interface, minimal effort required for interaction, and overall usefulness in meeting customer needs. These findings suggest that a user-centered mobile application can enhance convenience, streamline service, and strengthen customer engagement.

Keywords: Design Thinking Process · User Experiences · User Interface · Product-Market Fit Pyramid · Usability Test · Mobile Application · Coffee Shop

1 Introduction

D'Oro Coffee is a coffee shop franchise that aims to create a welcoming environment for customers while delivering quality products, reliable services, and a positive experience to the local coffee-drinking community. In today's market, many coffee shops have adopted mobile applications to provide fast, convenient services such as online ordering, checking promotions, and locating nearby branches directly through smartphones. These applications allow customers to choose options like pick-up-and-go, car-side delivery, or in-store collection—helping them save time and avoid waiting in line.

At the time of this study, D'Oro Coffee offered membership services through a web-based platform (Fig. 1), providing access to promotions, store locations, and loyalty points. However, this approach has several limitations: customers may miss important notifications about promotions or events, and the web interface requires multiple steps to check order status, reducing overall convenience. Importantly, these limitations are not unique to D'Oro Coffee; many coffee shops and similar businesses face comparable challenges when relying solely on web-based platforms instead of dedicated mobile

T. Dohi (Ed.): ICSED 2025, CCIS 2889, pp. 93–105, 2026.
https://doi.org/10.1007/978-981-92-0202-7_7

applications. This highlights a broader problem within the industry, where enhancing digital customer experiences has become essential for competitiveness and customer retention.

To address these challenges, this paper focuses on designing a dedicated mobile application for D'Oro Coffee, emphasizing user interface (UI) and user experience (UX) to enhance customer satisfaction. We analyzed D'Oro's market positioning as a middle-class brand, offering affordable prices to a broad customer base. Iterative user studies revealed that simplicity in design, minimal learning effort, and inclusion of only essential functions aligned with customer needs significantly improve satisfaction. The main contribution of this work is a mobile application design that enhances D'Oro's customer experience by bridging convenience, accessibility, and brand engagement.

The remainder of this paper is organized as follows. Section 2 reviews relevant theories, frameworks, and prior research. Section 3 describes the experimental methodology, while Sect. 4 presents and discusses the results. Finally, Sect. 5 concludes the paper and outlines directions for future work.

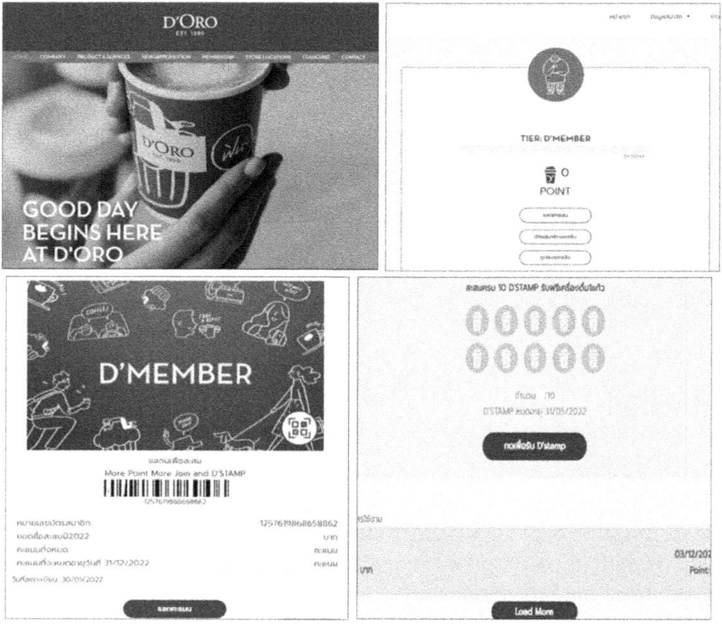

Fig. 1. D'Oro coffee website at the time of this study.

2 Related Work

2.1 Marketing and Customer Loyalty

To reach more customers and provide timely service, technology plays an important role. Promotional activities—such as coupons, discounts, freebies, and sweepstakes [1–4]—help retain customer loyalty and increase sales. A membership system that offers both monetary and non-monetary privileges is especially effective in building long-term brand loyalty [5–8]. Today's mobile applications further enhance this by enabling customers to access promotions, track orders, and receive notifications anytime, anywhere. Previous studies show how mobile apps can strengthen customer engagement and trust [9, 10].

2.2 Design Thinking

Design Thinking offers an innovation-driven, user-centered problem-solving approach [11]. By applying the Funnel Model—interviewing participants, selecting suitable tools, qualitative interpretation, and deep insight analysis—designers can identify pain points and refine solutions. This iterative process ensures the final product addresses real user needs.

2.3 Lean UX

Lean UX integrates Agile principles into UX design, emphasizing rapid iterations, hypothesis testing, and feedback loops [12]. Unlike traditional UX approaches that rely on extensive up-front documentation, Lean UX focuses on lightweight deliverables and collaborative practices, enabling teams to adapt quickly to changing requirements. The four-phase cycle—declaring assumptions, creating MVPs (Minimum Viable Products), running experiments, and collecting feedback—supports continuous refinement to ensure solutions align with user expectations. This approach reduces the risk of building unnecessary features by validating ideas early and often [13]. In practice, Lean UX encourages cross-functional collaboration, shared understanding, and evidence-driven decision-making, which makes it particularly suitable for fast-moving digital product environments such as mobile application design.

2.4 Product-Market Fit

Product-Market Fit (PMF) focuses on aligning product features with market needs [14–17]. Olsen's Product-Market Fit Pyramid [15] highlights five key layers: target audience, underserved needs, value proposition, feature set, and user experience. The "40% rule" is often used as a benchmark—if at least 40% of surveyed users would be "very disappointed" without the product, it suggests a strong PMF.

2.5 Usability Testing

Usability testing ensures prototypes meet user needs before full deployment. Small sample testing (at least four participants) can uncover up to 80% of usability issues [18–20]. Iterative testing and redesign, as recommended in [21], help refine UX, ensuring the final product is intuitive, efficient, and aligned with customer expectations.

3 Methodology

This study aims to develop a mobile application prototype for D'oro cafés and services. We applied the Product-Market Fit Pyramid [15] to identify target users, uncover underserved needs, and create an initial design. Usability testing was then conducted, followed by iterative modifications based on participant feedback.

3.1 Finding Underserved Needs

The goal of data collection was to identify the unmet needs of target users. To this end, we conducted face-to-face interviews with four participants to elicit their opinions and explore customer pain points in greater depth. The identified issues were then prioritized, with the most critical addressed first in the design process. The findings from this phase are presented in Sect. 4.1.

3.2 Usability Testing

Building on interview insights and user personas, we developed a prototype and asked participants (customers at D'Oro branches) to complete four key tasks: signing in, testing fast service and promotions, using essential features (e-coupons and point collection), and signing out. During these sessions, we observed user actions, clarified the intended use of the prototype when necessary, and collected feedback throughout the process. The procedure was repeated with additional participants (see Table 1), and all findings were used to refine the prototype. The number of participants in Table 1 follows the five-user rule [19], which suggests that three studies with five users each can uncover approximately 85% of usability problems in qualitative evaluations [20]. The results from the three iterative testing rounds are presented in Sect. 4.2.

Table 1. Interviewees and the purpose of each round of testing.

Test	Prototype	Interviewees	Purpose
1st	Version 1	5 D'Oro coffee's customer	Gathering opinion and information on prototype
2nd	Version 2	10 D'Oro coffee's customer	Verify corrections from previous comments and collect data
3rd	Version 3	10 D'Oro coffee's customer	Confirm improvements and receive comments for future developments

Table 2. Comparing the value propositions of the mobile application and website versions.

Benefit	Mobile application (Ours)	Website (Current)
Performance		
I- Fast service	High	N/A
Must-have		
I- E-coupon	High	N/A
I- Point collection	High	Low
I- Information	High	Low
Delight	-	-

4   Experimental Results

We applied the Product-Market Fit pyramid framework [15] to examine both the problem and solution spaces, with a focus on two specific parts of the pyramid: the lower part called Problem Space (Sect. 4.1) and the upper part called Solution Space (Sect. 4.2). The problem space encompasses target customers, underserved needs, and value propositions. One issue identified was the website access process, which requires multiple steps, feels inconvenient for users, and slows down service delivery. These challenges affect not only the problem space but also cascade into the solution space. To address them, we gathered data within the problem space, analyzed the issues, and developed early prototypes of a mobile application. These prototypes were iteratively refined to explore ways of enhancing usability and reducing service delays.

4.1   Problem Space

Results from User Interviews. We conducted interviews with four target users to understand their experiences with D'Oro coffee shops and identify pain points. Since D'Oro did not yet have a mobile application, users reported that subscriptions and point collection must be done through the website, which requires searching or bookmarking the site and manually logging in. Alternatively, points are collected via barcode scans or paper coupons, which are often forgotten. Overall, users found the process inconvenient, involving too many steps and consuming excessive time. Additional challenges (Fig. 2) included difficulty finding parking upon arrival (8/10), long waits and queues during peak hours due to slow service (7/10), items being out of stock (5/10), and limited awareness of current promotions (3/10), as users could not easily access updated information from home or mobile devices. These insights were used to develop user personas and guide the design of our mobile application prototype.

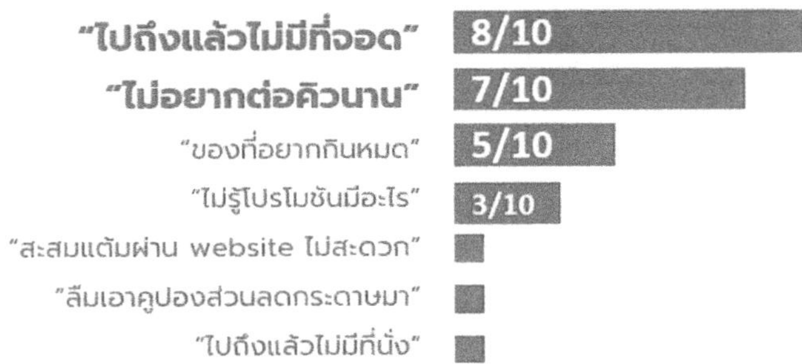

Fig. 2. Average Likert-scale ratings (1–10) from four interview participants. English translation from top to bottom are "No parking available when arriving (8/10)," "Don't want to wait in a long queue (7/10)," "The desired items are sold out (5/10)," "Unaware of promotions (3/10)," "Collecting points via website is inconvenient," "Forgot to bring paper discount coupons," and "No seats available when arriving."

User Persona. Based on the information gathered, we summarized one of our user persona as follows: Ms. Ane, a professional lady officer who values convenience and speed. Her primary frustration is having to wait for orders, especially when parking is difficult during peak hours or when queues are long. Her main goal is to order coffee and receive it quickly without delays.

Value Proposition. Based on the analysis of underserved needs, we identified the key benefits that will improve user comfort, address existing problems, and enhance the overall user experience. These benefits are organized into two categories: must-have benefits and performance benefits. Although delighter benefits were initially considered, they were omitted in this study to focus on the most critical aspects for the mobile application. The prioritized benefits are summarized in Table 2.

4.2 Solution Space

We developed our prototype using Figma, a tool for creating graphical mockups that can simulate interactive usage. This interactive prototype was employed in our usability testing to observe user interactions, collect usage data, and iteratively refine the application based on user experience feedback, following the diagram in Fig. 3.

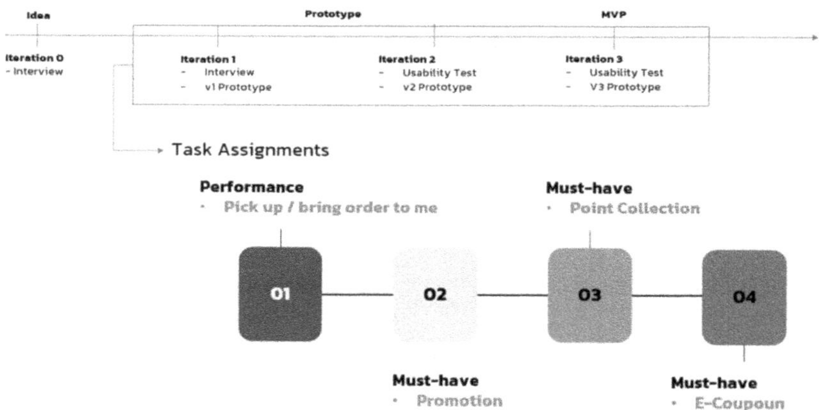

Fig. 3. Steps in our solution space.

Prototype Versions 0 and 1. To develop the mobile application, we focused on essential must-have features, specifically e-coupons and point collection, both implemented using QR codes. To address performance and meet users' underserved needs—convenience, speed, and timely updates—we added two key features: Pre-Order, allowing customers to confirm and pick up orders from home or at the store with hand-over service if no parking is available, and Promotion & Menu Availability, displaying updated promotions and menu information on the app's home page (see Fig. 4).

During usability testing (Fig. 4), participants completed four main tasks. First, users registered with email and password, and feedback suggested adding social sign-in options such as Facebook or Google. After signing in, users reached the home page, which highlights two main features: Fast Service and New & Promotion. Within Fast Service, the "Pickup at D'Oro" option was improved to show the nearest three branches first for convenience, and the delivery option was removed, as users preferred existing food delivery apps, reducing development costs. In New & Promotion, users requested that the navigation bar remain visible during scrolling and that promotion images could be used directly without returning to a previous screen, which was addressed in Version 1. Initially (Version 0), e-coupons and point collection were on separate pages, but users suggested displaying the point counter and D'stamp side by side, so Version 1 combined them on a single page, allowing users to choose their preferred option. The QR code clearly indicates eligible discounts, improving usability and clarity.

Prototype Version 2. In Version 2 (Fig. 5), several refinements were made based on user feedback to improve usability and align with natural workflows. The delivery option was replaced with "I'm here, please bring my order" to reflect that most D'Oro customers order directly at branches, pumps, or offices, emphasizing store pickup instead. QR codes were separated onto a dedicated scanning page to improve scanning accuracy, and a Favorites page was added to speed up ordering and enhance customer convenience. The order page was updated to include size and sweetness options, allowing users to personalize their drinks, and the payment button text was clarified from "True Money" to "True Money Wallet." Navigation was optimized by moving the Back button to the left side across pages to match natural user expectations, while the Confirm button remained on the right. These adjustments collectively enhanced user experience, streamlined interactions, and addressed key pain points identified during testing.

Fig. 4. Prototype versions 0 and 1.

Fig. 5. Prototype version 2.

Prototype Version 3. In Version 3 (Fig. 6), several refinements were made to improve clarity, usability, and user engagement. The "Pick up" text box was removed to prevent confusion with the button for picking up orders, and the graphic icon was updated from a battery to a coffee cup to better reflect the coffee shop theme. Contact buttons on order status and order success pages now allow users to call the branch directly, addressing situations such as traffic delays, melting ice, or difficulty locating cars. The menu was expanded to include both food and drinks for greater variety, and the ordering interface was improved by separating size and sweetness options for clearer visibility and easier selection. A sign-up option was added for users who cannot register in-store, and promotion items can now be ordered directly by clicking on the promotion photo. A "star" button was added to streamline saving favorite menu items, and a greeting message displaying expiring points was introduced to increase user awareness. Finally, the front-order button previously labeled "Delivery" was changed to "I'm here!! Please bring order to me" to better support pick-up orders. These updates collectively enhance usability, reduce friction in ordering, and provide a more intuitive and engaging experience for users.

Table 3 concludes user evaluations across each prototype iteration, where "+" and "–" indicate positive and negative feedback, respectively, and the percentages represent the proportion of users providing that feedback.

5 Conclusion

Most users provided positive feedback on our prototypes, highlighting the simplicity of the UI, the minimal effort required for interaction, and the overall usefulness in meeting customer needs. Unlike many mobile app designs that emphasize numerous features, our prototype differentiates itself by focusing on essential functions and context-specific solutions refined through iterative testing. This user-centered approach not only enhances convenience and engagement for D'Oro Coffee but also provides practical implications for the retail and food service industry, showing how streamlined, evidence-driven design can create mobile applications that balance simplicity, functionality, and customer value.

For future work, further studies could expand the scope of user testing to a larger and more diverse sample, incorporating quantitative methods such as surveys to validate and generalize the findings. In addition, future evaluations should include standardized usability metrics—such as task-completion rate, time on task, error rate, or validated scales like SUS and UMUX-Lite—together with pre-registered tasks and clear success criteria. Additional iterations could focus on developing a high-fidelity prototype or an MVP, integrating advanced features such as personalized recommendations, loyalty program optimizations, and push notifications for promotions. Exploring cross-platform compatibility, accessibility improvements, and real-time order tracking could further enhance the user experience. These steps would provide a more robust foundation for potentially launching a commercial mobile application that fully addresses the evolving needs of D'Oro Coffee customers.

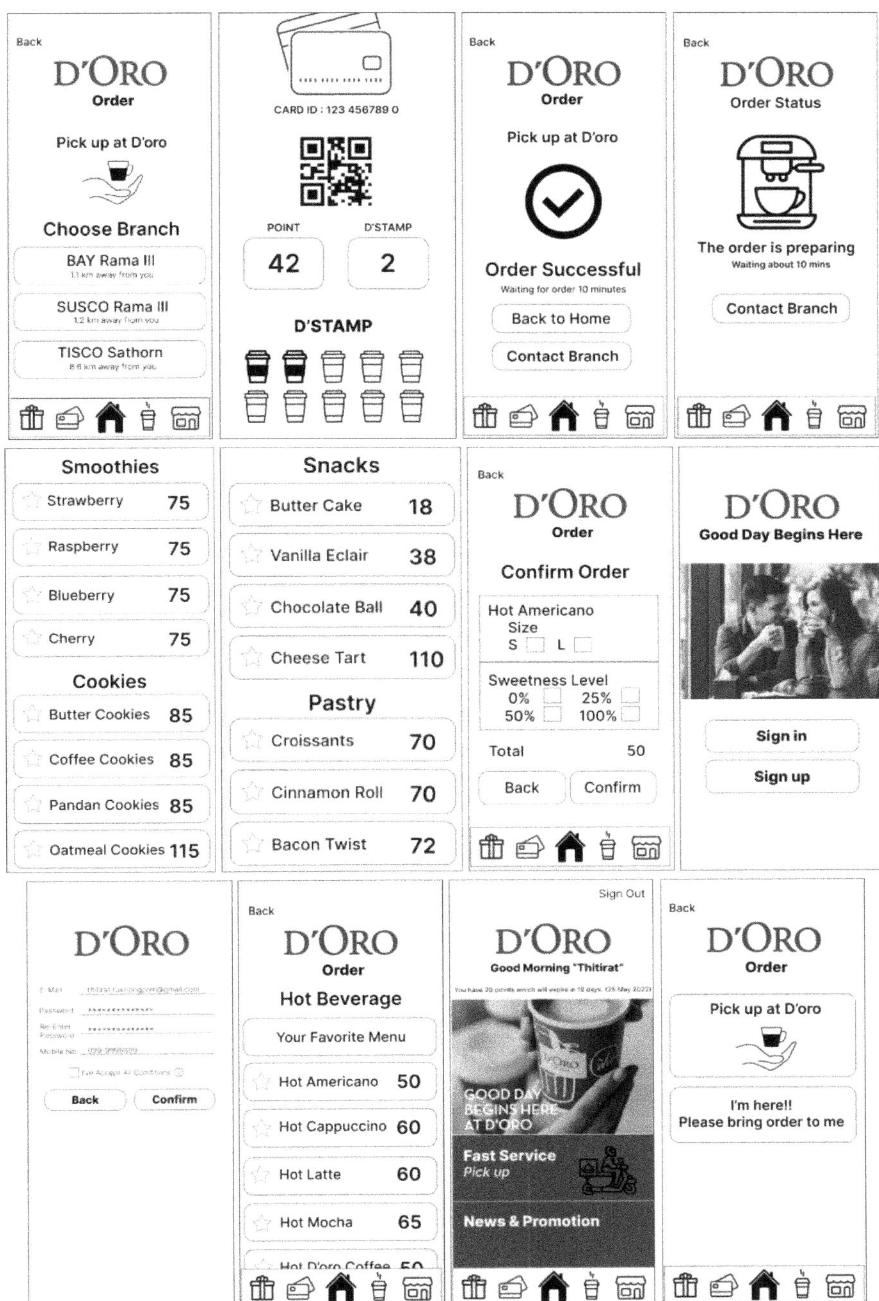

Fig. 6. Prototype version 3.

Table 3. Prototype evolution based on user feedback. Positive feedback is shown in bold, and percentage values indicate the proportion of users who provided that feedback.

Features [V1 prototype]		Features [V2 prototype]		Features [V3 MVP]	
(+) Self pickup	**60%**	**(+) Self pickup**	**70%**	**(+) Self pickup**	**80%**
(+) Promotion	**50%**	**(+) Promotion**	**50%**	**(+) Promotion**	**60%**
(+) Point collection	**50%**	**(+) Point collection**	**70%**	**(+) Point collection**	**70%**
(+) E-coupon	**40%**	**(+) E-coupon**	**40%**	**(+) E-coupon**	**50%**
(-) Delivery	10%				
(-) Seat availability	20%				
(-) Parking reservation	20%				
UX		UX		UX	
(+) Easy to use and uncomplicated	**60%**	**(+) Adding a favorite menu function helps speed up the ordering process**	**60%**	**(+) Displaying the customer's name and notifying about points nearing expiration shows attentiveness**	**80%**
(-) Normally do not sign out from the app	40%	(-) The QR codes of e-coupons are placed too close to each other, making scanning inaccurate	50%		
Message		Message		Message	
(-) Not serious about having a seat in the shop	40%	(-) Coffee customization should allow choices of size and sweetness	50%	**(+) Very easy to use and not complicated**	**80%**
(-) The menu is too extensive, which may cause delays in finding the desired item	60%	(-) The command buttons are difficult to use; for example, on the order confirmation page, the "Back" button should be on the left and the "Confirm" button on the right for better clarity	60%	(-) Provide a walkthrough on the first sign-in	40%
				(-) Add real images to the menu	40%
				(-) Provide a discount reminder when proceeding to payment	60%

References

1. Méndez, M.: Sales Promotion Effects on Brand Loyalty. Doctoral dissertation. Nova Southeastern University (2012). https://nsuworks.nova.edu/hsbe_etd/76/
2. Ade-Johnson, C.S.: An empirical investigation of the effectiveness of sales promotion in Maltina and Malta Guinness sales promotion strategies. J. Mass Commun. Journal. **4**(7) (2014)
3. Kotler, P., Armstrong, G.: Principles of Marketing. Pearson Prentice Hall, Boston (2012)
4. Tandoh, I., Sarpong, L.: The impact of sales promotions on the performance of auto-mobile industries in ghana: a case study of PHC motors (Accra-Ghana). Eur. J. Bus. Manag. **7**(11), 176–194 (2015)
5. Coursaris, C.K., Kim, D.J.: A meta-analytical review of empirical mobile usability studies. J. User Exp. **6**(3), 117–171 (2011)
6. Abu-Alhaija, A.S., Yusof, R.N.R., Hashim, H., Jaharuddin, N.S.: Determinants of customer loyalty: a review and future directions. Aust. J. Basic Appl. Sci. **12**(7), 106–111 (2018)
7. Liebermann, Y.: Membership clubs as a tool for enhancing buyers' patronage. J. Bus. Res. **45**(3), 291–297 (1999)
8. Madaan, K.V.S.: Fundamentals of Retailing. Tata McGraw-Hill Education Pvt. Ltd., Noida (2009)
9. Su, D.N., Nguyen, N.A.N., Nguyen, L.N.T., Luu, T.T., Nguyen-Phuoc, D.Q.: Modeling consumers' trust in mobile food delivery apps: perspectives of technology acceptance model, mobile service quality and personalization-privacy theory. J. Hosp. Market. Manag. **31**(5), 535–569 (2022)

10. Ramadanty, S., Widayanti, R.: Sale promotion and brand loyalty through mobile application Line official account. J. Crit. Rev. **7**(17) (2020)
11. Lee, S., etal.: Apply funnel model to design thinking process. In: 22st DMI: Academic Design Management Conference, Impact the Future By Design (2020)
12. Kartiko, C., Arrasyid, H.A., Wardhana, A.C.: Designing a mobile user experience student knowledge management system using Lean UX. J. Eng. Appl. Technol. **2**(1) (2021)
13. Tavichaiyuth, N., Foojinphan, N., Leelahakorn, P., Kanchanakul, S., Siriborvornratanakul, T.: Covid-19 travel planner mobile application design with lean product process framework. Augment. Hum. Res. **7**(1), 1–9 (2022)
14. Maples, M.: Andy Rachleff on "How to Know If You've Got Product Market Fit." Starting Greatness Newsletter. https://greatness.substack.com/p/andy-rachleff-on-how-to-know-if-youve. Accessed 24 Sept 2025
15. Olsen, D.: The Lean Product Playbook: How to Innovate with Minimum Viable Products and Rapid Customer Feedback. Wiley, Hoboken (2015)
16. Taghian, M., Shaw, R.N.: Market fit and business performance: an empirical investigation. J. Strateg. Mark. **18**(5), 395–415 (2010)
17. Albert, B.: Why UX professionals need to care about product-market fit. J. User Exp. **19**(4), 162–167 (2024)
18. Virzi, R.A.: Refining the test phase of usability evaluation: how many subjects is enough? Hum. Factors **34**(4), 457–468 (1992)
19. Nielsen, J.: Why you only need to test with 5 users. Nielsen Norman Group (NN/g) (2000). https://www.nngroup.com/articles/why-you-only-need-to-test-with-5-users/. Accessed 27 Sept 2025
20. Budiu, R.: Why 5 participants are okay in a qualitative study, but not in a quantitative one. Nielsen Norman Group (NN/g) (2021). https://www.nngroup.com/articles/5-test-users-qual-quant/. Accessed 27 Sept 2025
21. Dumas, J.S.: User-based evaluations. In: The Human-Computer Interaction Handbook: Fundamentals, Evolving Technologies and Emerging Applications, pp. 1093–1117 (2002)

AI-Based Intelligent Information Systems and Human-Computer Interaction Design

AI-Driven Framework for Enhancing Understanding of Object-Oriented Programming Concepts Among Novice Learners

Javier Dominguez, Oluwaseun Bamgboye$^{(\boxtimes)}$, Kehinde Babaagba, and Xiaodong Liu

School of Computing, Engineering and the Built Environment, Edinburgh Napier University, Edinburgh, UK
{o.bamgboye,K.Babaagba,x.liu}@napier.ac.uk

Abstract. Object-Oriented Programming (OOP) stands as a prevalent software development approach, yet students with a basic grasp of OOP often encounter challenges in comprehending abstract concepts like association, inheritance, and polymorphism. The verb/noun metaphor offers a means to alleviate these learning difficulties by transforming a list of requirements into classes. This involves converting nouns into objects with attributes and verbs into methods and associations. This research introduces an AI-driven approach designed to enhance students' comprehension of OOP concepts while facilitating the direct processing of user requirements. The proposed framework employs Natural Language Processing tools and incorporates sets of heuristic rules based on the verb/noun metaphor to process user requirements. The resulting output comprises pertinent OOP objects and entities, complete with relationships and accompanying metadata. The approach can produce a collection of classes and relevant OOP concepts derived directly from the requirements list, supported with detailed explanations to further enhance the students understanding and knowledge expansion.

Keywords: Artificial Intelligence · Natural Language Processing · OOP · User Requirements · Software Engineering

1 Introduction

In computing, emulating real-world situations entails the utilization of Object-Oriented programming concepts. This programming paradigm typically requires the organization of problem specifications into objects, encapsulating both descriptive data and executable actions pertinent to these objects. Such a structure closely mirrors the cognitive processes employed by humans when addressing analytical and computational challenges encountered in real-life situations.

Previous studies [1–3] have identified notable difficulties associated with the teaching and learning of OOP languages. Core concepts such as objects, inheritance, polymorphism, abstraction, and association are often challenging for students to comprehend. Similarly, the mapping of real-world scenarios to corresponding OOP constructs has been

T. Dohi (Ed.): ICSED 2025, CCIS 2889, pp. 109–122, 2026.
https://doi.org/10.1007/978-981-92-0202-7_8

reported as a significant obstacle for learners [4]. These difficulties hinder the development of appropriate programming logic and the implementation of effective, high-quality code among novice programmers and individuals with limited OOP experience.

Previous approaches [5–8] have predominantly focused on assessing the suitability of tools to facilitate OOP learning while neglecting the integral development of a dialogic process. This process should concurrently address user requirements and cultivate a profound comprehension of fundamental OOP concepts. The employment of verb/noun metaphors is acknowledged as highly efficacious in structuring the flow of OOP software, particularly in the translation of natural language requirements into Unified Modeling Language (UML) diagrams [9, 10]. Despite its merits, the utilization of UML may pose challenges, proving difficult for novice OOP learners and demanding considerable time for comprehension and application of associated concepts.

This research proposes an Artificial Intelligent-driven approach that leverages the verb/noun metaphor in conjunction with Natural Language Processing (NLP) techniques to enhance the learning and comprehension of OOP paradigms. The proposed method involves the utilization of an NLP classification algorithm, combined with various heuristic rules, to identify objects and metadata. The goal is to automate the construction of classes, providing corresponding explanations and appropriate descriptions. Through NLP, user requirements expressed in natural English can be tokenized and annotated, thereby improving the effectiveness of subsequent analysis.

The primary motivation for this research is to address persistent deficiencies in the learning and understanding of Object-Oriented Programming. By doing so, the objective is to improve students' knowledge and mastery of OOP principles, ultimately bridging gaps in their learning experience. The realization of this objective is guided by the following research questions:

- RQ1: To what extent does the integration of NLP influence the accuracy of tokens classification?
- RQ2: How effective is the proposed framework in achieving accurate OOP Class construction?

The remainder of the paper is organised as follows: Sect. 2 discusses the related work and explores some previous approaches to learning of OOP, Sect. 3 presents the overview of the proposed framework, Sect. 4 provides the details of the prototype implementation and testing of the approach, while the evaluation and discussion of the results are presented in Sect. 5. The conclusion and the future direction of the research are presented in Sect. 6.

2 Previous Approaches and Related Work

The adoption of tool-based approaches that integrate concepts such as gamification, augmented reality and visualisation has dominated the various approaches proposed by different researchers. This section considers a review of these approaches in the scope of improving the learning of OOP paradigm.

2.1 Tool-Based Approaches to OOP Learning

A common example of Computer-Aided Software Engineering (CASE) tools for facilitating learning and design of OOP is the use of UML, which serves as a cornerstone in focusing on the visualisation aspects inherent at early stages of learning and designing OOP. An example of such initiative is the visual learning environment presented in [11], conceived to aid students in the software development design phase. It helps students with foundational grasp of programming but lack theoretical conceptual knowledge. A similar tool centric approach that integrates graph trees and visualisation is the Prototype-based, Object-Oriented Interpreter (POOI) [12], specifically crafted to support the practical applications of OOP rather than delving into the intricate core concepts.

The recent surge in the adoption of gamification has emerged as a popular strategy for developing tools that foster a conducive learning environment, presenting challenging and abstract concepts in a more engaging and user-friendly manner. This approach posits that users can enhance their understanding and visualisation of complex ideas, coupled with heightened motivation, through game-based interactions. For instance, "Ztech de Object-Oriented" [13] has been designed for students to navigate through mini puzzles to learn specific programming concepts. However, this approach lacks flexibility for learners to autonomously monitor their progress and track the acquired knowledge.

Other attempts at incorporating gamification into the learning of Object-Oriented Programming (OOP) include the utilisation of games such as Sifteo cubes [6] and Serious Games (SG) [14] to address challenges in grasping the basics of OOP. These tools primarily focus on identifying classes, methods, objects, and relations. Despite its acceptance, it faces skepticism due to the limited empirical evidence, often stemming from evaluations involving small student cohorts. Some alternative tools proposed a blend of traditional and gamification techniques, such as Multiuser Programming Pedagogy for Enhancing Traditional Study (MUPPETS) [15]. Consequently, practitioners tend to dismiss this approach, although certain aspects may still inform the design of metadata displays in related tools.

The contemporary trend in simplifying the challenges associated with learning OOP involves the application of Augmented Reality, as evidenced in recent approaches [5, 16]. These endeavors predominantly emphasize visualization and gamification to facilitate mobile and collaborative learning among novice learners. However, the development of these tools primarily relies on the Unity framework, which, while conducive for fast prototyping, lacks robust support for OOP categories such as C++ and C#.

2.2 Application of NLP in Learning Systems

Natural Language Processing (NLP) as a branch of Artificial Intelligence (AI) has consistently experienced significant growth, exemplified by prominent instances such as the large graph models proficient in generating text and images on user's request. It is also prominent in voice recognition software like Siri and Alexa.

In contemporary times, NLP has become a pivotal tool in diverse academic and professional domains. One notable application involves the analysis of sentences produced by language learners, coupled with the creation of automated correction and scoring system, as observed in previous research [17]. Another application involves the generation of tailored exercises and tests designed to meet the unique needs of individual language learners. These instances merely scratch the surface of the manifold possibilities afforded by this advancing technology.

In terms of enhancing the understanding of OOP concepts with NLP, the tool Graphic Object-Oriented Analysis Laboratory (GOOAL) [18] offers an interface allowing users to input sentences that are subsequently translated into the 4W language, which later generates dynamic UML diagrams while aiming to accelerate software development. Similarly, architecture proposed in a related study [19] relies on preprogrammed grammatical and semantic rules. The architecture processes textual user input and generate a class diagram to visually represent the requirements of a given problem. While this tool lays the groundwork for an NLP-based learning tool, it was primarily conceptual at the time of publication.

An alternative approach [20] involves utilizing NLP to create a graphical class diagram from a requirements list. This method combines NLP techniques with a classification algorithm. The NLP involves input parsing and tokenization while the classification algorithm then forms a trio of NOUN-VERB-NOUN and their relationships. However, it is important to note that the applicability of the algorithm to a broader context remains unexplored and is currently validated for only specific requirements. Therefore, existing studies underscore the unexplored potential of research and applications in using NLP to support the learning of OOP concepts.

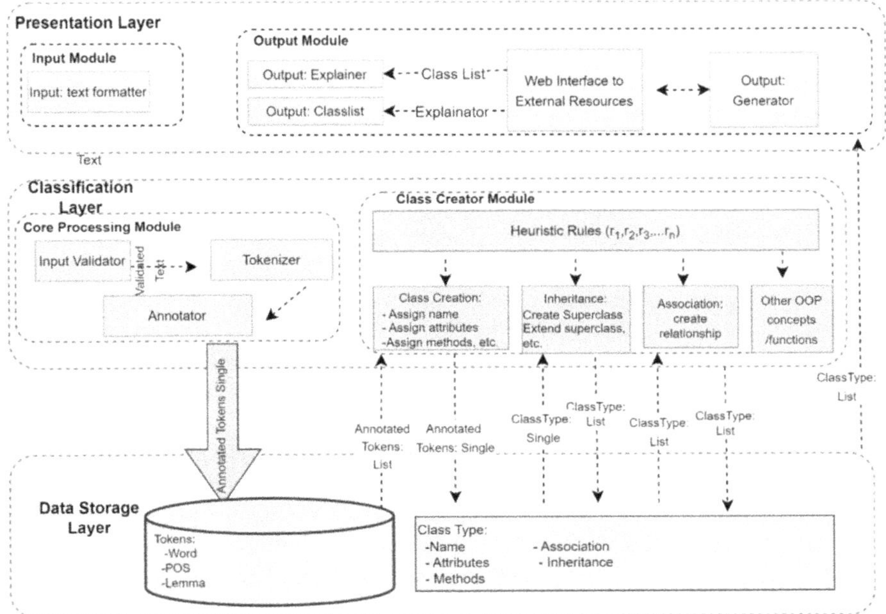

Fig. 1. Layered AI-driven Framework for understanding of OOP Concepts

3 AI-Driven Framework

This section describes the proposed AI-driven framework designed to alleviate challenges encountered by students in comprehending the OOP concepts. It incorporates a robust layered software architectural pattern shown in Fig. 1 to facilitate development and enhance the understanding of key OOP concepts. Employing the principle of layering in software engineering, this technique aims to mitigate software system complexity and ensures a clear separation of concerns, without compromising the integrity of the remaining layers. Data input and transfer between the layers of the framework is achieved in a top-bottom approach while output from the system is produced in a bottom-up approach.

3.1 Presentation Layer

The Presentation layer comprises two different modules: the user input module and the output module. Input to the architecture is achieved through the User Input Module, while the result from processing is received by the Output module of the presentation layer. The user input module provides the user interface for the text input with the associate text box. Specific description of software development task is provided using plain English language. The description of the task serves as data used by the underlying NLP components to generate equivalent program classes and methods. This module allows the user to define the program requirements necessary for the program design and implementation. It also provides an Application Programming Interface (API) for direct exchange of data between the module and the lower Classification layer. Inputs to this module can take the form of regular English language expressions separated by dots (full stops). Each expression must follow the NOUN-VERB(s)-NOUN(s) structure and can be in active or passive form, always considering that mixing both forms in the same sentence will not make sense grammatically.

The output module communicates with the underlying data storage layer and is responsible for the formatting and displaying of the outputs from processing the user requirements, using the appropriate read/write program libraries. It consists of components such as the Output Explainer, Output Classlist, Output generator, as well as web interface to appropriate web resources to support the class/class hierarchy construction and explanation of the OOP concepts in each program. The Output generator is responsible for formatting the output generated by the Classification Layer, subsequently persisting it in the Data Storage Layer. It also differentiates OOP keywords from other identifiers using various font colours. The Output Explainer is tasked with furnishing comprehensive explanations for each of the diverse Object-Oriented Programming (OOP) concepts, elucidating the" what" and "how" aspects. Additionally, it retrieves supplementary information through the Web interface to enhance the descriptions of specific concepts, including class creation, association, inheritance, and polymorphism. The classlist is required for the hierarchical descriptions of the program classes and their relationships. This helps to achieve some modularity in Object-Oriented program development. The structure of this module has been configured to enable the comparison of user requirements lists, derived from the input module, with the displayed results.

3.2 Classification Layer

The Classification Layer consists of the CoreNLP module and the Class Creator module. The CoreNLP Module can use libraries such as the Stanford CoreNLP library [21], comprising three key components: the Input Validator, Tokenizer, and Annotator. The Input Validator ensures the accuracy of the text and user input by verifying against transcription errors. Subsequently, the text is tokenized, generating a list of annotated tokens that include the words, Part-Of-Speech, and lemma. During annotation, the Annotator component utilizes the Tokens Module from the lower layer, referencing a tag dictionary for the English language and assigning corresponding tags to known words. Unknown or ambiguous words are tagged based on statistical probabilities derived from pretrained models.

Rule #1: In active sentence, first noun is the subject and thus the name of the class.
Rule #2: In active sentence, other nouns except the first are objects and attributes of the class.
- *Example: The user can update their names and addresses*
- *Result: class name = user; attributes = name, addresses.*
Rule #3: In passive form sentence, the first noun following the word "by" is the subject and thus the name of the class.
Rule #4: in a passive form sentence that contains the word "by", all nouns that are not immediately after "by" are objects and thus attributes of the class.
- *Example: Names and addresses can be modified by user*
- *Result: class name = user; attributes = name, addresses.*
Rule #5: in a passive form sentence that does not contain the word "by", the first noun is the noun is the subject and thus the name of the class.
Rule #6: in a passive form sentence that does not contain the word "by", all nouns that are not the first are objects and thus attributes of the class.
- *Example: User's names and addresses can be modified*
- *Result: class name = user; attributes = name, addresses.*
Rule #7: the nouns "program", "system", "software" and "code" when used as objects and thus class name, are changed to main.
- *Example: The system can modify names*
- *Result: class name = main; attributes = name.*
Rule #8: in a sentence in active form, all verbs are methods of the class.
- *Example: The user can access and update their names*
- *Result: class name = user; methods = access, update.*
Rule #9: in a sentence in passive form, only verbs in past participle form are methods.
- *Example: Names are accessed and updated by users*
- *Result: class name = user; methods = access, update.*
Rule #10: two classes with the same name are the same class
- *Example: Users can modify name. A user can update their address.*
- *Result: class name = user; attributes = name, address; methods = modify, update.*
Rule #11: two classes are subclasses of a superclass if they have at least one attribute in common.
- *Example: Users can modify name. Admin can update name.*
- *results: class name = superclass; attributes = name.*
  class name = user; methods = modify; extends superclass.
  class name = admin; methods = update; extends superclass.
Rule #12: two classes are subclasses of a superclass if they have at least one method in common.
- *Example: Users can modify name. Admin can modify address.*
- *Results: class name = superclass; methods = modify.*
  class name = user; attributes = name; extends superclass.
  class name = admin; attributes = address; extends superclass.
Rule #13: the main class would never be a subclass.
Rule #14: two classes would be associated if the name of one is an attribute in another.
- *Example: User can modify name. Admin updates user.*
- *Results: class name = user; attributes = name; methods = modify.*
  class name = admin; methods = update; associates to user.
Rule #15: when two classes associate, if the second is subclass of a superclass, then only the first class and the superclass associate

Fig. 2. Heuristic Rules

Once tokenized and annotated, the classification algorithm utilizes the list of annotated tokens to create classes, inheritances, and associations. This process is facilitated by applying a set of heuristic rules from the Class Creator Module, aligning with the verb/noun metaphor. The classification algorithm comprises four distinct sections that incrementally modify the output by applying rules based on the verb/noun metaphor.

The Class Creation Module complements the Classification Module by employing a set of heuristic rules illustrated in Fig. 2. These rules aid in class creation, emphasizing code reusability for class and method inheritance, and defining associations between classes. The outcome of this process is directed at the ClassType module of the Data Storage layer.

The initial step in class creation involves identifying the subject, verb(s), and object(s) of each sentence, treating each sentence as a potential class. Rules #1 to #9 are applied, searching for Part-Of-Speech tags and saving the lemma or base root of the word when rules apply. The result is an expanding list of potential classes, each containing a name, a list of attributes, and a list of methods, isolated from the rest.

Subsequently, class refinement employs Rule #10, merging classes with the same name defined in separate sentences, resulting in a consolidated list of classes where duplicates are disregarded.

The class inheritance phase, guided by Rules #11 to #13, creates super classes when two classes share at least one attribute or method. These super classes, named" super" plus the name of one of the classes with common features, are added to the list of classes. This work currently limits the inheritance level between classes to 2. The strategy for class inheritance ensures that compatibility between sub class (subtype) and super class (subtype) by adapting methods like Hearst patterns and implemented through provision of additional heuristic rules.

The final stage involves searching for associations using Rules #14 and #15. Classes are associated if the name of one appears as an attribute of another, indicating that the methods of the second class invoke actions on the first. The resulting classes form associations, often one-to-many but not exclusively. For this project, associations are signaled but not explicitly detailed.

The output of this classification algorithm is a list of classes with details such as name, attributes, methods, inheritance (if applicable), and associations (if applicable). This list is then formatted and presented in the Presentation layer.

3.3 Data Storage Layer

The Data Storage layer represents the lowest layer of the framework and contains modules that describe the token type and the class type. The token type generates objects from annotated words processed through the Natural Language Processing library, while the class type generates objects adhering to the standard format of Object-Oriented Programming (OOP) objects, encompassing attributes, methods, inheritance, associations, and a name.

These structures serve as the foundation for generating result lists through specific methods invoked from the Classification layer. These results are categorized based on OOP identifiers and concepts and subsequently stored. These stored results are then employed in the Explanators and classlist, each in their respective applications.

4 Prototype Implementation and Testing

To enhance comprehension of the proposed framework developed within our approach, we have implemented and tested a prototype system. The system underwent testing based on a set of requirements defined by a tutor and several students in a Java programming class. The development process adhered to the Agile methodology, involving iterative cycles where prototype requirements were reviewed, followed by implementation and testing phases.

The prototype system's implementation is based on the Stanford CoreNLP library [22], which facilitates the classification and annotation of textual inputs representing specific system requirements. This foundation is further enriched with a set of heuristic rules tailored to the specific context.

In applying the verb/noun metaphor to user input, the CoreNLP pipeline consolidates all necessary information into a single *CoreDocument*. Each grammatical sentence in the user's input is considered a potential Java class, and the CoreNLP creates the *CoreDocument* as a list of sentences separated by punctuation marks such as periods, line changes, question marks, or exclamation marks. Subsequently, each sentence is tokenized by spacing each word, and the tokens are labeled with their Part-Of-Speech (POS) through the annotator "pos" utilizing a maximum entropy approach. To address challenges in identifying relationships between classes arising from different sentences using the same noun in singular or plural or the same verb in different tenses, the annotator "lemma" is introduced. This annotator obtains the base forms of each token, facilitating comparisons of classes, attributes, and methods. Ultimately, each sentence in a *CoreDocument* becomes a list of annotated tokens containing the word, Part-Of-Speech, and lemma.

Following tokenization and annotation, the classification methods are applied through a four-section algorithm that incrementally modifies the output. This algorithm employs a list of rules based on the verb/noun metaphor. The system iterates through the list of tokens, identifying the first verb in the sentence. If the verb is in the form of "to be" and there are other verbs in the rest of the sentence in past participle form, the sentence is flagged as passive. In the case of a passive sentence, it is divided into two partitions. The first partition searches for a noun following the word" by" and adds it to the noun list as the first (Rule #3). For verbs in past participle form, they are assigned as methods (Rule #9). The second partition adds every noun to the noun list. If the object has been found in the previous list, Rule #4 applies; if not, Rule #5 applies. The remaining nouns are considered subjects per Rule #6. For sentences in the active form, the system traverses the token list again, adding nouns and verbs to their respective lists in order. The first noun is the subject (Rule #1), the rest are objects (Rule #2), and the verbs are methods (Rule #8). In all cases, if a noun is found belonging to the list specified in Rule #7, it is changed to" main." Finally, the first noun on the list is assigned as the class name, the rest as attributes, and all the verbs as methods. This list continues to expand if there are valid sentences in the *CoreDocument* created by the pipeline.

The implementation phase adhered to a test-driven development approach, encompassing Integration and Unit tests. The detailed low-level implementation of the prototype is depicted by the graphical window, as illustrated in Fig. 3. The graphical user interface presents a sample output in the form of Java class structure created from the specified requirements, accompanied by descriptions of the associated OOP concepts. The concepts description is facilitated by the relevant buttons on the GUI for the understanding of various Object-Oriented Programming (OOP) concepts. There are separate provisions to augment comprehension of classes, Association, Polymorphism, and Inheritance. These descriptions also include associated links to supplementary learning resources on the web. For instance, a detailed description of a class created by the tool based on the user's input can be accessed through the" Explain Classes" button built in the prototype.

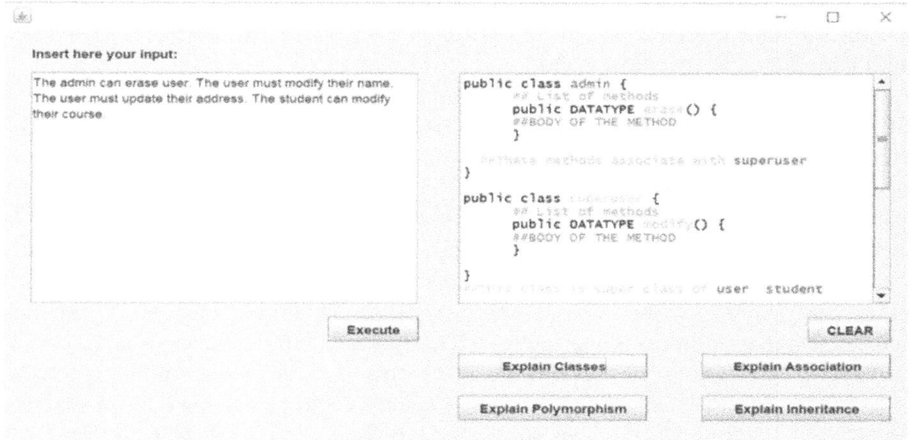

Fig. 3. Prototype Implementation

5   Evaluation and Results

RQ1: *To what extent does the integration of NLP influence the accuracy of tokens classification?*

To provide response to RQ1, we evaluate the accuracy of the framework and its implementation using a set of requirements based on various programming issues from *beecrowd* forum [23]. It is a repository for diverse programming challenges with more than two thousand issues and program requirements, grouped into nine distinct categories that provides coding challenges in over 25 different programming languages. A total of 100 random samples were selected from the various programming challenges across the 9 categories.

The quantitative evaluation employs the accuracy metric in Eq. 1 to compute the ratio of correct outputs or predictions to the total number of predictions obtained through a comprehensive analysis. The utilization of accuracy is a standardized and well-established method for evaluating CoreNLP [21], particularly suitable for assessing discrete datasets.

$$Accuracy = \frac{No\ of\ correct\ Outputs}{\sum_{i=1}^{n} Total\ no\ of\ Outputs} \tag{1}$$

The evaluation of accuracy is computed on three different aspects of the approach: the result of the Natural Language Processing tool, the result of the classification of tokens, and the result of the creation of classes (provided in response to RQ2). The correctness of CoreNLP is quite straight forward; a token is correctly annotated if the annotators match the expected result. As the approach only classifies nouns and verbs, it does not consider adverbs in this context. Similarly, the classification of the annotated tokens is measured in terms of the correct and incorrect classifications. The values of the correct annotated NLP and the correct classification are later evaluated against the Expected and Total classification respectively. Table 1 contains the total number of tokens generated for the analysis.

$$Accuracy\ NLP = \frac{1061}{1092} = 0.971611 \tag{2}$$

$$Accuracy\ Classification = \frac{1056}{(1056 + 58)} = 0.947935 \tag{3}$$

Table 1. Analysis of Tokens

Analysis	Tokens				
	Expected	Correct NLP	Incorrect NLP	Correct Classification	Incorrect Classification
Total	1092	1061	31	1056	58

The accuracy of the integrated NLP toolkit in this context and the classification of the tokens created by the proposed framework are separately evaluated. The accuracy of NLP (as shown in Eq. 2) is estimated at 97.1611%, which is consistent with the result of accuracy of the pipeline provided in [24]. This indicates that a little above 97% of the input processed by the proposed framework is correctly tagged as the appropriate *Part-of-Speech*. Similarly, the accuracy of the token classification is 94.7935% as computed in Eq. 3. The result shows that more than 9 out of 10 inputs will be correctly identified as nouns and verbs by the proposed approach.

$$Accuracy\ Class\ Construction = \frac{251}{(251 + 27)} = 0.90287 \tag{4}$$

Table 2. Analysis of Classes

Analysis	Classes			
	Expected	Actual	correct	Incorrect
Total	257	272	251	27

RQ2: *How effective is the proposed framework in achieving accurate OOP Class construction?*

From a technical perspective, a generated output necessitates evaluation by a human expert, who judges its correctness based on its adherence to Java syntax and structure. Accuracy of the Java class construction has been computed using Eq. 1 and validated by the human expert. A Java class is deemed accurate when it is appropriately constructed and applies the relevant Object-Oriented Programming (OOP) concepts. For example, If the concept of Association or Inheritance is expected in a class but not shown, the class will be considered incorrect even if it has the appropriate name, attributes and methods. Table 2 shows the analysis of the total Java classes currently constructed from the sample dataset in the evaluation. The accuracy is later computed in Eq. 4. The result of the accuracy for Java class construction is estimated as 90.2877%. This renders the framework reasonably accurate in both class construction and description, with just under 10 percent of the outcomes displaying some degree of inaccuracy. The evaluation's validity is further established through human expert assessment, particularly in terms of the anticipated output corresponding to inputs, encompassing the classification methods contingent on the accurate application of the classification rules.

The findings indicate that the framework is sufficiently accurate to bolster students' comprehension of Object-Oriented Programming (OOP) concepts and enhance their confidence in developing OOP programs with the requisite principles. Additionally, it can be inferred that a learning tool that imparts inaccurate information has the potential to confuse novice learners in Object-Oriented programming, causing them to erroneously perceive misrepresented OOP concepts as authentic and valid. This, in turn, could contribute to a more challenging learning experience.

By comparison, prior approaches, such as BlueJ[1] and Greenfoot[2], which are widely used in educational environments for teaching OOP, the proposed framework exhibits comparable performance. While tools like BlueJ emphasize visualization and interactivity, they rely heavily on instructor-guided exploration and often lack automated validation of OOP concepts from natural language inputs. As a result, students may still struggle with translating problem statements into accurate class structures without substantial scaffolding. In contrast, the proposed framework integrates heuristic rule sets with NLP classification to parse natural language and extract relevant programming constructs. This endows it with a higher degree of adaptability and semantic comprehension. Its ability to generate classes not only syntactically correct but also semantically aligned with OOP principles distinguishes it from prior systems.

Finally, the proposed framework surpasses many existing educational and automation tools in terms of accuracy, semantic precision, and relevance to pedagogical outcomes. Its high performance supports its potential as a practical aid for improving learners' understanding and application of OOP concepts.

6 Conclusion and Future Work

This study presents an effective approach, incorporating a well-designed framework, capable of enhancing the learning and understanding of Object-Oriented Programming (OOP) concepts by creating a more engaging and interactive learning environment. The

---

[1] https://www.bluej.org/.

[2] https://www.greenfoot.org/door.

framework successfully implements a Computer-Aided Software Engineering (CASE)-based solutions, offering solutions to programming problems and explanations of essential OOP concepts alongside traditional learning methods. This dual approach enables users to comprehend the practical application of various OOP concepts while simultaneously grasping the associated theoretical foundations. The framework's evaluation is grounded in the accuracy of results compared to expected outputs, a crucial aspect for effective student learning of OOP concepts, fostering increased engagement with tools and enhancing the learning process. Furthermore, the integrated API's flexibility in the framework facilitates the creation of simplified online learning resources for tutors.

There are possibilities for future enhancements, particularly in refining classification techniques without necessarily altering or eliminating the reliance on CoreNLP. Potential improvements involve the addition of other linguistic components, such as adjectives or adverbs, to the rule set, thereby enabling more extensive processing of complex requirements. Additionally, the classification algorithm could be expanded to consider complex verb tenses for refining methods within classes, or the introduction of a set of forbidden words to prevent the creation of inconsequential attributes or methods.

References

1. Sim, T.Y., Lau, S.L.: Review on challenges and solutions in novice programming education. In: IEEE International Conference on Computing (ICOCO), Kota Kinabalu, Malaysia, pp. 55–61 (2022)
2. Xinogalos, S.: Object-oriented design and programming: an investigation of novices' conceptions on objects and classes. ACM Trans. Comput. Educ. (TOCE) 15(3), 1–21 (2015)
3. Kolling, M.: The problem of teaching object-oriented programming. Part 1: Lang. J. Object-Oriented Program. 11(8), 8–15 (1999)
4. Yan, L.: Teaching object-oriented programming with games. In Proceedings of the 6th International Conference on Information Technology: New Generations (ITNG 2009), Las Vegas, NV, USA, pp. 969–974 (2009)
5. Abidin, Z.Z., Zawawi, M.A.A.: OOP-AR: learn object oriented programming using augmented reality. Int. J. Multimed. Recent Innov. (IJMARI) 2(1), 60–75 (2020)
6. Corral, J.M.R., Balcells, A.C., Estevez, A.M., Moreno, G.J., Ramos, M.J.F.: A game-based approach to the teaching of object-oriented programming languages. Comput. Educ. 73, 83–92 (2014)
7. Lotfi, E., Mohammed, B.: Teaching object oriented programming concepts through a mobile serious game. In: Proceedings of the 3rd International Conference on Smart City Applications, pp. 1–6 (2018)
8. Su, J.M., Hsu, F.Y.: Building a visualized learning tool to facilitate the concept learning of object-oriented programming. In: International Congress on Advanced Applied Informatics (IIAI-AAI), pp. 516–520 (2017)
9. Boyd, N.: Using natural language in software development. JOOP 11(9), 45–55 (1999)
10. Drechsler, R., Soeken, M., Wille, R.: Formal specification level: towards verification-driven design based on natural language processing. In: Proceeding of the 2012 Forum on Specification and Design Languages, Vienna, Austria, pp. 53–58 (2012)
11. Tsai, C.Y.: Improving students' understanding of basic programming concepts through visual programming language: the role of selfefficacy. Comput. Hum. Behav. 19, 224–232 (2019)
12. Perez-Schofield, B.G., Ortin, F.: A didactic object-oriented, prototype-based visual programming environment. Sci. Comput. Program. 176, 1–13 (2019)

13. Seng, W.Y., Yatim, M.H.M.: Computer game as learning and teaching tool for object oriented programming in higher education institution. Procedia Soc. Behav. Sci. **123**, 215224 (2014)
14. Abbasi, S., Kazi, H., Kazi, A.W., Khowaja, K., Baloch, A.: Gauge object oriented programming in student's learning performance, normalized learning gains and perceived motivation with serious games. Information **12**(3), 101 (2021)
15. Phelps, A.M., Egert, C.A., Bierre, K.J.: MUPPETS: multi-user programming pedagogy for enhancing traditional study: an environment for both upper and lower division students. In: Proceedings Frontiers in Education 35th Annual Conference, pp. S2H-8 (2005)
16. Hang, L.Y., Romli, R., Muhaiyuddin, N.D.M.: AR-OOP: augmented reality-based mobile learning application for learning object-oriented programming. Multidiscip. Appl. Res. Innov. **4**(1), 116–121 (2023)
17. Meurers, D.: Natural language processing and language learning. In: Encyclopedia of Applied Linguistics, pp.4193–4205 (2012)
18. Perez-Gonzalez, H.G., Kalita, J.K.: GOOAL: a graphic object oriented analysis laboratory. In: Companion of the 17th Annual ACM SIGPLAN Conference on Object-Oriented Programming, Systems, Languages, and Applications, pp. 38–39 (2002)
19. Bajwa, I.S., Naeem, M.A., Riaz-Ul-Amin, M.A.C.: Speech language processing interface for object-oriented application design using a rulebased framework. In: 4th International Conference on Computer Applications (2006)
20. Tripathy, A., Rath, S.K.: Application of natural language processing in object oriented software development. In: 2014 International Conference on Recent Trends in Information Technology, pp. 1–7 (2014)
21. Toutanvoa, K., Manning, C.D.: Enriching the knowledge sources used in a maximum entropy part-of-speech tagger. In: 2000 Joint SIGDAT Conference on Empirical Methods in Natural Language Processing and Very Large Corpora, pp. 63–70 (2000)
22. Manning, C.D., Surdeanu, M., Bauer, J., Finkel, J.R., Bethard, S., McClosky, D.: The Stanford CoreNLP natural language processing toolkit. In: Proceedings of 52nd Annual Meeting of the Association for Computational Linguistics: System Demonstrations, pp. 55–60 (2014)
23. Azevedo Filho, J.O., Barboza, C.R., Santos, J.M., Tonin, N.A., Bez, J.L.: beecrowd. https://www.beecrowd.com.br. Accessed 25 Jan 2024
24. Gessler, L.D., Peng, S., Liu, Y., Zhu, Y., Behzad, S., Zeldes, A.: Overview of AMALGUM–large silver quality annotations across English genres. Soc. Comput. Linguist. **4**(1) 2021

Optimizing Data Placement in Hybrid Cloud for Efficient AI Training

Hardik Ruparel[1]($\boxtimes$) (iD), Harshal Daftary[2], and Pramod Kumar[1]

[1] San Jose, USA
`hruparel@uci.edu`
[2] Seattle, USA
`hdaftary@cs.stonybrook.edu`

Abstract. Hybrid cloud environments provide a scalable and cost-effective solution to train large-scale AI models by dynamically allocating computational resources and optimizing data placement strategies. However, training efficiency in these environments is significantly influenced by multiple interdependent metrics such as data locality, network bandwidth, latency, computing power, storage cost, scalability, public cloud API cost, memory utilization, GPU utilization, and energy efficiency. Tuning one of these parameters often leads to trade-offs in others. For instance, increasing bandwidth usage might result in higher energy consumption, whereas minimizing latency by co-locating data and compute may escalate transfer or storage costs. For the scope of this paper, we consider "Model Training Efficiency" as a multi-faceted metric that can be interpreted differently depending on the priority—whether optimizing for cost-effectiveness, minimizing energy consumption, or achieving the fastest model convergence. In this study, we propose a novel mathematical model to quantify training efficiency while capturing these trade-offs, thereby enabling informed data placement decisions. Furthermore, we also present real-world case studies illustrating how different strategies such as data caching, replication and cloud bursting can mitigate these trade-offs. Our goal is to provide a generic mathematical framework that enables organizations to strategically balance computational performance, cost, and resource efficiency for training AI models in a hybrid cloud configuration.

Keywords: Hybrid Cloud · Data Placement · AI Training Optimization · Mathematical Model · Sustainability

1 Introduction

By combining public cloud resources with on-premises private infrastructure, hybrid cloud systems enable businesses to use "the best of both worlds" for their

---

H. Ruparel, H. Daftary and P. Kumar—Independent Researcher.

T. Dohi (Ed.): ICSED 2025, CCIS 2889, pp. 123–136, 2026.
https://doi.org/10.1007/978-981-92-0202-7_9

workloads [1]. Regulatory or security requirements, cost restrictions, and performance requirements are the primary considerations that influence the location of applications and data in such configurations [1]. Furthermore, organizations are increasingly using Hybrid Cloud to support AI/ML workloads. One of the key driver is the sheer computing and data demands of AI many enterprises are turning to hybrid architectures to meet these needs [2]. Global hybrid cloud market alone is expanding rapidly, reflecting this trend. Hybrid Cloud market size was valued around $81 billion in 2022 and is forecasted to reach $348 billion by 2031, showing a growth of 17% CAGR [3].

Furthermore, many industries like finance, healthcare and federal face strict regulatory and privacy requirements that dictate how and where data can be handled. A hybrid cloud strategy is often critical for compliance [4]. Sensitive data and portions of AI training that involve regulated information can be kept on-premises or in a private cloud to meet compliance standards, while less sensitive components leverage public cloud resources [4]. This "compliance by design" approach allows precise control over data locality, ensuring that protected data never leaves their secure environment, even as they harness cloud-based AI services for other tasks. For example, a bank could train models on anonymized data in the public cloud but keep customer-identifiable data and final model tuning on-prem for regulatory reasons. Hybrid setups thus provide "the best of both worlds": the cloud's scalability and innovation, together with on-prem control to satisfy governance, security, and compliance mandates [5].

2 Key Metrics Impacting Training Efficiency

Several core metrics that influence the performance and cost of training in a hybrid cloud environment are outlined below.

2.1 Data Locality

The proximity of data storage to the computational resources that require that data is referred to as data locality. Maintaining data close to the point of computation, or high data locality, speeds up training as it significantly cuts down the data transfer time. In hybrid cloud setting, data can either be kept on-premises, in the cloud, or replicated across both. Systems may utilize data replication for moving the data to the computing site or data virtualization techniques which involves avoiding the data movement and remotely accessing it from on-premises or cloud data stores whenever required [6].

2.2 Scalability

Scalability is a system's ability to add or remove resources in order to accommodate the training workload requirements. In hybrid clouds, scalability refers to utilizing the cloud's elastic resources when local infrastructure maxes out typically through cloud bursting or distributing the training across environments. High scalability can improve training efficiency either by distributing work among multiple servers (horizontal scaling) or by adding more resources to a single server to handle larger models or data (vertical scaling).

2.3 Bandwidth Availability

The network bandwidth between on-premises and cloud, or across cloud regions, determines how quickly big datasets may be migrated or accessed remotely. Training may be slowed down by a bottleneck caused by insufficient bandwidth if the model often retrieves data from a distant repository. Reducing dependency on constant data transfers or guaranteeing sufficient bandwidth are key factors in hybrid cloud performance [7]. Network congestion and slowdowns occur when bandwidth is constrained and many requests are made to access the same data. Dedicated network links may help expand bandwidth, but will be more costly.

2.4 Latency

Network latency is the round-trip time delay in data communication. Even with high bandwidth, high latency can degrade performance, especially for iterative training that requires frequent synchronization or data access across sites. Each time a training process fetches a batch of data over a WAN link, latency adds to the iteration time. Thus, reducing latency by placing data closer to compute or using faster networks improves training throughput. Many hybrid cloud solutions co-locate data and compute to address "data gravity" concerns—the idea that large datasets attract applications to stay near them [1]. Using cloud regions adjacent to on-prem data centers or vice versa can cut latency, as seen in setups where on-prem infrastructure is placed in co-location facilities with direct high-speed links to cloud providers [7].

2.5 Computation Power

The speed at which machine learning models are trained is significantly dependent on the processing capacity of the underlying computing hardware including CPUs, GPUs, and TPUs. While public clouds offer specialized computational resources on demand, on-premises installations could have limited or outdated hardware [1]. Although increasing computational power reduces training durations, performance optimization requires efficiently feeding data and models to these computer resources.

Efficient memory utilization directly influences computational throughput of the underlying system. Training large language models is a memory-intensive task, as the large parameter sets, gradients, and optimizer states often exceed GPU memory. For instance, a transformer with billions of parameters often exceed the memory capacity even on high-end GPUs [8]. Techniques like model parallelism, memory offloading, and dynamic memory management (e.g., DeepSpeed ZeRO) enable training larger models within constrained memory resources but may introduce overheads such as increased inter-device communication or slower memory access due to offloading [8–10].

Similarly, ensuring high GPU utilization and efficient data pipelines is fundamental for optimal AI training performance. Poor pipeline performance can cause expensive GPUs to sit idle that in turn significantly diminishes the overall compute throughput. Analysis indicates that inefficient data loading can reduce GPU utilization to as low as 1030% [11,12]. Optimizations such as caching the frequently accessed data in GPU or RAM, pre-fetching, parallel data loading, and advanced scheduling methods in distributed setups can help minimize GPU idle times, thereby maximizing its throughput [13].

2.6 Storage Cost

The cost of storage varies depending on the placement decision. Storing large training datasets in a public cloud can be expensive over time, as the cloud providers typically charge based on utilized storage size (GB per month) along with additional charges for data access. This means that storing the same size of data in multiple files is generally more costly to access than accessing a single large file due to the increased API access costs associated with multiple requests [14]. These expenses associated with storing massive datasets in the cloud can become unaffordable, motivating some organization to move workloads back on-premises [15]. On-prem storage has an upfront capital cost and maintenance overhead but might be economical for large volumes in the long run. In a hybrid scenario, frequently used "hot" data may be kept on expensive, fast storage near compute, while offloading "cold" archival data to cheaper storage even if it's in the cloud. The key challenge is to minimize cost without hurting performance.

2.7 Energy Efficiency

Energy usage is an increasingly important metric that affects running expenses as well as the impact on the environment. Data centers consume a lot of electricity, and moving data across networks requires a lot of energy [16]. To improve training efficiency, excessive energy usage shouldn't be required. Performance-per-watt and Joules per training iteration are two examples of energy efficiency metrics. Compared to typical company data centers, public cloud data centers are often far more energy and carbon efficient [16]. Azure services, for instance, are up to 98% more carbon efficient and up to 93% more energy efficient than a typical company datacenter [17].

3 Related Work

The problem of optimizing data placement and scheduling in hybrid clouds has been thoroughly explored in both industry and academia. According to the theory of *data gravity*, because data transfer is expensive, huge datasets tend to bind applications near them [1]. Accenture notes that many enterprises adopt hybrid strategies where they keep highly transactional, data-intensive applications on-premises or in private clouds for performance, and use the public cloud for other workloads [1]. Numerous frameworks for workload and data placement decisions have been developed to select the best environment depending on the nature of the workload [7].

Transferring some workloads to the cloud can save energy for training jobs. However, energy is also used when moving data from on-premises to the cloud or through clouds. Recent studies on sustainable computing focus on measuring end-to-end carbon costs of computations. We require comprehensive sustainability criteria that take data center operating and embodied energy costs into consideration. We should encourage more environmentally friendly computing processes by allocating sustainability charges to each activity [18]. Earlier research has already examined the trade-offs between data virtualization and data replication. With virtualization, data remains at its source and is combined on the fly, which avoids duplication increases latency [6]. Replication creates data copies in the target environment, which improves local access speed but increases extra storage costs and synchronization overhead [6]. Thus, many systems use a hybrid approach that replicates static data for fast reads and virtualizes dynamic data to reduce network latency. Additionally, intelligent caching and data orchestration frameworks such as Alluxio provide distributed caching layers bridging on-prem and cloud storage [19]. By intelligently caching frequently accessed data, such systems eliminate redundant data transfers and reduce egress costs, effectively improving data locality and bandwidth utilization. A performance study by Alluxio demonstrated up to 3× improvement in data access performance in hybrid cloud scenarios with such a caching layer. Recent proposals even include predictive, optimization-based strategies for data placement in hybrid environments. Additionally, energy efficiency is also a key consideration when deciding where to store data due to the increase in demand for sustainable computing [18]. For hybrid cloud-edge systems, Symvoulidis et al. (2023) [20] created a deep learning-based data placement technique that uses user mobility pattern classification to optimize data location while balancing migration overhead and latency. By pre-positioning data based on user behavior estimates, their predictive technique shortened access path lengths by 50% and decreased data access costs by up to 60%. In order to reduce work tardiness/performance, private cloud energy consumption, and public cloud prices, Sun et al. (2023) define hybrid cloud scheduling as a multi-objective optimization problem [21]. Their strategy, which combines cutting-edge optimization methods like greedy heuristics and swarm intelligence, provides notable energy savings while preserving cost and quality of service, proving the efficacy of resource scaling and intelligent workload allocation. In order to balance VM placement and resource provisioning, reduce SLA violations, and improve load distribution, Simaiya et al. (2024) offer a dynamic scheduling system [22] that combines a hybrid PSO-GA optimization with LSTM-based CPU load prediction. Sun et al. (2023) [21] presents a privacy-aware multi-workflow scheduler that uses a two-phase algorithm to optimize energy and cost that outperforms current data placement approaches in hyrbid cloud environments. This algorithm first finds Pareto-optimal solutions using a salp-swarm algorithm and then refines them with an iterative greedy search. Another approach, Achieving Performance by Cost-Effective Replication (APER) dynamically adds or removes the data replicas in a geo-distributed cloud setting based on the frequency of data access. This approach helps in optimizing database query performance, thereby adhering to the response time service level objectives (SLO). Furthermore, one more way to reduce latency includes dynamic data placement mechanism that adds or removes replicas based on active users' proximity. Time series-based De-duplication and Optimal data Placement Strategy (TDOPS) enhances data storage efficiency by using time series-based de-duplication, preventing redundant data copies and optimizing placement based on data center load and transfer costs. Together, these strategies improve cloud efficiency by reducing query times, optimizing storage, and balancing cost-performance trade-offs [23].

In summary, existing research provides a solid foundation and emphasizes balancing latency, bandwidth and cost. However, a comprehensive model that includes all key metrics in guiding data placement is still required. We address this gap by formulating an optimization model for data placement in hybrid cloud for training AI models.

4   Proposed Model

To optimally place data in a hybrid cloud for efficient training, we propose a mathematical model that captures the influence of each key metric on overall training efficiency. We define training efficiency, y, as a quantitative figure that increases when training is faster, cheaper and more sustainable. Our goal is to maximize y by choosing where to store each portion of data (on-premises vs. cloud) and how to provision network and compute resources.

Let:

- L: Data Locality Factor ($0 \leq L \leq 1$).
- B: Network Bandwidth (in Gbps).
- τ: Network Latency (in seconds).
- P: Computation Power (reflecting Data Processing Rate).
- C_s: Storage Cost Factor (reflecting cost for chosen data placement).
- S_c: Scalability Factor (reflecting number of parallel compute resources that can be used).
- E_e: Energy Efficiency Metric ($0 \leq E_e \leq 1$) with 1 being highly efficient.
- M_u: Memory Utilization Efficiency ($0 \leq M_u \leq 1$ reflecting effective use of fast memory relative to model size).
- G_u: GPU Utilization and Data Pipeline throughput ($0 \leq G_u \leq 1$ reflecting GPU active time and effective data loading rate).

We propose an efficiency function:

$$y = f(L, B, \tau, P, C_s, S_c, E_e) \tag{1}$$

One possible formula expresses the effective training throughput as a function of these factors normalized by cost and energy penalties. Consider a model that processes data of total size D (per iteration or epoch). If a fraction L is local, it is processed at high speed, while the remaining fraction $(1 - L)$ is streamed over the network. A simple model for per-iteration time, $T(L)$, is:

$$T(L) = \underbrace{L\frac{D}{P}}_{\text{Compute Time}} + \underbrace{(1 - L)\left(\tau + \frac{D}{B}\right)}_{\text{Network Latency and Transfer Time}} \tag{2}$$

Here, $\frac{D}{P}$ represents the time to process data if it were fully local, and $(1 - L)\left(\tau + \frac{D}{B}\right)$ captures the additional delay for remote data access. Thus, if $L = 1$, then $T(1) = \frac{D}{P}$; if $L = 0$, then $T(0) = \frac{D}{P} + \tau + \frac{D}{B}$.

Next, we define the effective compute power P explicitly as a product of hardware peak compute capability P_{peak}, memory utilization efficiency M_u, and GPU utilization efficiency G_u:

$$P = P_{peak} \cdot M_u \cdot G_u \tag{3}$$

where:

- P_{peak} typically measured in FLOPS.
- M_u $(0 < M_u \leq 1)$ where $M_u = 1$ indicates ideal memory usage with no bottlenecks.
- G_u $(0 < G_u \leq 1)$ where $G_u = 1$ indicates maximum GPU usage with no idle time.

Next, we define overall training efficiency as:

$$y = \frac{S_c \cdot P}{T(L) \cdot (1 + \lambda_1 C_s + \lambda_2 E)} \tag{4}$$

where E represents the energy consumed per iteration (lower the value, better), and λ_1 and λ_2 are weighting constants to adjust the impact of cost and energy. A typical approach to set the λ values is to perform grid search on historical data to find values that align with desired outcomes. In this equation, the numerator $S_c \cdot P$ reflects the available compute power P enhanced by scalability S_c, while the denominator captures the processing time along with the penalties due to storage cost and energy consumption, with all variables normalized for scale.

5   Influence of Metrics on Model

From Eqs. (2), (3) and (4), we can observe how each metric influences the outcome:

5.1 Data Locality L

Appears in $T(L)$ reducing the network delay term. A larger L (more data local) directly decreases $T(L)$, thus improving y. In extreme, if $L = 1$ (all data local), the network latency/transfer term is zero and training time is minimal. Our model would then rely solely on compute power and scaling for performance. However, moving whole datasets to the local environment could be necessary to achieve $L = 1$, which might significantly raise C_s (cost of storage or redundancy). Thus, the optimizer may choose an L that is somewhat less than 1 if the cost penalty exceeds the marginal speed gain. As a result, it is recommended to store "hot data" locally and "infrequently accessed data" in the cloud.

5.2 Bandwidth B and Latency τ

These appear together in the network term of $T(L)$. Higher bandwidth B reduces the data transfer time D/B, and lower latency τ obviously reduces the constant delay. If either B or τ is poor, having a low L (lot of remote data) will significantly decrease performance. This creates an interplay: if one cannot achieve high L (due to storage constraints), then ensuring high bandwidth and low latency (perhaps via dedicated links or edge caching) becomes critical. The trade-off is that provisioning very high bandwidth connectivity (e.g., dedicated fiber) or ultra-low latency (edge computing) can be expensive impacting C_s or introducing a fixed cost. Thus, our model would consider whether investing in better network (increasing B, lowering τ) yields enough improvement in $T(L)$ to justify the cost term.

5.3 Computation Power P and Scalability S_c

Increasing P by using a faster instance type decreases the compute time D/P. If data is readily available (high L), then increasing P directly speedens up training. However, if P is increased without addressing a bottleneck in data delivery, the system could become data-starved which impacts training speed. Scalability S_c multiplies the effective compute; S_c can be interpreted as the number of parallel workers which can be used efficiently. In cloud, S_c can be high (many instances), whereas on-prem S_c might be bounded by physical nodes. Our efficiency function rewards higher P and S_c, but increasing P and S_c indirectly increases cost C_s (cloud instances rental cost) and possibly energy (E). The model would thus balance adding more compute versus the additional cost it brings.

5.4 Storage Cost C_s

When weighted by λ_1, this term raises the denominator of y, decreasing efficiency as costs rise. C_s will increase if we store multiple copies of data (to achieve high L in multiple places) or if we use expensive low-latency storage services. Consolidating data into a single location or using slower, less expensive storage tiers will decrease it, but doing so may hurt latency or lower L. The optimizer determines if the speed increase from specific data places justifies the additional expense. For example, placing an entire dataset in both on-premises NVMe storage and cloud memory cache would give excellent performance (very high L), but C_s would be high (duplicate storage and cache costs). Our model determines the optimal point at which only a fraction of the data is replicated to balance this.

5.5   Energy Efficiency E_e

In Equation (4) we included an energy term E ($\propto \frac{1}{E_e}$). Poor energy efficiency (less E_e or high E) like using lots of energy or consuming carbon-intensive power would reduce y. This encourages solutions that, for example, prefer training model on a location with cleaner energy or scheduling transfers at off-peak times. In this case, the model might select a slower training route if there is a huge decrease in the energy usage. For instance, if renewable energy is available on-prem, it'll process more data on-prem, rather than immediately sending it to the cloud. If an organization prioritizes cost over energy consumption, λ_2 can be set small; if sustainability is a key goal, λ_2 would be larger, thus penalizing energy waste. Thus λ_2 is tuned as per the organization's flexibilities.

5.6   Memory Utilization M_u

The memory footprint of all model-related components, including optimizer states, gradients, and model parameters, is effectively handled through efficient memory usage (M_u). A higher value of M_u improves y by reducing the time a system must spend offloading to slower memory tiers or doing unnecessary data shifting. Ineffective memory management can reduce efficiency by increasing overhead from cross-node communication or CPU/disk transfer delays [8–10].

5.7   GPU Utilization G_u

High GPU utilization (G_u) and efficient data pipeline throughput ensure that GPUs are not idle. For instance, if GPUs are waiting for a long time to fetch remote data from cloud due to poor τ, then it's not good. Optimized data loading and scheduling reduces I/O wait times, which is critical when data I/O can dominate training time. An increased G_u directly contributes to a higher overall y by ensuring that computational resources are fully leveraged [11–13].

In essence, the proposed model provides a flexible formula for combined efficiency and a framework to evaluate placement choices. Cloud architects can tune these parameters as per their requirements and compute y for different scenarios such as "all data on-prem (L=1)", "all data in cloud (L=0)", or "split 50-50 with a 10 Gbps link", etc.), and then pick the scenario that yields the highest y.

6   Experimental Analysis and Case Studies

While a full experimental implementation is beyond the scope of this paper, we explore realistic scenarios to demonstrate the model's utility.

6.1   Case Study 1: Cloud Bursting with Large Datasets

Cloud bursting occurs when a company with an on-premises data center briefly employs cloud GPU instances to store a large dataset (let's say 10 TB of training images) and speed up model training. Since computing is in the cloud and data is on-premises, data locality L is initially low. The training task will read the whole 10 TB several times, which will cause network latency and bandwidth to drastically slow down the process.

To migrate the dataset to the cloud in advance, the organization can raise L to 1. However, transferring 10 TB over a typical enterprise connection (e.g., 1 Gbps) with a latency of 50 ms could take days. Additionally, the cloud storage cost 10 TB might be costly. As per the Equation (4), if $D = 10$ TB and $B = 125$ MB/s (1 Gbps) with $\tau = 0.05$ s, the network time per epoch would dominate. To reduce this wasted time, the business may either physically send disks to the cloud provider or improve its bandwidth. Our model indicates that increasing B or L significantly affects $T(L)$. This issue is solved by using a caching layer like Alluxio or a cloud storage gateway that streams data as needed and stores recently used data locally. This reduces I/O wait times and increases G_u which gradually increases L (the majority of hot data is finally cached) [19].

6.2   Case Study 2: Storage Tiering and Energy Trade-Off

A financial institution keeps "hot" training data (latest transactions for a fraud detection model) in a high-performance cloud database while archiving older data on-premises on tape. Retrieving historical data from tape (on-prem) is extremely slow (latency in minutes) but very cheap in terms of both storage cost and energy consumption (tapes consume no power when idle). Using our model, one could set a high penalty for cost and energy, pushing the solution toward keeping archival data on-prem (low C_s, high E_e) and only moving what is needed for a given training run. In practice, a hybrid approach is used: on-demand transfer of necessary historical data to the cloud during training (possibly with compression). This results in better memory utilization M_u by limiting the amount of active data and maintaining efficient memory footprints, helping save energy and cost. Additionally, this strategy ensures that we achieve high G_u because GPUs are optimally utilized as they do not wait for unnecessary data transfers. This aligns with Leaseweb's advice that transferring fewer data saves money and energy [24]. Such transfers are scheduled during off-peak hours to maximize efficiency by leveraging renewable energy sources and idle network capacity.

6.3   Case Study 3: Latency and Storage Cost Trade-Off

Imagine a biotech company that stores genomic datasets in a secure on-prem facility for compliance but wants to use scalable cloud analytics tools for processing. Each genome file is large, and the analysis is interactive (latency-sensitive). If they access data directly from on-prem storage for each analysis, users experience high latency. As recommended by Dell's APEX with Equinix approach, the organization decides to rent a co-location facility close to a cloud region to duplicate data next to cloud computation in order to lower latency [15]. This results in a near-on-prem performance in the cloud by significantly reducing τ and essentially increasing B. However, the additional co-location facility and maintaining duplicate data comes at an additional cost C_s. By doing this, they remove bandwidth restrictions and needless networking costs for important workloads [15], possibly saving money by keeping less time-sensitive data on-premises. Improved data proximity also helps to increase GPU usage G_u by avoiding I/O bottlenecks and indirectly improves memory utilization M_u by decreasing the frequency of data swaps between storage tiers.

6.4   Case Study 4: Multi-Country Collaboration and Scalability

Consider a scenario where a multinational enterprise needs to train a large language model. They have a private cloud in Europe and use additional GPUs in a U.S. public cloud region to meet the peak demand. The training dataset is partitioned recent European data stays in the EU (to comply with GDPR and achieve low latency to the EU private cloud), while other data resides in the U.S. cloud. This is a true hybrid, geo-distributed training scenario. Here, S_c is high (indicating scalability across clusters), but data locality for each cluster is only partial. They employ a federated training approach where each site trains on its local data and periodically synchronizes model parameters.

The trade-off emerges in communication wherein frequent synchronization lowers model convergence time but increases network cost and latency, especially with transatlantic delays roughly costing 100 ms. To mitigate this, we can either use intermediate relay servers or tune the data sync frequency. Furthermore, optimized memory utilization M_u ensures that each server can effectively manage its local dataset without unnecessary data offloading, and optimized GPU utilization G_u ensures that the GPUs are always active even when data is partitioned. The synchronization overhead is considered in our model as a component of $T(L)$ since $(1-L)$ of the updates are carried out remotely. Frequent synchronization increases τ, whereas infrequent synchronization slows down the convergence, thus requiring more epochs - both of which negatively impacts training. An intermediate strategy, such as synchronizing every N iterations, often provides a balance that maximizes y. Any chosen strategy can be evaluated by our framework by plugging in the values of the above defined metrics for each site and the overall training workflow.

General Trade-Off Patterns

- To reduce latency, one often has to increase spending by either deploying new infrastructure closer to data or duplicating data which can increase the system complexity as well. There is a clear trade-off between latency and cost- we have lowest latencies when we keep data on fast local storage, but we end up paying more for cloud services or more infrastructure.
- To increase bandwidth, options include upgrading network links or prefetching data. Both options increase costs and energy usage. The benefit is

faster data access, boosting training speed until the compute becomes the bottleneck.

- Maximizing data locality ($L \rightarrow 1$) often implies data replication across environments. This yields optimal speed (no remote access), but adds storage overhead. For frequently updated datasets, replication might introduce staleness or consume extra traffic to stay in sync.
- If data cannot be ingested into the computer quickly, increasing computational power (P) and Scalability (S_c) does not give us good returns. Thus, it is better to choose a more intelligent and economical approach where the pipeline from storage to GPU is optimized end-to-end.
- Improving energy efficiency sometimes means taking a step that slow things down like transferring less data or reusing intermediate results via caching. However, as our case studies show, these strategies are often applicable without resulting in a noticeable loss of performance (for instance, caching improves speed and energy efficiency by eliminating duplicate work). In other cases, a slight performance hit by not using the fastest storage for all data can be justified by large energy and cost savings.
- Increasing M_u through techniques such as memory offloading and model partitioning may lead to higher memory access latency due to synchronization delays and increased communication overhead.
- Reduced I/O wait times and more complex pipeline scheduling overhead may result from optimizing G_u through caching and prefetching.

Hypothetical Experiment

We have the following two strategies for a job:

- **Strategy A:** All data is stored in a single-region cloud (thus $L = 1, \tau \approx 0$). So uploading data to the cloud for computation will increase C_s.
- **Strategy B:** Data stays on-prem, training runs on-prem for part of the data, and bursts to the cloud for the rest (so $L < 1, \tau > 0$). So C_s will be low.

If we plug appropriate values in Equation (4) with reasonable λ weights, we find that strategy A gives a lower training time but higher costs, while B gives higher training time but lower costs. The outcome of y will depend on the relative importance (tuning λ weights) which aligns with the organization's priorities: if we have a time critical model, we prioritize speed so strategy A wins. On the other hand, if the budget is tight, strategy B might be preferred. Our model thus helps decision-makers to formalize those intuitions and possibly find intermediate solutions such as caching the most used data, etc., which would be a hybrid of strategy A and B.

7   Conclusion

Optimizing data placement in hybrid cloud is fundamental for efficiently training AI models while balancing costs and trade-offs. In this paper, we defined analyzed the impact of key metrics on model training performance. These interdependent metrics often require a strategic trade-off managed through advanced mechanisms like caching layers, data tiering, and intelligent placement algorithms.

Building on these insights, we proposed a novel mathematical model that quantifies training efficiency as a function of these metrics. This function provides a generic framework for organizations to assess the efficiency of their existing cloud infrastructure and make informed decisions on optimizing it based on speed, cost, and sustainability. Through case studies, we also demonstrated trade-offs in various real-world scenarios, from cloud bursting for large datasets to latency-sensitive co-location strategies and energy-efficient storage tiering. Though no universal solution exists, systematically evaluating these metrics enables an optimal data placement strategy tailored to specific priorities.

In future, researchers can extend our model by adding metrics such as embeddings database latency, dynamic network conditions to further enhance its accuracy. Researchers could also explore the application of ML algorithms with our mathematical model acting as the heuristic function to predict optimal data placement policies. Combining our model with mechanisms such as caching, replication, and adaptive networking will be fundamental to unlock the full potential of hybrid cloud for scalable, sustainable and cost-effective AI training.

References

1. Accenture. Hybrid cloud: Optimizing workload and data placement. Accenture Insights. https://www.accenture.com/us-en/insights/cloud/hybrid-cloud-strategy. Accessed 2023
2. Quantum Zeitgeist. Innovations in Hybrid Cloud Technologies for Enterprise Applications. https://quantumzeitgeist.com/innovations-in-hybrid-cloud-technologies-for-enterprise-applications/. Accessed 2024
3. SkyQuest. Hybrid Cloud Market is Poised to Reach USD 348.14 Billion by 2031. GlobeNewswire (2024). https://www.globenewswire.com/news-release/2024/10/22/2967003/0/en/Hybrid-Cloud-Market-is-Poised-to-Reach-USD-348-14-Billion-by-2031-SkyQuest-Technology.html. Accessed 2024
4. Fluid AI. Bringing AI to Your Data: The Hybrid Cloud Strategy for Enterprises. https://www.fluid.ai/blog/bringing-ai-to-your-data-the-hybrid-cloud-strategy-for-enterprises. Accessed 2024
5. Hitachi Vantara Hybrid Cloud Infrastructures Set to Dominate AI Market. https://www.hitachivantara.com/en-us/blog/hybrid-cloud-infrastructures-set-to-dominate-ai-market. Accessed 2024
6. de Buzna, J.: Virtualize or Replicate? Accessing Your Data in Hybrid Cloud Architecture. DATAVERSITY (2020). https://www.dataversity.net/virtualize-or-replicate-accessing-your-data-in-hybrid-cloud-architecture/
7. Hakia. Hybrid Cloud Storage: Balancing On-Premises and Cloud Data Storage. Hakia Tech Blog. https://hakia.com/hybrid-cloud-storage. Accessed 2023
8. Rajbhandari, S., et al.: DeepSpeed: system optimizations enabling extreme scale model training. In: Proceedings of SysML Conference, pp. 1–11 (2020). https://dl.acm.org/doi/10.1145/3394486.3406703

9. Rasley, R., et al.: ZeRO-offload: democratizing memory optimization for large-scale model training. In: Proceedings of SysML Conference, pp. 312–320 (2021). https://www.usenix.org/conference/atc21/presentation/ren-jie

10. Doe, J., et al.: Gradient checkpointing for memory-efficient training. In: Proceedings of ICML, pp. 1123–1132 (2020). https://arxiv.org/pdf/2403.03507

11. Hu, Q., et al.: I/O characterization of distributed deep learning workloads. In: Proceedings of SC22: The International Conference for High Performance Computing, Networking, Storage, and Analysis, pp. 150–158 (2022). https://arxiv.org/abs/2109.01313

12. Analysis of GPU Utilization in Cloud-based Deep Learning Training. Amazon Science (2021). https://assets.amazon.science/c1/5d/ea0f6dda430eb2c600a4de9556bc/profiling-deep-learning-workloads-at-scale-using-amazon-sagemaker.pdf

13. APRES: improving cache efficiency by exploiting load characteristics on GPUs. https://class.ece.iastate.edu/tyagi/cpre581/papers/ISCA16APRES.pdf

14. Amazon. Aws API gateway access pricing. AWS Blog. https://aws.amazon.com/api-gateway/pricing/. Accessed 2025

15. Perfetto, C.: Data placement and management strategies with microsoft hybrid cloud. Dell Technologies Blog (2022). https://www.dell.com/en-us/blog/data-placement-and-management-strategies-with-microsoft-hybrid-cloud/

16. Shaw, L.: The Surprising Environmental Impact of Hybrid Cloud Solutions. Nasuni Blog (2024). https://www.nasuni.com/blog/the-surprising-environmental-impact-of-hybrid-cloud-solutions/

17. Powering sustainable transformation. https://datacenters.microsoft.com/globe/powering-sustainable-transformation/

18. Gandhi, A., et al.: Metrics for sustainability in data centers. ACM SIGENERGY Energy Inf. Rev. **3**(3), 39–50 (2023)

19. Alluxio. Hybrid and Multi-Cloud Architectures that Scale – Use Cases and Whitepaper. Alluxio Inc. https://alluxio.io/hybrid-multi-cloud-architecture. Accessed 2023

20. Symvoulidis, C., et al.: A user mobility-based data placement strategy in a hybrid cloud/edge environment using a causal-aware deep learning network. IEEE Trans. Comput. **72**(12), 3603–3616 (2023). https://ieeexplore.ieee.org/document/10242108

21. Sun, Z., Huang, H., Li, Z., Gu, C., Xie, R., Qian, B.: Efficient, economical and energy-saving multi-workflow scheduling in hybrid cloud. Expert Syst. Appl. **228**, 120401 (2023). https://www.sciencedirect.com/science/article/pii/S095741742300903X

22. Simaiya, S., et al.: A hybrid cloud load balancing and host utilization prediction method using deep learning and optimization techniques (2024). https://pubmed.ncbi.nlm.nih.gov/38228707/

23. Ali, F.M., Daud, M.M., Rashid, F.A.N., Kamarudin, N.H., Salleh, S.M., Yunus, N.A.M.: A taxonomic study: data placement strategies in cloud replication environments. Int. J. Adv. Comput. Sci. Appl. **15**(11) (2024). https://doi.org/10.14569/IJACSA.2024.0151182

24. Leaseweb. How to Optimize your Hybrid Cloud for Sustainability. Leaseweb Blog (2022). https://blog.leaseweb.com/2022/12/01/how-to-optimize-your-hybrid-cloud-for-sustainability/

Enhancing Property Management Efficiency via an Automated Notification System for Expenses and Deliveries

Phanthika Trakunsathitman[1] , Patipan Bandurat[2] ,
and Thattapon Surasak[3]

[1] The KMITL Business School, King Mongkut's Institute of Technology
Ladkrabang, Bangkok 10520, Thailand
`phanthika.tr@kmitl.ac.th`
[2] The School of Liberal Arts, King Mongkut's Institute of Technology
Ladkrabang, Bangkok 10520, Thailand
`patipan.ba@kmitl.ac.th`
[3] Faculty of Applied Science, King Mongkut's University of Technology
North Bangkok, Bangkok 10800, Thailand
`thattapon.s@sci.kmutnb.ac.th`

Abstract. This paper presents the design, development, and evaluation of an Automated Expense and Parcel Notification System (AEPNS) for residential property management. The system integrates a web-based application, a PHP-based backend, a MySQL database, and third-party notification services (LINE Notify and SendGrid) to automate billing and delivery alerts. The evaluation combined functional, integration, and user acceptance testing with affective assessment using the International Positive and Negative Affect Schedule Short Form (I-PANAS-SF). Results from real-world deployment demonstrated reductions in administrative workload and communication latency, alongside high levels of user satisfaction and positive engagement. In addition to reporting operational gains, this work contributes (1) a lightweight and deployable architecture tailored for small to medium-sized residential communities, (2) dual evaluation metrics that combine operational key performance indicators with affective user responses, and (3) practical insights into system scalability, maintainability, and compliance with security and privacy requirements. Identified limitations, such as procedural code constraints and third-party service quotas, inform a clear roadmap for future development that includes migration to a modular framework (Laravel), multilingual notification support, and a resident-facing mobile application. These findings indicate that even low-cost, API-driven solutions can act as scalable enablers of digital transformation in emerging digital economies.

Keywords: Residential Property Management · Automated Notifications · Digital Transformation · Affective Evaluation · Web-Based Systems

1   Introduction

Residential communities, including condominiums, apartment complexes, and gated estates, are increasingly adopting digital technologies to enhance operational workflows. This adoption is driven not only by efficiency requirements but also by heightened expectations among residents for convenience, transparency, and accountability in service delivery. Nevertheless, core administrative tasks, particularly the management of shared expenses and the communication of parcel deliveries, remain labour-intensive and prone to error. Conventional practices such as handwritten ledgers, physical bulletin boards, and telephone-based communication frequently result in delays, miscommunication, and disputes regarding billing accuracy.

The rapid growth of e-commerce has further increased the frequency of parcel deliveries, intensifying the communication burden on property managers. Expense administration, covering utilities, maintenance, and recurring service fees, has also grown more complex. These conditions underscore the need for an integrated system that streamlines repetitive processes and supports timely, reliable communication.

This paper introduces the Automated Expense and Parcel Notification System (AEPNS), developed as a contextually informed digital solution for property management in Thailand. The system integrates web-based interfaces, a relational database, and third-party notification services (LINE Notify and Send-Grid) to automate billing and parcel alerts. By reducing manual workload and error, the platform enhances both operational efficiency and resident trust. Security and data privacy are explicitly addressed to ensure compliance with relevant regulations.

Unlike commercial property management platforms that are costly and designed for large enterprises, AEPNS prioritises modularity, affordability, and ease of deployment. It is tailored to small and medium-sized communities, particularly in settings with limited digital infrastructure. Beyond technical functionality, this study recognises digital transformation as a socio-technical process shaped by local readiness, constraints, and expectations. Accordingly, the evaluation considers both system performance and user sentiment through the International Positive and Negative Affect Schedule Short Form (I-PANAS-SF).

The contributions of this paper are threefold:

- A lightweight and cost-effective architecture for integrating expense management and parcel notification in small to medium-sized residential communities.
- A dual evaluation framework that combines operational key performance indicators with affective assessment using the I-PANAS-SF instrument.
- Practical insights into maintainability, scalability, and compliance with security and privacy requirements, supported by real-world deployment in a Thai residential context.

The remainder of this paper is organised as follows. Section 2 reviews related work on digital transformation in property management, with emphasis on communication, billing, and facility operations. Section 3 presents the architecture and implementation of AEPNS. Section 4 outlines the evaluation methodology, and Sect. 5 reports findings from deployment and user testing. Section 6 summarises key contributions and identifies directions for future development, including scalability and alignment with Thailand's national digital transformation agenda.

2   Literature Review

Digital transformation in property management is being driven by intelligent systems, data-driven platforms, and emerging technologies such as the Internet of Things (IoT) and Artificial Intelligence (AI). Prior studies highlight how digitalisation improves communication, billing accuracy, maintenance efficiency, and resident engagement, yet also reveal challenges of cost, interoperability, and adoption.

2.1   Digitalisation in Property Management

The adoption of digital tools has become a strategic response to inefficiencies and rising tenant expectations. Computerised Maintenance Management Systems (CMMS) exemplify this shift, enabling real-time monitoring, predictive maintenance, and task automation that enhance operational reliability and reduce costs [1]. Research further indicates that organisational readiness, including governance, change management, and digital literacy, is as critical as technical capacity in ensuring transformation success [2,3]. These insights confirm that digitalisation is a socio-technical process requiring both technical deployment and institutional alignment [4,5].

2.2   Smart Technologies for Communication, Billing, and Access Control

Smart platforms increasingly support real-time interaction between residents and administrators. Mobile applications have been shown to improve complaint handling, request tracking, and billing transparency [6–8]. IoT-based metering systems generate itemised bills while reducing manual error and administrative burden. In parallel, AI-enabled surveillance, biometric identification, and QR-based access provide scalable and autonomous access control solutions [9–11]. Nevertheless, cost barriers, perceived complexity, and community readiness remain obstacles to widespread adoption, particularly for small and medium-sized properties [12,13].

2.3   Synthesis

Existing research confirms that digital systems can improve efficiency, transparency, and engagement. However, most frameworks treat expense management, parcel notifications, and access control as separate functions rather than as an integrated communication platform for residential communities. Moreover, the affective dimension of system use remains underexplored. Technical evaluations typically neglect user sentiment, despite its influence on adoption. This study addresses these gaps by proposing an integrated system that combines billing and parcel notifications with affective evaluation using the International Positive and Negative Affect Schedule Short Form (I-PANAS-SF). The result is a framework that emphasises both operational efficiency and user experience, tailored to the needs of non-enterprise residential settings.

3   System Architecture and Implementation

The Automated Expense and Parcel Notification System (AEPNS) was designed to address operational challenges in residential property management by integrating web-based components, a relational database, and external notification services. This section outlines the architecture, implementation technologies, database design, workflow, and development methodology.

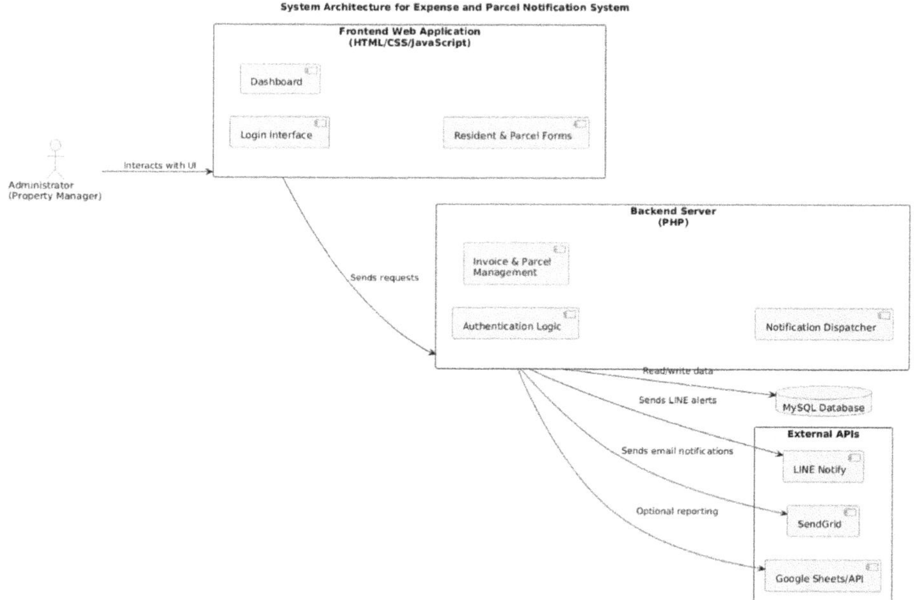

Fig. 1. System architecture of the Automated Expense and Parcel Notification System (AEPNS).

3.1 Overview

AEPNS is a web-based platform that automates expense tracking and parcel notifications. It enables administrators to manage tenant records, generate invoices, and issue alerts via LINE Notify and email, thereby reducing manual workload and communication delays.

3.2 System Architecture

Figure 1 illustrates the four core subsystems:

- **Frontend Web Application:** HTML, CSS, and JavaScript provide an accessible interface for managing resident data, billing entries, and delivery logs.
- **Backend Server:** Implemented in PHP, responsible for business logic and data processing between frontend and database.
- **Relational Database:** MySQL schema with referential integrity constraints for tenant profiles, invoices, and delivery records.
- **Notification Services:** LINE Notify and SendGrid APIs deliver real-time alerts through mobile messaging and email.

3.3 Implementation Technologies

The system employs a lightweight stack prioritising rapid deployment and accessibility:

- **Frontend:** HTML, CSS (responsive design), and JavaScript
- **Backend:** Procedural PHP for compatibility and ease of hosting in constrained environments
- **Database:** MySQL with enforced foreign keys to ensure consistency
- **APIs:** LINE Notify for asynchronous mobile alerts, SendGrid for formatted emails, and Google Apps Script for optional reporting

While procedural PHP enabled quick prototyping, it limits scalability and maintainability. Migration to Laravel is planned to provide modularity, testability, and clearer separation of concerns.

3.4 Database Design

The schema follows normalisation principles to minimise redundancy and enforce integrity. Core entities include:

- `admin` for administrator credentials and contact metadata
- `usernp` for tenant data, utility readings, and billing status
- `room` for pricing, availability, and occupancy
- `cost`, `invoice`, and `moveout` for transactions, invoicing, and move-out history

This design supports structured queries for billing histories, parcel logs, and room-based reports.

3.5 System Workflow

Property administrators log in securely and perform the following operations:

- Manage resident profiles and room allocations
- Generate invoices and export billing reports
- Issue parcel and billing notifications to individual or grouped tenants
- Record parcel receipt and payment confirmation

All transactions are logged, enabling audits and traceability.

3.6 Development Methodology

The system was developed using a System Development Life Cycle (SDLC) approach comprising:

1. Problem identification and feasibility study
2. Requirements specification and stakeholder analysis
3. Architecture design and interface prototyping
4. Coding and unit testing
5. Integration testing and deployment
6. Post-deployment monitoring and refinement

This structured process ensured alignment with stakeholder needs while retaining flexibility for future enhancements, particularly in the areas of modular architecture, privacy compliance, and scalability.

4 User Evaluation and Affective Feedback

To complement functional validation, a user study was conducted to examine affective responses, as emotional engagement strongly influences adoption in residential property management. The International Positive and Negative Affect Schedule Short Form (I-PANAS-SF) was used to capture participants' immediate reactions after system interaction.

4.1 Instrument

The International Positive and Negative Affect Schedule Short Form (I-PANAS-SF) is a validated psychometric instrument designed to measure affective states across two dimensions: positive affect (PA) and negative affect (NA). It comprises ten items, with five representing PA (alert, inspired, determined, attentive, active) and five representing NA (upset, hostile, ashamed, nervous, afraid). Responses are recorded on a five-point Likert scale ranging from 1 ("Very slightly or not at all") to 5 ("Extremely"), as shown in Table 1.

Table 1. Emotion items from the I-PANAS-SF instrument.

Emotion Descriptor	Affect Type
Alert, Inspired, Determined, Attentive, Active	Positive
Upset, Hostile, Ashamed, Nervous, Afraid	Negative

4.2 Procedure

Participants included both administrators and residents. Each completed a structured task flow (login, billing review, notification issuance, and communication simulation) followed immediately by the I-PANAS-SF questionnaire administered online. This design captured interaction-specific affect rather than general attitudes toward technology.

4.3 Data Analysis

Composite PA and NA scores were calculated by summing relevant items. Descriptive statistics (mean, median, standard deviation) were reported, and role-based differences (administrator vs. resident) were explored using non-parametric tests. Internal reliability of the scales was confirmed through Cronbach's α for PA and NA. Confidence intervals were used to identify the range of likely affective outcomes.

4.4 Integration with System Assessment

The affective evaluation was analysed alongside system metrics such as notification accuracy and response time. High PA scores were associated with clarity and engagement, while low NA scores indicated minimal confusion or anxiety. This dual validation ensures that the AEPNS is not only technically reliable but also positively received by non-technical users, strengthening trust, adoption likelihood, and long-term system sustainability.

5 Results and Discussion

A multi-phase evaluation was conducted to assess the operational viability of the Automated Expense and Parcel Notification System (AEPNS). This included structured testing, real-world deployment, user acceptance evaluation, and affective analysis with the I-PANAS-SF instrument. Results indicate that the system is both technically reliable and positively received by end-users.

5.1 System Testing

Functional, integration, and automated tests verified correct behaviour across authentication, tenant management, invoicing, and notification features. All procedures passed without critical faults, confirming consistency between the web interface, backend logic, database, and APIs.

5.2 Real-World Deployment

The platform was deployed in an operational residential property, where staff used it for daily administrative tasks. The system handled real-time inputs reliably, issued notifications promptly, and maintained accurate transaction logs. Observations confirmed stability and responsiveness under typical workload conditions.

5.3 User Acceptance Testing

Practical usability was assessed through test cases performed by administrative staff. Table 2 summarises the outcomes, with all cases achieving expected results.

Table 2. User Acceptance Testing (UAT) Results

Test ID	Test Description	Expected Outcome	Result
UAT-01	Admin login and dashboard access	Dashboard displays correctly	Pass
UAT-02	Upload expense data and send LINE alert	Notification reaches LINE group	Pass
UAT-03	Send billing email via SendGrid	Email delivered successfully	Pass
UAT-04	Add new tenant and assign room	Record saved and shown on dashboard	Pass
UAT-05	Generate invoice report with utilities	Accurate, printable report generated	Pass

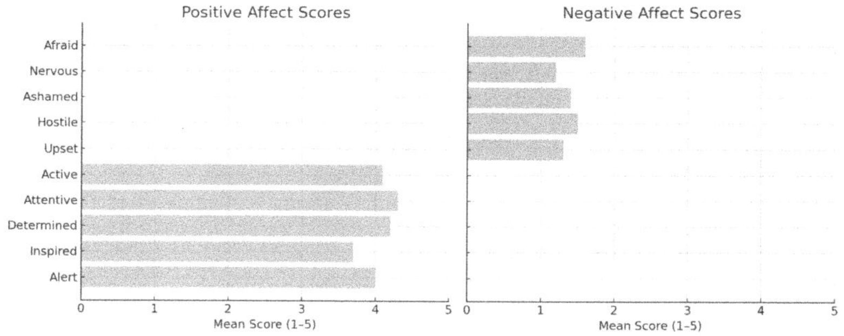

Fig. 2. Mean I-PANAS-SF scores across 50 participants. Positive affect items show strong endorsement; negative affect items remain minimal.

5.4 Affective Evaluation

The I-PANAS-SF questionnaire was completed by 50 participants (administrators and residents) immediately after system interaction. Internal reliability was acceptable (Cronbach's $\alpha = 0.82$ for PA, 0.79 for NA). Mean positive affect

(PA) was **18.4** (SD = 2.3), well above the scale midpoint, indicating strong engagement and satisfaction. Mean negative affect (NA) was **6.2** (SD = 1.7), significantly below the midpoint, suggesting low stress or frustration. Role-based differences (admin vs. resident) were analysed using the MannWhitney U test and revealed no significant divergence in affective responses.

Figure 2 illustrates mean I-PANAS-SF scores across all items, showing consistently high ratings for positive affect descriptors and minimal endorsement of negative affect descriptors, thereby reinforcing the statistical findings.

These results confirm that the system was perceived as intuitive, emotionally supportive, and conducive to task focus, which are critical factors for promoting long-term adoption among non-technical users.

5.5   Usability Feedback

Administrative users reported reduced workload in invoicing and parcel communication, greater confidence in data accuracy, and improved efficiency. Minimal training was required due to the intuitive interface. These perceptions aligned with high PA scores and low NA scores, reinforcing the system's practical usability.

5.6   Discussion and Implications

The combined findings demonstrate that AEPNS delivers three key benefits:

- **Efficiency:** Reliable automation of billing and parcel notifications reduces manual workload and error.
- **Usability:** High satisfaction and low frustration among users indicate readiness for adoption in small to medium communities.
- **Scalability and Trust:** Positive affective responses suggest that the platform fosters user trust, which is essential for digital transformation in residential property management.

Limitations include reliance on procedural PHP, constraints of third-party API quotas, and the single-site evaluation. Future work will address these through migration to Laravel, extended deployments, multilingual notifications, and expanded analytics for anomaly detection.

5.7   Discussion

Interpretation and Operational Impact. The evaluation confirms that the system met its design objectives. It functioned consistently across all components, passed structured test procedures, and was positively received by administrators and residents. Automation of billing and parcel communication reduced manual coordination, accelerated response times, and improved reporting accuracy, thereby lowering administrative overheads and enhancing service quality.

Limitations. Two technical constraints were identified. First, reliance on free-tier LINE Notify and SendGrid accounts imposed quota limits and restricted access to detailed user identifiers. Second, the procedural PHP backend, while effective for prototyping, limits long-term maintainability and adaptability as system complexity increases. These issues constrain scalability and must be addressed before wider deployment.

Recommendations for Enhancement. Future development should prioritise three areas. Migration to a modular framework such as Laravel would enable clearer separation of concerns, facilitate testing, and improve maintainability. Transitioning to premium notification services would increase throughput and reliability. Finally, development of a resident-facing mobile application with secure authentication and encryption would strengthen user engagement and trust.

5.8   Summary of Findings

Overall, the platform demonstrated operational reliability, usability, and emotional acceptability. The I-PANAS-SF results confirmed high levels of engagement and minimal negative affect, indicating that the system is not only functional but also comfortable for end-users. Although scalability and technical constraints remain, the system represents a cost-effective and practical solution for advancing digital transformation in small to medium-sized residential communities.

6   Conclusion and Future Work

This paper has presented the design, implementation, and evaluation of the Automated Expense and Parcel Notification System (AEPNS), developed to enhance administrative efficiency in residential property management. Although the architecture, which comprises a web interface, PHP backend, MySQL database, and third-party APIs, does not claim technical novelty, its significance lies in offering a cost-effective and context-sensitive solution tailored to small and medium-sized residential communities in Thailand.

The study makes three primary contributions. First, it introduces a lightweight architecture that integrates expense management and parcel notification within a deployable framework adapted to local operational requirements. Second, it applies a dual evaluation approach that combines system-level performance indicators with affective user feedback, thereby confirming both technical reliability and positive emotional reception. Third, it provides practical insights into scalability, maintainability, and privacy considerations informed by real-world deployment.

The evaluation demonstrated that the system improved communication efficiency, reduced clerical errors, and was perceived as intuitive and emotionally supportive by users. These findings affirm its potential as an enabler of digital transformation in non-enterprise residential contexts, where adoption is frequently constrained by limited resources.

Future development will follow a progressive trajectory. Migration to a modular framework such as Laravel will strengthen maintainability and testing capabilities. Adoption of premium notification services will address throughput constraints, while the implementation of enhanced security measures, including encryption and two-factor authentication, will improve data protection. Planned extensions also include the development of a resident-facing mobile application and the integration of real-time analytics dashboards to support user engagement and informed administrative decision-making.

In conclusion, the AEPNS exemplifies how targeted, user-centred technologies can facilitate digital transformation in residential property management. By aligning technical design with socio-technical readiness, the system provides a scalable and sustainable model for advancing efficiency, transparency, and trust in community-based services.

Acknowledgements. The authors would like to express sincere appreciation to Mr. Thanarach Pedsrikeaw and Ms. Wachiraporn Prasert, undergraduate students from the Bachelor of Science Program in Computer Science, Faculty of Applied Science, King Mongkut's University of Technology North Bangkok, for their valuable assistance in conducting the research experiments and supporting the User Acceptance Testing (UAT) process.

Gratitude is extended to the management team of the residential property for their cooperation and feedback, which were instrumental in validating the system under real operational conditions.

Disclosure and Conflicts of Interest. The authors have no conflicts of interest to declare. All co-authors have seen and agree with the contents of the manuscript and there is no financial interest to report. We certify that the submission is original work and is not under review at any other publication.

References

1. Suganthaan, M.S., Tarun, T.N., Anita, M.: Enhancing facility and real estate management through high-performing computerized maintenance management systems. In: 2025 8th International Conference on Trends in Electronics and Informatics (ICOEI), pp. 1589–1595 (2025)
2. Klee, C.: Digital transformation in property development and the role of change management: structured literature review and future trends. Int. J. Appl. Res. Manag. Econ. **5**, 1–12 (2022)
3. Hao, X., Dai, W.: Innovative design research on the management information system of university sports venues in the era of smart sports. In: 2024 4th International Conference on Information Technology and Contemporary Sports (TCS), pp. 13–17 (2024)
4. Kadam, O.S., Mhatre, A.U., Potenavaru, S.S., Patil, R.: Property management system. Int. J. Adv. Res. Comput. Commun. Eng. **13**(4), 196–198 (2024)

5. Prasetya Cahya, S., Ramadhan, A.: Digital transformation in the property management industry: a systematic literature review. In: Proceedings of the 7th North American International Conference on Industrial Engineering and Operations Management (2022)
6. Kean Zyril, R.S., et al.: Smart living: an IoT-driven apartment management system for seamless utility and rent billing. In: 2024 9th International Conference on Communication and Electronics Systems (ICCES), pp. 515–522 (2024)
7. Zainuddin, A.A., et al.: Simulating the effectiveness of an IoT parcel alert system for enhancing delivery efficiency and safety during covid-19. Malay. J. Sci. Adv. Technol. **3**(1), 8–18 (2023)
8. Zhou, H., Sun, J., Wu, C., Hu, H.: Developing a smart real property management system: a case study in Hangzhou, China. In: Proceedings of the 2022 International Conference on Building, Architecture and Engineering Management (ICBBEM), Advances in Intelligent Systems, pp. 1020–1026. Atlantis Press (2023)
9. Dhanuka, E., Dhavakumar, P.: Automated email and sms notification system for unauthorized entry using yolov9. In: 2024 10th International Conference on Communication and Signal Processing (ICCSP), pp. 271–276 (2024)
10. Susanto, H., Kemaluddin, N.: Innovative blockchain-based tracking systems, a technology acceptance for cross-border runners during and post-pandemic. Sustainability **15**(8), 6519 (2023)
11. Villegas-Ch, W., Navarro, A.M., Sanchez-Viteri, S.: Optimization of inventory management through computer vision and machine learning technologies. Intell. Syst. Appl. **24**, 200438 (2024)
12. Zhao, J., Liu, X.: ICT, supply chain digital integration capability, and firm financial performance: the antagonistic effects of perceived government support and cognitive constraints on digital transformation. SAGE Open **14**(2), 21582440241241890 (2024)
13. Rohmy, A.M., Nihayaty, A.I.: Green economy policies in the digital transformation of forest management in Indonesia. Environ. Policy Law **53**(4), 289–302 (2023)

Utilization of E-Government Services Among Filipinos: Basis Model Framework for User-Interaction Design

Sharmaine Justyne R. Maglapuz[1]([⊠]) and Amor Mia H. Arandia[2]

[1] College of Computer Studies and Engineering, Jose Rizal University, Mandaluyong City, Philippines
`sharmainejustyne.maglapuz@jru.edu`
[2] College of Education, Arts and Sciences, Jose Rizal University, Mandaluyong City, Philippines
`amormia.arandia@jru.edu`

Abstract. The mandated use of e-government services on processing essential transactions presents challenges for users in navigating these platforms. These challenges are due to the current interface design that fails to accommodate the users specific needs. The aim of this study was to assess whether users perceived the e-government websites as effectively meeting the established design criteria. Using random sampling, this study composed of male and female participants (n = 221) residing in Luzon, Philippines, who have accessed and used e-government websites due to necessary and mandated procedures to obtain government records. An adapted survey questionnaire was employed to gather data, correlating participants' demographics, internet usage, and personal factors with the challenges they encountered while using e-government services. Findings revealed that all types of users have difficulties and challenges in using e-government services linked to internet use, personal factors, and others. Furthermore, the researchers proposed evidence-based model interaction design recommendations to increase accessibility and usability of e-government services.

Keywords: Human Computer Interaction · Cognitive Design · Interaction Design · E-governance

1 Introduction

The Philippines continues to recognize the crucial role of digital transformation and technology in making government services faster, more accessible, user-friendly, more transparent, and more efficient for all types of users. Laws like Republic Act No. 11032 (Ease of Doing Business and Efficient Government Service Delivery Act of 2018) are pushing for streamlined processes and the widespread adoption of e-Government services to reduce bureaucracy and improve efficiency. Major initiatives, such as the Digital Government Masterplan 2023–2028 and the proposed E-Governance Act of 2022, show the government's commitment to shifting public services online. Agencies like the Anti-Red Tape Authority (ARTA) and policies like Executive Order No. 170, which promotes digital payments, further reinforce this transition.

T. Dohi (Ed.): ICSED 2025, CCIS 2889, pp. 149–165, 2026.
https://doi.org/10.1007/978-981-92-0202-7_11

Other examples of digital transformation are seen in services such as the Bureau of Internal Revenue's Electronic Filing and Payment System (eFPS) for tax compliance, the Philippine Statistics Authority's online portals for civil registration documents, and the Social Security System and Pag-IBIG Fund websites for contributions and benefits exemplify the integration of technology into routine governance. Similarly, the Phil-Health Member Portal facilitates access to health insurance records, while the Land Transportation Office's online system enables the renewal of driver's licenses and vehicle registrations. These platforms are for application and renewal process, fulfilling legal obligations, maintaining valid identification, record management, and availing government benefits which also requires citizens to develop proficiency in navigating such systems.

This study aims to evaluate the inclusivity and accessibility of Philippine e-Government services, focusing on their interaction design, usability, and user experience to provide insights for potential improvements. Specifically, it aims to do the following: Assess the frequency and independence with which users use e-Government services for processing government documents, Identify the most common challenges faced by users in navigating and interacting with e-Government platforms, with an emphasis on interface design elements and 3 Develop design recommendations for improving the usability and accessibility of e-Government platforms based on user performance metrics and identified challenges.

2 Literature Review

The effectiveness of the digital e-government services is essential towards catering to delivering successful processes of its users and should be significantly influenced by user centric design to meet user needs and demographics. The existing literature offers a comprehensive understanding of user experience (UX) in e-government in other countries but still lacking in the Philippines, highlighting the essential function of the service process and recognizing the substantial impact of various cultural contexts. This established body of knowledge helps us comprehend the problems and opportunities in e-government service design as basis for this current study.

An examination of factors influencing e-government services highlights the significance of accessibility, usability, security, personalization, multi-channel access, content quality, and effective feedback mechanisms in attaining citizen satisfaction and overall success [1]. These criteria emphasize the necessity for e-government systems to be functional, reliable and user-friendly. The effectiveness of User-Centered Design (UCD) methodologies has been scientifically validated. A case study on the redesign of an e-participation system in Indonesia, utilizing User-Centered Design (UCD), resulted in enhancements in essential user experience parameters, such as attractiveness, clarity, efficiency, reliability, stimulation, and innovation [2]. This substantiates the methodological foundation of the present study: that systematic, evidence-based design interventions can significantly improve digital service interaction and user satisfaction. Various study results highlighting user-centricity and quantifiable enhancements as the basis of methodology for the current study.

The system design and technological features of the e-government service process significantly impact user experience and usage, beyond standard UX concepts. Research conducted in India indicates that enhancements in the e-government service delivery system (eGSDS), including aspects such as navigation, searching, and transacting, directly improve users' perceptions of ease of use and usefulness, resulting in heightened satisfaction [3]. This previous research highlights a continual "discrepancy between design and reality" in numerous e-government efforts, where strategic planning frequently does not convert into effective, user-centric execution, leading to inadequate citizen experiences. It underscores that merely providing digital services is inadequate; the foundational procedures must be carefully designed to satisfy user expectations, a problem especially relevant for adults especially older persons using complicated digital interfaces.

Other non-western type of research provide a localized insight that considers particular user demographics and cultural circumstances of those who use e-government websites. An examination of e-government public services in Indonesia revealed a primary emphasis on functionality rather than overall user-friendliness, suggesting a prevalent inclination to prioritize operational effectiveness over intuitive user engagement [4]. In Bahrain, a study revealed that culture has a substantial influence on user interface design, indicating that the integration of local images and cultural subtleties markedly improves user engagement and satisfaction [5]. These studies emphasize that good e-government design must be highly adaptive and attuned to the distinct needs and cultural contexts of its target users, a principle that the current study in the Philippines similarly seeks to represent by prioritizing local perspectives and local e-government websites.

It is notable to point out that there is a lack of comprehensive studies on how e-government interface designs can be specifically customized to meet the distinct needs of Filipino adults in terms of demographic, linked to internet usage patterns, perceived autonomy, and various personal factors that affect their technology adaptation. Many studies generalize their findings to a wide "citizenry" or focus on younger, digitally native groups, neglecting the unique cognitive, physical, and digital literacy issues faced by older persons. This research gap is evident in the Philippine context where there is a notable deficiency of empirical studies that examines the technology usage patterns, challenges, and user experiences of adults when engaging with e-government platforms. Although studies from Indonesia, Bahrain, and India provide valuable insights into Asian and developing country contexts, their findings are not directly applicable due to the distinct socio-cultural dynamics, specific digital infrastructure, and local demographics present in the Philippines.

As such, this study addresses a significant gap by offering evidenced based insights after examining the relationship among internet usage, autonomy, personal variables, and the obstacles faced by adult individuals in the use of e-government services. Lastly, the researchers provide a foundational model framework for user-interaction design aimed at improving the accessibility and usability of e-government services for Filipino adult users.

3   Research Methodology

This study employed quantitative methods to assess the usability, accessibility, and user experience of Philippine e-Government services Filipino users. The respondents were male and female (n = 221) Filipino adults, living in Luzon area, who had prior interaction with e-Government platforms such as the Bureau of Internal Revenue (BIR), Social Security System (SSS), and PhilHealth, selected through random sampling. The study primarily sought the participants' opinions and experiences regarding their use of e-government websites, ensuring their responses were voluntary, confidential, and based on their personal views.

An online adapted survey questionnaire answered on a likert scale was used to collect quantitative data on user challenges, perceptions, and interaction design issues. The researchers validated the appropriateness of the adapted survey questionnaire by conducting expert interviews with 3 older adults. An invitation was sent to 8 experts but only 3 have willingly agreed to participate in the interview. An expert interview design in a qualitative interview method is aimed at acquiring information about exploring a specific field of action [2]. Using snowball sampling, the criteria for choosing these 3 experts are those who 1) have often used e-government services 2) are willing to express their process knowledge of e-government services use and 3) who can identify problems in the use of e-government services.

The survey questionnaire adapted were developed based on Human-Computer Interaction (HCI) design standards and ISO 9241-11 Ergonomics of Human-System Interaction to address specific user needs in accessing E-government websites. The survey evaluated respondents' perceptions of the design quality of the platforms they had used. The survey was disseminated through online forms and community networks.

The collected data was analyzed using descriptive statistics, in terms of identifying trends in user experience, ease of navigation, and accessibility barriers. Correlation was applied to explore relationships between age, digital literacy, and perceived usability and the weighted mean was used to evaluate the design criteria based on the users' perception to identify whether the e-government websites were performing in accordance with design standards collected during the literature review. These include Physical Challenges, Cognitive Challenges, Emotional and Psychological Barriers, Lack of Familiarity and Experience, Interface Design Issues, Resistance and Negative Perceptions, and Privacy and Trust Concerns, which led to the developed framework.

Ethical considerations were strictly observed to protect participant confidentiality and ensure voluntary participation. No personally identifiable information was collected, and all responses were used solely for research purposes. Informed consent was obtained before respondents can answer the survey and data privacy and security was employed. The research posed minimal risk to participants and was approved by the Ethics Review Board of Jose Rizal University. No participants were subjected to any harm, discomfort, or undue influence during the study proper.

4   Results and Discussion

The study's primary objective was to evaluate the inclusivity and accessibility of Philippine e-Government services through the lens of interaction design, usability, and user experience; the analysis integrated both demographic variables, user behavior patterns and their evaluation of the user interfaces using standard design principles. This approach provided a perspective on how different user segments engage with e-Government platforms, revealing potential disparities in access, satisfaction, and ease of use.

4.1 The Frequency and Independence with Which Users Use e-Government Services for Processing Government Documents

Key gaps were revealed when the study compared established design and usability standards with user challenges found in e-Government platforms. To measure engagement and digital proficiency, the frequency of use and the degree of independence in completing transactions were evaluated. The findings highlighted the need for more understandable, user-friendly interfaces, with 55.41% of users completing tasks without assistance and 44.59% requiring it. Relatives (n = 107) and friends (n = 68) were the primary sources of assistance for 99 respondents (n = 166), followed by spouses (n = 10), children (n = 19), and occasionally strangers (n = 9). These results show that a considerable percentage of users depend on close social networks, especially intergenerational support, to successfully access government systems due to difficulties in navigating services on their own.

These results show that e-government interfaces need to be easy to use and include people with different levels of digital skills. Even though 55.41% of users finished tasks on their own, 44.59% needed help, which shows that users' freedom was limited. Of the 99 people who asked for help (n = 166, and some respondents answered more than once), the most common answer was a relative (n = 107), followed by a friend (n = 68), a child (19 times), a spouse (n = 10), and a stranger (n = 9). This pattern shows that people still rely on close, often intergenerational networks. This makes the case for clearer interaction design that follows usability and accessibility standards, as well as community-oriented digital literacy efforts and easy-to-find support (tutorials, live chat, guided prompts) to help people use technology with confidence and independence.

Independence also depends on getting ready for the transaction. A majority (62.61%) read written instructions before using e-government sites, which suggests that they aren't very intuitive or that they prefer detailed instructions. 19.82% watch instructional videos, and 15.32% don't do anything to prepare, which could mean they trust or are familiar with the site. Less than 1% of people ask their families for help or try other methods, like following rules, going to school, or getting evaluations. These behaviors show that different people need different kinds of preparation and show how important it is to keep both text-based and visual learning resources while making on-page guidance better. This way, users can do important tasks without help from outside sources.

4.2 Common Challenges Faced by Users in Navigating and Interacting with e-Government Platforms, with an Emphasis on Interface Design Elements

To address the objective of identifying the most common challenges in navigating and interacting with e-Government platforms, the discussion that follows examines evidence from the survey conducted by the researchers, among the discussed areas are as follows: users' device and connectivity context, reported independence versus need for assistance, pre-use preparation behaviors, and age-/education-related correlation patterns.

User Profile, Access Conditions and Device Patterns

Findings of user profile, access conditions and device patterns showed that the majority were aged 18–24 years (n = 176; 79.6%), while 20.4% (n = 14) were aged 25–64. Access is primarily mobile-first: 62% of people only use cell phones, 30.3% use more than one device (most often a laptop and cell phone together), and smaller groups use only a desktop (5.4%), a laptop (5.4%), or a tablet (0.9%). These patterns show how important it is to make sure that e-platforms work on all devices whether phone or laptops.

Mobile data is the most popular way to connect, followed by fiber or post-paid subscriptions. Some people also use free public Wi-Fi, Piso Net, or internet cafés. Slow or unstable connections can slow down transactions, make sessions expire, and make it hard to get to resources like forms or instructional videos. This can make people angry, be dependent on others, and lower their confidence in technology. To make e-government access truly open to everyone, we need to fix these infrastructure problems and make design improvements at the same time.

Website Usage by Document and Process Priority

The survey shows that people mostly use high-priority platforms. As shown in Fig. 1, PhilSys (n = 70 users; 15.62%), SSS (n = 59; 13.17%), and PSA (n = 59; 13.17%) are the most popular because they keep records of identity, contributions, and civil registrations that are important for jobs, banking, and claims.

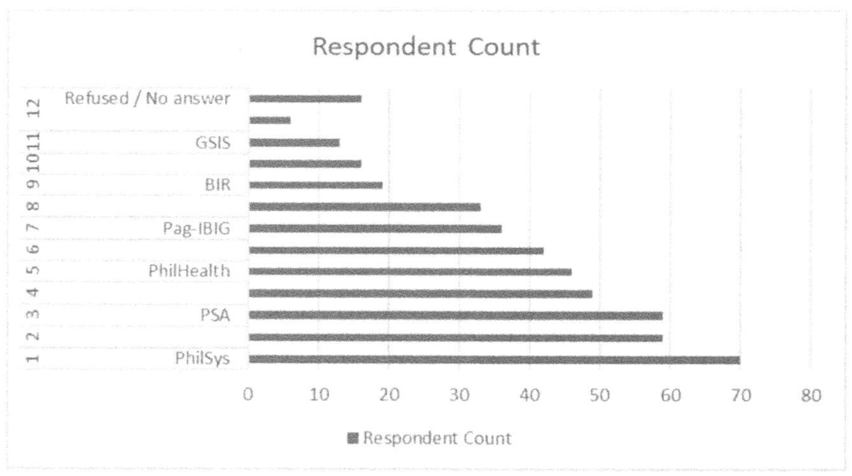

Fig. 1. Respondent Count per Website

A second tier—COMELEC (n = 49; 10.94%), PhilHealth (n = 46; 10.27%), LTO (n = 38; 8.48%), and Pag-IBIG (n = 36; 8.04%)—supports election, health, licensing, and housing needs that aren't used as often but are still very important. The lower numbers for GSIS (n = 13; 2.90%) and PRC (n = 6; 1.34%) are due to cyclical or specialized needs, not because they are less important.

In general, among the 205 people who answered (448 selections), usage shows the priority of the documents: routine, high-stakes records lead to frequent visits; periodic needs lead to moderate access; and specialized platforms serve smaller groups on predictable cycles. Because many transactions require these documents, only 7.2% (n = 17) did not answer these platforms.

Correlation of Demographics on the Interface Barriers
As provided in Fig. 2, the demographics are correlated with the design factors, older respondents are *slightly* more experienced and confident using e-government sites (experience $r = 0.164$; $r = 0.137$), yet they trust the platforms less and feel more dissatisfied—the strongest effect is lower perceived data safety (r = −0.195), followed by higher dissatisfaction ($r = −0.167$). Their pain points line up with design factors: needing extra explanations ($r = −0.177$), struggling when layouts change (r = −0.164), feeling overloaded/pages too complex ($r = −0.10/−0.04$), finding feedback unclear ($r = −0.092$), text hard to read (r = −0.043), touch interactions less comfortable ($r = −0.134$), and multi-step memory load (recall $r = −0.090$). These are small effects, but they consistently point to the interface, not just user constraints.

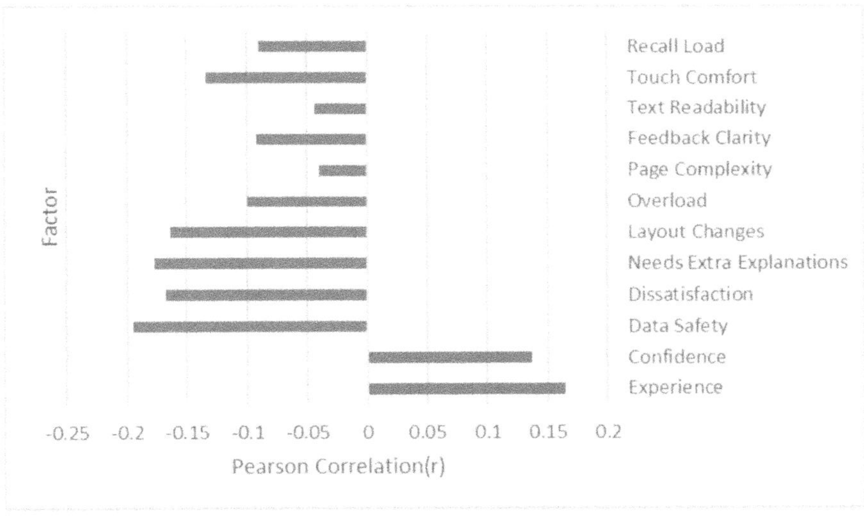

Fig. 2. Correlation of Factors with Age

As illustrated in Fig. 3, higher education relates to slightly greater experience ($r = 0.073$) and confidence ($r = 0.148$), but also tougher privacy scrutiny: lower perceived data safety ($r = −0.184$) and lower comfort sharing personal information ($r = −0.106$). In practice, better-educated users want clearer, on-screen explanations of why data are collected and how they're protected.

On Users' Device Preference And Access Behaviors.
The demographic profile of the responses indicates that 79.6% are within the 15–24 age bracket, highlighting the considerable engagement of younger individuals with e-government platforms. The representation of elder respondents (ages 25–64) exceeding 20% underscores the imperative of guaranteeing accessibility for users across all

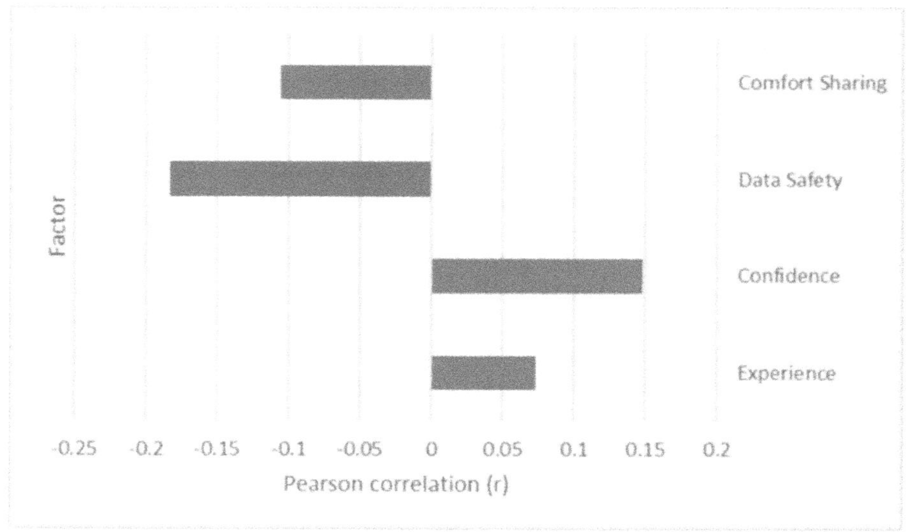

Fig. 3. Correlation with education level

generations. The dominance of mobile data as the principal method for accessing these services illustrates the wider technology environment in the Philippines, characterized by prevalent mobile-first behavior. The utilization of mobile devices by 62% of respondents underscores the imperative for mobile-optimized platforms that are swift, responsive, and tailored for smaller screens [6].

Notably, the 30.3% of individuals who reported utilizing both mobile and desktop/laptop devices suggest that users quick transition between platforms based on context or government process complexity. This multi-device functionality facilitates the same user experience across several platforms.

On the Dependence of Older Adults to Navigate e-Government Website Interfaces.

The findings show that several users refer to instructional resources prior to utilizing e-government websites. This proactive activity indicates a readiness to utilize public digital services, yet it also highlights a deficiency in the inherent intuitiveness of these platforms. That 44.59% of respondents need assistance—primarily from family (107 references) and friends (68 mentions)—indicates that utilizing these websites frequently necessitates external support. This is especially applicable to less technologically proficient individuals, including senior citizens.

This need for human support networks for digital navigation underscores a continuing digital divide. Intergenerational support is crucial for closing digital divides, although it also highlights the inadequacies of existing systems in promoting autonomous usage [7]. Addressing this necessitates enhanced interface design and investment in community-oriented digital literacy initiatives and onboarding tools customized for individuals with diverse digital skills.

On the Effect of Infrastructure Lapses Towards the Accessibility of Systems and Users' Frequency of Use.

The dependence on mobile data and restricted access to high-speed internet via fiber or broadband highlight persistent infrastructure issues. Inconsistent connectivity may hinder service accessibility, especially when forms, videos, or pop-up instructions do not load correctly. These constraints increase customer dissatisfaction and increase reliance on others for effective transaction fulfillment. Enhancing infrastructure must be prioritized concurrently with platform development to provide genuinely inclusive digital government [8].

The research indicated that the majority of users visit e-government websites at least annually, demonstrating a trend of sustained participation rather than isolated contacts. This underscores the assertion that e-government platforms should be engineered for both usability and sustained performance. As these systems become crucial for accessing identification, healthcare, financial, and civic services, enhancing their reliability and user experience is imperative.

On E-Government Websites Popularity.

The frequency of access to various e-government websites seems to closely correspond with users' daily requirements. The Social Security System (SSS), PhilSys (national ID), and PhilHealth platforms exhibited the highest utilization rates, highlighting consumers' prioritization of financial security, identity authentication, and healthcare access. These services are essential for personal and professional security and so constitute high-priority digital touchpoints.

In contrast, a lower involvement with websites such as GSIS and PRC may be attributed to the demographic attributes of the respondents—many may not be government employees or licensed professionals presently necessitating these platforms. Nonetheless, its diminished utilization does not signify irrelevance; instead, it indicates differing levels of requirement contingent upon user profile and life stage.

On the Trust Towards E-Government Websites.

Confidence in utilizing e-government services was inconsistent, with 45.05% indicating "Not Much" confidence, implying a persistent challenge with confidence in the use of e-government websites. Merely 22.07% expressed a high level of confidence. This range highlights a disparity in digital empowerment that necessitates modification through better designing and support strategies.

Older users had somewhat increased trust and experience stemming from regular encounters with services like PhilHealth or SSS; nevertheless, this was coupled with heightened concern regarding data security. Correlational study indicated that as age increases, there is a heightened concern over data safety ($r = -0.195$) and privacy, along with increasing dissatisfaction with website usability ($r = -0.167$). These findings corroborate prior research indicating that elderly users exhibit more risk aversion and require elevated levels of transparency and reassurance in online settings [9].

Users with advanced educational backgrounds exhibited greater confidence ($r = 0.148$) but simultaneously demonstrated heightened mistrust regarding data protection ($r = -0.184$). This indicates that greater education may enhance critical knowledge of dangers, highlighting the necessity for improved communication of security measures and privacy rules on the platforms.

Usability and Age Related Barriers.

Usability issues were predominantly associated with age. Older respondents had a greater tendency for discomfort in information sharing (r = −0.089), challenges in adapting to website modifications (r = −0.164), and a greater need for additional clarifications (r = −0.177). The data revealed heightened challenges in memory recall (r = −0.090), issues with tactile input devices (r = −0.134), and dissatisfaction with interface complexity and information overload.

These problems underscore the necessity of incorporating cognitive and physical accessibility into design. Concise text, easy design, uniform navigation, and segmented information display are essential for minimizing user fatigue and enhancing understanding. The limited awareness of tutorials and support systems (support awareness r = −0.075; instructional helpfulness r = −0.017) indicates a deficiency in proactive communication techniques or onboarding design that might assist users in navigating processes with confidence.

4.3 Design Recommendations Based on Processed Data

The findings address both functional and experiential aspects of digital engagement. Key issues include navigation difficulties, unclear interface elements, and limited on-screen guidance, all of which reduce efficiency and heighten frustration. Despite broad access, design-related barriers persist, underscoring the need for stronger user-centered design in government platforms.

Drawing from these struggles, a systematic design framework was developed. Mobile-first use and age-linked discomfort with touch and pop-ups reflect physical challenges, while information overload, memory-heavy steps, and extra explanations point to cognitive strain. Uneven confidence and dissatisfaction reveal emotional barriers, and heavy reliance on manuals, videos, or assistance highlights gaps in familiarity. Layout inconsistencies, unclear feedback, and cluttered navigation surface interface design flaws, while sensitivity to changes reflects resistance and negative perceptions. Finally, lower trust in data security—especially among older, educated users—raises privacy concerns. These patterns justify the design recommendations in the next section.

5 Conclusions and Recommendations

This study examined the usability, accessibility, and user perceptions of e-government service websites among a local population, integrating quantitative data to achieve an in-depth understanding of user experience. The findings indicated significant trends regarding usage frequency, confidence levels, sources of support, and demographic associations, underscoring essential usability issues, particularly among senior users.

This study's findings indicate significant usability and accessibility issues in e-government service websites [10]. A significant number of users continue to seek assistance, frequently depending on family or social networks, which underscores the ongoing challenge of independently navigating these platforms. Many users have poor confidence in utilizing the sites, hindered by obstacles such as unreliable internet connectivity and reliance on mobile data, which further complicate their experience. The most commonly utilized websites are those directly associated with financial and social services, reflecting consumers' pragmatic incentives. Infrequent utilization of other platforms may indicate either a lack of awareness or a perception of complexity.

Correlational investigation indicated that the users experience diminished confidence about data privacy and exhibit heightened irritation when utilizing e-government websites. They also indicate diminished comfort with website modifications, task recollection, and interface interactions, implying that age-related usability factors require attention. Users with higher education levels exhibit increased confidence alongside heightened scrutiny over data privacy, signifying a demand for more transparent and safe solutions. These conclusions highlight the necessity for a user-centric model framework that fosters transparent, supportive, and adaptable interfaces, while enhancing digital trust and reducing user dependency through inclusive and intuitive design standards.

The study must be interpreted with several constraints. The study used random sampling; a larger and more diverse sample would strengthen the findings and offer a broader view of factor–demographic relationships. The survey may also benefit from more distinct results based on qualitative data and answers from the users to address more specific concerns. Coverage of the respondents also explores the results based on the respondents' capability on accessing the websites, however, it is also important to note that the country also has individuals requiring the government processes and documents, but has no access to any form of technology - to which are currently underrepresented in the study. Lastly, the study was made based on the generalization of websites being used, and a perspective per website may provide more detailed insights on how users perceive the interfaces based on the document or process it provides.

Through discovery of problems encountered and major issues by the users as discussed in the sections above, a framework based on a localized context on the improvement of Philippine E-Government Websites is developed.

The developed UI/UX Framework for Philippine E-Government Websites as illustrated in Fig. 4. Integrates fundamental HCI concepts with user input to tackle the issues found in the results section of this paper, addressing the human need for a user centered design - considering multiple factors that hinder the users from fully utilizing and embracing the websites that are supposed to provide them with basic government documents. Performance-Centered Design was emphasized in response to recurrent user complaints regarding slow loading times and system failures. Privacy-Centric Transparency can reduce data safety issues by incorporating visible security indicators and streamlined privacy policies in Filipino, hence enhancing user confidence and informed consent. Accessible and intuitive design will address problems associated with complex layouts and inadequate mobile responsiveness. Language and comprehension were essential in addressing digital literacy disparities, employing language toggles, icons, and audio-visual aids to improve clarity and inclusivity. Users expressed a significant demand for assistance, leading to the incorporation of Help & Guided Support features, including tooltips, live chat, and step-by-step walkthroughs, which can contribute to a decrease in drop-off rates. Remote-friendly interaction, encompassing remote identification verification and family-assist modes, can eliminate access obstacles for customers in underserved regions, or simply due to the inability to proceed to actual government sites for such purposes, while queue tracking can enhance service efficiency. The Feedback &

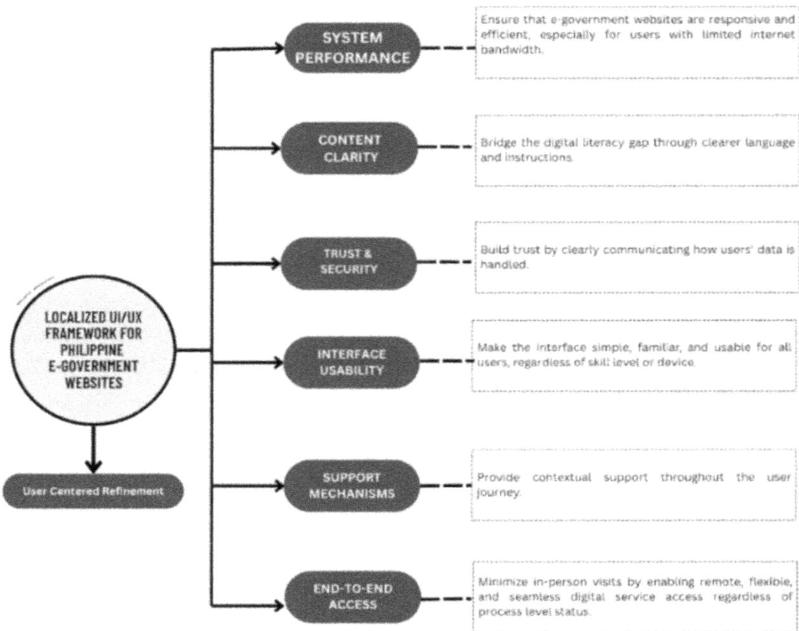

Fig. 4. UI/UX Framework for Philippine E-Government Websites

Iterative Design component underscores ongoing enhancement via post-interaction surveys, transparent updates, and consistent user testing to implement more user centered refinements.

This study offers significant contributions to the field of Human-Computer Interaction (HCI), especially in the relatively under-explored area of local government digital services in the Philippines. Despite the increasing importance of digitalization in public services, the application of HCI principles in government websites remains limited. This research highlights the potential of HCI to improve the design and functionality of e-government platforms, emphasizing the importance of usability, accessibility, and user-centered design.

By identifying the challenges users face, the study underscores how incorporating HCI methodologies [11] can create more intuitive, inclusive, and effective digital services. The integration of HCI into the design process allows government websites to better meet the needs of diverse users, ensuring accessibility and ease of use for people across different age groups, technological competencies, and abilities. This approach is crucial for enhancing the user experience and facilitating the adoption of digital services.

Furthermore, this research lays the groundwork for future studies exploring the systematic application of HCI to e-government services. It demonstrates that HCI is not just a theoretical concept but a practical framework that can directly improve accessibility and user satisfaction. By adopting HCI principles, local government agencies can design more efficient, effective, and user-friendly digital services, ultimately advancing public sector digitalization and fostering a more inclusive experience for all citizens.

To apply the developed framework, a section of the PhilSys website (https://philsys. gov.ph/) was replicated to demonstrate how content clarity could be enhanced using the proposed framework. This was achieved by adding direct Filipino instructions alongside the English instructions, arranged neatly and in accordance with the users' line of sight. Providing bilingual instructions allows users to refer to an alternative language when they experience difficulty understanding the content, particularly for technical procedures.

It was observed that the website provides instructions on what users need to do prior to the National ID application process. However, these instructions are presented entirely in English, which may pose challenges, especially for users who are not fully proficient in the language. Additionally, some of the instructions may be overwhelming for certain users due to the amount of information presented. As part of the framework's implementation, additional contextual instructions were added to improve clarity and guide users more effectively through the required steps.

Another design mockup was developed to address the Trust and Security design concerns identified by users of the PSA Online website (https://psahelpline.ph). Although the site complies with data privacy laws, its reliance on dense legal jargon and lengthy policy text hinders user understanding. Currently, no concise, plain-language summary is integrated into the user flow, making this redesign necessary and highlighting a gap in the existing implementation. While disclaimers regarding data usage and data privacy are present on the website to inform users that their information is secure, these disclosures are not presented in a manner that is easily understandable to the general public.

The interface of eBIRForms, a free desktop software provided by the Bureau of Internal Revenue (BIR), is currently utilized by taxpayers to file required tax forms. However, the existing offline system remains confusing and stores files locally on the user's device. As a result, file management and record keeping are entirely dependent on the device being used. If users change devices, they are unable to retrieve their previous records. Apart from this, the feedback feature of the software only sends out an approval number and a copy of the file generated by the user will only be available should the user saves it as a file. Backups are not available, and tracing old files is nearly impossible. To address this, as part of the Interface Usability, the application must be running on the cloud so that any reports saved by the users are easily retrievable according to their TIN number. Data retrieval and archiving would be more effective this way, and more users may be able to properly document their reported files. To improve interface usability, the filing process should be more understandable. On screen instructions can be added since the process of filing is complex in itself already. The data entry process must also translate the jargon that may be foreign to its users.

While the e-government platforms have been introduced for members convenience and ease, it is important to examine its impact, dynamics, and performance to ensure its relevance and maintain its purpose in helping others. Research on interface designs, website performance, can certainly help the government identify user experience and satisfaction with e-government service and later on review and fine tune. The results of the study revealed that a significant number of individuals are dissatisfied with their interactions, contrary to the primary goal of e-government services to meet user needs. This underscores the importance of recognizing unique user expectations, enabling policymakers to better understand the factors that influence user satisfaction. Prior research similarly stressed that technical efficiency alone is insufficient; sustainable e-government adoption also depends on infrastructure, legal frameworks, and digital competence among officials [12]. Moreover, users are more likely to have a gratifying experience when e-government websites are responsive, attentive, and reliable throughout the access process and in subsequent interactions with citizens.

This underscores the value of a design framework that government agencies can use to build e-government websites that are not only functional but also user-centered and responsive to the needs of Filipino users. Like the study on Indonesia's e-government enterprise system proposed the Zuma's e-Government Framework (ZEF), which synergizes Service-Oriented Architecture (SOA) and Business Process Management (BPM) to address dynamic policy changes across central and local governments. By organizing legacy, component, technical, and business layers, ZEF supports integration of common and specific rules, fostering systems that are more flexible, adaptable, and capable of delivering reliable, higher-quality digital services. [13] By aligning interface standards with how people actually understand and navigate these services, the framework can standardize and streamline key interactions, improve comprehension and task flow, and ultimately reinforce the purpose and public value of the platforms.

This research serves as a starting point for future studies that can explore how HCI can be systematically applied to the design and improvement of e-government services. It provides evidence that HCI is not just a theoretical framework but a practical tool that can directly impact the accessibility and user satisfaction of public sector websites. By incorporating HCI guidelines into public sector website design, local government units can significantly enhance the efficiency, reach, and effectiveness of their digital services, ultimately fostering a more inclusive and user-friendly experience for citizens.

In conclusion, the framework demonstrates that integrating technical solutions with localized, user-informed design principles fosters a more inclusive, reliable, and accessible e-government experience for Filipinos. Successive revisions will continue to integrate user feedback to address evolving requirements. Given the ongoing nature of this research, a separate paper is already in progress to present the qualitative analysis of interview data and open-ended survey responses, providing a more in-depth understanding of user perceptions.

Appendix A – Survey Questionnaire

A. Questions on Demographics

1. Device Used in Accessing E-Government Services
2. What did you do before accessing the e-government device?
3. Do you own the device that you used the last time you accessed e-government services?
4. If it was not your device, who owns the device?
5. What is your estimated household income in Pesos?
6. Did you ask for assistance in accessing the e-government service?
7. If you asked for assistance, who helped you?
8. What type internet did you use in accessing e-government?
9. How frequent have you experienced filing e-government service?

10. Have you experienced manual filing of any government documents like BIR, Land-bank (Banking Applications), DFA, NBI, SSS/GSIS Portal, PhilHealth Portal, PAGIBIG Portal, LTO?
11. Which e-government website among the following have you tried accessing/ used?
12. Please enter your age

B. E-government Website Design Questions

What is your level of self-confidence in using e-government service?

1.1 How easy is it for you to read the text on e-Government websites?

1.2 How clear and helpful do you find the feedback provided by Filipino e-Government websites, such as error messages or confirmation messages, when completing tasks like tax filing or benefit claims?

1.3 How comfortable are you with using input devices (e.g., mouse, touchscreen) for precise actions like clicking or dragging on these websites?

2.1 How well can you follow the steps to complete tasks, like applying for government documents or submitting forms, on Filipino e-Government websites such as BIR, SSS, or PhilHealth?

2.2 How often do you find it hard to remember steps for using e-Government websites without assistance?

2.3 How quickly do you adapt to changes in the layout or structure of e-Government websites?

3.1 How confident do you feel when using e-Government websites independently?

3.2 How often do you feel frustrated due to the difficulties in using e-Government website interfaces?

3.3 How worried are you about making mistakes, causing prob-lems or deleting something while using e-Government platforms?

4.1 How familiar are you with the components you see like but-tons, menus, or dropdowns on e-Government websites?

4.2 How familiar are you with the steps required to complete tasks (e.g., applying for documents or paying fees) on e-Government websites?

4.3 How often do you need additional explanations or instruc-tions to understand how to use specific features or complete tasks on e-Government websites?

5.1 How often do you struggle to notice or understand pop-ups, alerts, or other messages on e-Government websites?

5.2 How helpful are the tutorials, guides, or instructions provided on e-Government websites for understanding how to use their features?

5.3 How aware are you that support resources, such as FAQs, help sections, or customer support, are available on e-Government websites and can assist you if needed?

6.1 How often do you feel overwhelmed by the amount of information, options, or technical jargon on e-Government websites?

6.2 How much do you believe that mandated e-Government websites are too complicated or unnecessary for tasks you are required to complete?

6.3 How useful are government websites for helping you complete tasks like paying taxes or getting benefits?

7.1 How comfortable are you sharing personal information on government websites to complete required tasks?
7.2 How confident are you that your personal information is safe from unauthorized access on government websites?
7.3 How satisfied are you with the privacy protection provided by e-Government websites?

1. Ano ang mga naging challenges or difficulties mo sa paggamit ng e-government service website?
2. Ano ang gusto mong baguhin nila sa e-government service website?
3. Anong maisusuggest mo para mas maging maayos ang paggamit ng e-government service website?

References

1. Alazemi, N.N., Al-Shehab, A.J.: Factors affecting user experience of e-government services: an exploratory review. Int. J. Adv. Trends Comput. Sci. Eng. **13**(2), 80–83 (2024). https://doi.org/10.30534/ijatcse/2024/07132202
2. Döringer, S.: The problem-centred expert interview: combining qualitative interviewing approaches for investigating implicit expert knowledge. Int. J. Soc. Res. Methodol. **24**(3), 265–278 (2020). https://doi.org/10.1080/13645579.2020.1766777
3. Hasim, W., Wibirama, S., Nugroho, H.A.: Redesign of e-participation using user-centered design approach for improving user experience. In: Proceedings of the 2019 International Conference on Information and Communications, pp. 1–6. Universitas Gadjah Mada, Yogyakarta (2019)
4. Sachan, A., Kumar, R., Kumar, R.: Examining the impact of e-government service process on user satisfaction. J. Global Oper. Strateg. Sourc. (2018). https://doi.org/10.1108/JGOSS-11-2017-0048
5. Sukmasetya, P., Santoso, H.B., Sensuse, D.I.: Current e-government public service on user experience perspective in Indonesia. In: Proceedings of the 2018 International Conference on Information Technology Systems and Innovation (ICITSI), pp. 1–6. IEEE, Bandung–Padang (2018)
6. Aljasmi, L., Alobaidy, H.: The cultural impact on user interface design: the case of e-government services of Kingdom of Bahrain. In: Proceedings of the 2018 International Conference on Innovation and Intelligence for Informatics, Computing, and Technologies (3ICT), pp. 1–10. IEEE, Sakhier (2018). https://doi.org/10.1109/3ICT.2018.8855739
7. Newsbytes.PH: Survey: Pinoys Inseparable from Their Smartphones, Spend 86% of Day on Mobile Device. Newsbytes.PH (2023). https://newsbytes.ph/2023/11/29/survey-pinoys-inseparable-from-their-smartphones-spend-86-of-day-on-mobile-device/
8. Konrath, S.N., et al.: Intergenerational effects on the impacts of technology use in later life: insights from an international, multi-site study. Int. J. Environ. Res. Public Health **17**(16), 5711 (2020). https://www.mdpi.com/1660-4601/17/16/5711
9. Development Academy of the Philippines: The Philippine Government's Digital Transformation through DICT's E-Government Initiatives. DAP Compendium of Innovation (2025). https://coe-psp.dap.edu.ph/compendium-innovation/the-philippine-governments-digital-transformation-through-dicts-e-government-initiatives/

10. O'Connor, L.D., Balebako, R.A., Schoenebeck, S.Y., Vitak, J.: "Warn them" or "just block them"?: investigating privacy concerns among older and working age adults. In: Proceedings of the Privacy Enhancing Technologies Symposium (PETS), vol. 2021(1), pp. 282–302 (2021). https://petsymposium.org/popets/2021/popets-2021-0016.pdf
11. International Organization for Standardization: ISO 9241-11:2018 Ergonomics of Human-System Interaction—Part 11: Usability: Definitions and Concepts. ISO, Geneva (2018). https://www.iso.org/standard/63500.html
12. Rachmawati, U.A., Sensuse, D.I., Suhartanto, H.: Initial model of indonesian e-government grid services topology. Int. J. Comput. Theory Eng. 4(4), 656–661 (2012)
13. Zuma, N.A., Sensuse, D.I., Suhartanto, H.: Synergizing service-oriented architecture (SOA) and business process management (BPM) for Indonesian e-government enterprise system. Int. J. Comput. Theory Eng. 5(2), 369–374 (2013)

Language Modeling and Semantic Analysis

Conveying Natural Language Descriptions Into Meta-Language-Defined Structures

Alexander Fischer[✉][iD], Louis Burk[iD], Christoph Scharnagl[iD],
Ramin Tavakoli Kolagari[iD], and Uwe Wienkop[iD]

Nuremberg Institute of Technology, Nuremberg, Bavaria, Germany
{a.fischer,louis.burk,christoph.scharnagl,ramin.tavakolikolagari,
uwe.wienkop}@th-nuernberg.de

Abstract. We propose a meta-language-based approach that enables Large Language Models (LLMs) to generate structured, machine-readable outputs (MLDS) tailored to domain-specific needs. Unlike conventional methods tied to fixed formats like JSON or XML, our approach embeds a freely definable schema, called Meta-Language-defined Structure Instruction (MLDSI), directly into the prompt, guiding LLMs to produce valid outputs. We evaluated the method in two domains: 3D scene generation and automotive security modeling. Across 320 generated MLDS artifacts, we achieved a structural validity rate of 89.1%, with most errors linked to minor parsing issues. Compared to frameworks such as LangChain and Pydantic, our MLDS approach reduced setup complexity by over 80%, while maintaining comparable structural accuracy. The artifacts were readily usable and adaptable, either manually or through further prompting, demonstrating the method's flexibility. MLDSI-guided prompting thus provides an efficient bridge between natural language and formal tool input, enabling rapid prototyping and easier integration of generative models into domain-specific workflows.

Keywords: Meta-Language-defined Structures · Structured Prompting · Domain-Specific Modeling · Large Language Models

1 Introduction

Generative AI systems, in particular Large Language Models (LLMs), are increasingly employed to support the creation of structured content across a wide range of application domains. However, integrating such models into industrial software environments remains challenging: proprietary formats, complex toolchains, and the lack of standardized schemas significantly hamper the productive use of generative AI.

A. Fischer and L. Burk—Both authors contributed equally to this work.

© The Author(s), under exclusive license to Springer Nature Singapore Pte Ltd. 2026
T. Dohi (Ed.): ICSED 2025, CCIS 2889, pp. 169–183, 2026.
https://doi.org/10.1007/978-981-92-0202-7_12

A promising approach to address this problem is the use of so-called Meta-Language-defined Structure Instructions (MLDSI). These are formal specifications defined in a domain-specific meta-language, which serve as a schema for the desired target structure. Based on such an MLDSI, an LLM can generate a structured, machine-readable artifact, a so-called Meta-Language-defined Structure (MLDS). An MLDS thus results from a targeted transformation of natural language while adhering to the structural rules specified in the MLDSI.

However, the manual creation of MLDSI requires technical expertise and thus represents a substantial barrier to entry. In this paper, we propose an approach whereby MLDSI can be derived automatically from natural-language descriptions and a small number of structural examples. This makes it possible to first express the desired target structures in everyday language and then generate a formal, machine-processable specification that allows precise guidance of LLMs.

To evaluate this method, we conduct a comprehensive study in which we investigate the applicability, robustness, and structural correctness of the generated MLDSI and the resulting MLDS artifacts across different domains.

Whether and under which conditions this MLDS approach is practical and beneficial is examined by means of the following central research question:

Which prerequisites must be met for automatically generated MLDSI to serve as a bridge between natural-language descriptions and machine-processable structures, thereby enabling the integration of LLMs into industrial toolchains?

This central question is specified by the following three subquestions:

R1 How can MLDSI be generated automatically from natural-language descriptions and structural examples?
R2 To what extent do LLMs produce valid MLDS artifacts based on automatically derived MLDSI?
R3 How usable and adaptable are the resulting MLDS artifacts in various industrial tooling environments?

To ensure transparency and reproducibility, we make all relevant research artifacts, including evaluation results, domain-specific meta-languages, and generated MLDS artifacts, publicly available in our GitHub repository [5].

Organization of the Paper. The remainder of this paper is organized as follows. In Sect. 2, we explain the technical background and motivation for automating MLDSI. Sect. 3 provides an overview of related work. In Sect. 4, we describe the architecture of our tool and the procedure for MLDSI generation. A comprehensive evaluation is presented in Sect. 5. Sect. 6 discusses the key findings and delineates potential limitations. Section 7 offers insights into future work. Finally, Sect. 8 summarizes our contributions and outlines directions for further research.

2 Background and Motivation

In many technical and design-oriented domains, initiating a new project presents a significant challenge. This phenomenon, commonly referred to as the blank-page syndrome [8], describes the difficulty users face when attempting to create an initial meaningful draft in the absence of any predefined structure or guidance. In complex industrial tool environments, this can lead to substantial efficiency losses.

Moreover, while many professionals possess deep domain expertise, they are often tightly bound to specific tools or processes. In such scenarios, it is frequently necessary to wait for preliminary work from other team members before contributing independently. The simultaneous need for structural logic and tool compatibility further complicates flexible and autonomous collaboration.

The creation of structured artifacts typically requires programming skills or at least familiarity with markup and structuring languages such as JSON, XML, or YAML. This requirement poses a considerable barrier to entry, particularly for non-technical experts. Even modern AI-based chatbots offer limited support in this regard: without targeted adaptation or domain-specific knowledge, LLMs often generate linguistically plausible but structurally inadequate results.

Existing approaches to LLM-based structure generation typically rely on frameworks such as Pydantic or LangChain [3,4]. However, these require in-depth knowledge of the respective technologies as well as substantial configuration effort. As a result, their applicability in many industrial contexts remains limited.

Our approach takes a different path: instead of constraining the models to specific formats or toolchains, we utilize a configurable meta-language to define structured content that can be explicitly generated by LLMs. The resulting artifacts, referred to hereafter as Meta-Language-defined Structures (MLDS), can be directly passed to industrial tools or manually refined if necessary.

To ensure that an LLM correctly implements the requirements of the meta-language, we introduce Meta-Language-defined Structure Instructions (MLDSI). These instructions describe the desired target schema at a structural level and serve as a guiding blueprint for the model during generation.

The tool presented in this work enables the automated creation of such MLDSI from natural-language problem descriptions and example artifacts. This eliminates the need to manually define the underlying meta-language, a crucial step toward making LLM-based structure generation broadly accessible in domain-specific contexts.

3 Related Work

LLMs have seen growing interest in structured output generation. Early methods like Grammar Prompting [13] and PICARD [12] ensure outputs conform to formal grammars (e.g., BNF, SQL) by constraining the decoder. While reliable, these techniques require tight integration with decoding, such as limiting token choices or using validator hooks and depend on predefined rules.

Recent work refines decoder-level constraints. Park et al. [11] propose Grammar-Aligned Decoding (GAD), which respects grammar without distorting token probabilities. Zhang et al. [14] incorporate logic via Hidden Markov Models to enforce complex constraints. Although effective, these approaches still modify the decoding algorithm.

Other strategies avoid altering the decoder entirely. Beurer-Kellner et al. [2] use regex prompts and lightweight parsing to generate schema-compliant JSON with minimal overhead. Li et al. [9] integrate pushdown automata into prompts, guiding valid multi-step plans without fine-tuning.

Prompting has also been shown competitive with fine-tuning. Bassamzadeh and Methani [1] find optimized prompts rival trained models for DSL tasks. Our approach builds on this by using a prompt-embedded meta-language, supporting flexible and domain-specific structures beyond standard formats.

Benchmarking efforts like Geng et al. [7] evaluate decoding frameworks for efficiency and compliance. They show tools like Outlines and XGrammar ensure 100% JSON validity but often at the cost of speed or usability. Recent improvements include automata compression and speculative decoding.

In model-driven engineering, Netz et al. [10] show that LLMs can produce UML diagrams and structured artifacts, but their approach depends on toolchains like MontiGem. Other domains use fixed schemas (e.g., GeoJSON), which limit adaptability.

Our method avoids fixed notations or frameworks. Using Meta-Language-Defined Structure Instructions, users define arbitrary structures, e.g., Virtual Reality (VR) scenes or security models, directly in prompts. The LLM then generates machine-readable, human-legible outputs accordingly.

Comparison to Prior Work. Compared to grammar-controlled decoding [11–13], our method avoids modifying the model and remains decoder-agnostic. Unlike tool-dependent pipelines (e.g., LangChain), our meta-language requires only a one-time, declarative schema definition, readable and modifiable by domain experts.

While prompt-based generation may yield slightly higher error rates than hard-constrained decoding, it offers faster iteration and greater adaptability. Overall, our approach bridges formal rigor and flexible prompting through a universal, low-intrusion framework for structured output generation.

4   Methodology

This section outlines our five-step approach for generating structured, tool-compatible artifacts using LLMs and a custom meta-language: (1) analyzing domain constraints, (2) defining a meta-language, (3) generating MLDS via prompts, (4) refining the output, and (5) importing the result into target tools (cf. Fig. 1). The method supports iterative user guidance and ensures transparency by using clearly defined, reusable structures.

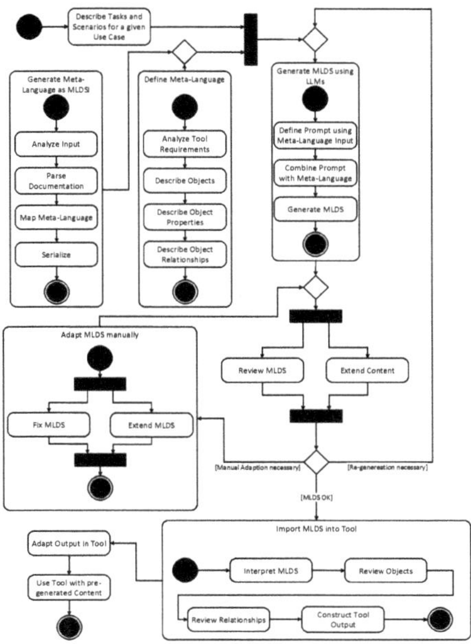

Fig. 1. Workflow for generating Meta-Language and LLM-based structure generation.

4.1   Conception of the Meta-Language

Our meta-language captures tool- and domain-specific requirements in a concise, readable schema. It enables the definition of custom object types, relationships, and value constraints, without relying on standards like JSON or XML. This serves as a binding contract between LLM and human experts.

The development follows three stages: First, domain concepts are identified and modeled semantically; second, they are converted into typed object definitions with explicit attributes and constraints; third, relationships are formalized to express hierarchies and dependencies. These relations (e.g., `contained_in`, `next_to`) guide the structure and semantics of MLDS generation.

Why a Meta-Language? LLMs are generally unaware of domain-specific formats. Our meta-language addresses this by:

- Allowing domain-specific object and relation types.
- Defining valid ranges to reduce ambiguity.
- Providing a consistent, interpretable schema for LLMs and humans alike.

Designing Domain Concepts. We begin with an analysis of the target system. In VR domains, typical concepts include rooms, avatars, or interactions; in automotive security, ECUs, assets, and attack steps. For each, we define attributes (e.g., layout, version, criticality), admissible values, and logical constraints.

Defining Structure. Objects are linked via typed relations with cardinality and semantics. This enables nested or lateral compositions and ensures that MLDS artifacts reflect real tool expectations.

MLDSI Examples. Consider a top-level `scene` object with dimensions and contained items; subordinate objects (e.g., a `table`) define relative positions; nested hierarchies can be built using `children`. These mechanisms are generic and apply across domains.

4.2   Generation and Adaptation of MLDS

The generation of a MLDS begins with the formulation of a composite prompt that combines a meta-language definition with a natural-language scenario. This prompt is processed by a LLM, which uses the embedded structural guidance to produce syntactically correct and schema-compliant output. In more advanced configurations, a two-step prompting approach is used to enhance transparency and enable the reuse of structural schemas across different scenarios. All outputs undergo automatic validation to ensure structural correctness prior to integration into downstream systems.

Once generated, the MLDS serves as a human-readable draft that can be refined iteratively. Domain experts are able to review, validate, and manually correct the results, or they may instruct the LLM to make targeted adjustments. This enables a hybrid workflow in which the generative capabilities of LLMs are effectively combined with human domain knowledge, leading to both efficient and trustworthy outcomes.

4.3   Gerneration of the Meta Language-Defined Structure Instructions

To enable the structured generation of domain-specific content from natural language, we introduce a multi-stage process that constructs a formal MLDSI. This MLDSI serves as a reusable language specification guiding LLMs in producing valid tool inputs based on documented structural and semantic constraints.

The process begins with an input analysis, comprising two components: a natural-language prompt defining the user's goal and a textual specification, such as documentation, templates, or interface definitions. The prompt conveys the intent to generate a structured MLDSI, while the specification defines expected formats, syntax, datatypes, and constraints.

In step two, our tool systematically parses the documentation to extract key structural features: hierarchical sections (e.g., `PARAMS`, `AGENTS`), root elements (e.g., `SCENARIO`), and recurring patterns like `Key: Value` or `@<Time>s -> <Action>`. It also derives attribute types, value ranges, and symbolic conventions (e.g., `@`, colons, indentation). Contextual constraints, such as exclusivity or ordering, are similarly captured. The result is a structured representation of the target's input logic, encoding both syntax and semantics.

From this representation, the third step generates the actual MLDSI: a formal, modular specification describing how valid inputs must be structured. It defines root elements (e.g., `SCENARIO:`), allowed substructures, and placeholder templates with associated types and constraints (e.g., `@<Time>: int`, `Action: enum`). References, cardinalities, and context rules can also be embedded. The MLDSI is kept abstract and example-free, designed for reuse and integration into prompt chains.

In the fourth step, the MLDSI is serialized into a well-structured, YAML- or JSON-like format, prioritizing consistency, clarity, and LLM compatibility. It uses key-value logic, indentation-based hierarchies, and typed placeholders to balance machine interpretability with human readability.

Finally, the MLDSI is made available for application and reuse. As a standalone schema, it guides LLMs in generating domain-specific outputs from natural language, without requiring example corpora or fine-tuning. By externalizing structural logic into a declarative format, the generation pipeline becomes modular and adaptable. MLDSIs can be updated independently of the model or prompt, enabling transparent control and domain flexibility.

In summary, MLDSIs make a tool's structural expectations explicit and operable in generative pipelines. They formalize previously implicit format knowledge into a reusable, machine-readable schema, bridging natural language and domain-specific tooling.

4.4   Generation and Verification of the MLDS

Once a valid MLDSI is created, it can guide the generation of a concrete, tool-compatible structure, the Meta Language-defined Structure. This artifact represents a domain-specific output such as a configuration file, model definition, or scenario layout that fully conforms to the syntactic and semantic rules in the MLDSI.

The process begins with a natural-language scenario description provided by the user. This is combined with the MLDSI into a composite prompt. Because the MLDSI defines structure, types, value ranges, and relations, the LLM can generate outputs that are not only syntactically correct but also semantically aligned with the domain model.

In its simplest form, the MLDSI is embedded directly into the prompt. The LLM is then instructed to instantiate an MLDS that matches the described scenario while adhering to all formal constraints. This enables rapid, consistent generation of structured outputs across varying use cases.

To ensure correctness, our toolchain includes an automated verification step. After generation, the MLDS is parsed and validated against the MLDSI. This check ensures structural completeness, correct keyword usage, proper typing, valid cardinalities, and fulfillment of context rules. Errors or ambiguities are returned to the user or corrected via refinement.

By combining prompt-driven generation with rule-based validation, the system produces reliable MLDS artifacts. This hybrid method, merging LLM flexibility with formal schema guidance, forms a foundation for tool integration and real-world deployment.

5   Evaluation

5.1   Problem Statement and Approach

Many data-driven processes in technical and design disciplines fail not due to a lack of elaboration but due to difficulties in getting started: missing structure, no defined entry point. To address this dilemma, we propose a method in which LLMs generate a domain-specific structure based on a meta-specification. The resulting MLDS offer a formalized, machine-processable framework, serving as a productive starting point. We validate this approach in two fundamentally different application domains: the automated generation of virtual environments and the model-based security assessment of vehicle systems.

5.2   Case Study 1: Automated Generation of Virtual Scenes

In the field of 3D scene creation, there is often a disconnect between conceptual ideas and technical implementation. Our system enables the transformation of a natural-language description, such as "A meeting room with ten chairs", into a structured JSON representation that serves as a blueprint for constructing a Unity scene. Instead of starting from scratch, developers receive a fully defined room structure with spatially arranged placeholder objects. This enables an accelerated design process that blends automated generation with manual fine-tuning. Across more than 200 generation runs, hierarchical object relationships were correctly represented. One example is shown in Listing 1.1, where a conference table and its associated chair are encoded as a structured object group. This object structure can be extended either through new prompts or directly via manual editing of the MLDS. The transition from an AI-generated proposal to user-specific refinement is seamless.

5.3   Case Study 2: Modeling Security-Critical Threats

Structured entry points can also significantly reduce the effort required in security engineering contexts. In this case study, we address threat modeling for connected embedded systems in the automotive domain [6]. LLMs are used to convert descriptive risk expressions, such as "OTA attack via unsecured connection", into formal JSON models. These MLDS models can be directly imported into existing security tools that, for example, calculate risk levels or derive protective countermeasures. An excerpt of an automatically generated threat model is shown in Listing 1.2. Such MLDS structures serve as a foundation for initial risk assessments, which can subsequently be refined or extended by security experts. This enables a hybrid workflow in which machine-generated proposals and human expertise interact synergistically.

```
1   { "objectId": "table_main_c1",
2     "objectType": "conference_table",
3     "assetName": "asset_table_glass",
4     "position": {"x": 1.5, "y": 0.5, "z": -2.5},
5     "dimensions": {"width": 3.5, "height": 0.9, "
            depth": 1.2},
6     "group": "interior",
7     "children": [ {
8         "objectId": "chair_main_r1",
9         "objectType": "chair",
10        "assetName": "asset_chair_swivel",
11        "relativePositioning": {
12          "referenceObject": "table_main_c1",
13          "relation": "right_of_positive_x",
14          "distance": 1.1
15        },
16        "dimensions": {"width": 0.5, "height": 0.8, "
                depth": 0.5},
17        "group": "interior" } ] }
```

Listing 1.1. VR: Linked Objects

```
1   { "Name": "Tampered OTA Update via Unsecured
            Transport",
2     "AccessRequired": "Remote",
3     "AttackComplexity": "(M)edium",
4     "PrivilegesRequired": "(L)ow",
5     "Urgency": "(H)igh",
6     "UserInteraction": "(N)one",
7     "AvailabilityImpact": "(H)igh",
8     "ConfidentialityImpact": "(H)igh",
9     "IntegrityImpact": "(H)igh",
10    "SafetyRelevance": "(H)igh",
11    "vulnerabilities": [ {
12      "Name": "Missing Update Channel Encryption"
13    } ] }
```

Listing 1.2. Security: Attack Model

5.4 Systematic Evaluation

For both application domains, the method was evaluated using several language models (including GPT-4o mini, GPT-o3 mini, DeepSeek R1, and R1 14B offline). The generated structures were automatically validated against their respective meta-specifications. The success rate in terms of syntactic correctness exceeded 95%, with most minor errors attributable to incomplete API responses or prompt-related inaccuracies. In terms of content, even complex scenarios were consistently translated into structured and usable formats.

The evaluation revealed several key findings. First, the MLDS files exhibited high structural fidelity, closely adhering to the defined formal specifications. Second, the process enabled productive initialization, as the automated output effectively replaced the typical blank starting point with an editable, structured foundation. Third, the artifacts showed strong refinability, allowing for easy manual adaptation or iterative improvement through prompt-based interaction. Finally, the method demonstrated clear cross-domain applicability; it is not limited to the evaluated domains but can also support structured outputs for educational content, logical systems, workflows, or digital twins.

For quantitative evaluation, a total of 320 automatically generated MLDS files were analyzed using a custom parser to check for compliance with the rules. Validation was performed directly against the corresponding domain-specific schema.

5.5 Evaluation Setup

The evaluation dataset consisted of 320 generated files, divided into two complexity levels: easy and medium. Each complexity level had two variants: one using semantic validators (withValidator) and one without (withoutValidator). Validators were applied downstream and verified semantic integrity (e.g., object overlap), while syntactic structure was independently analyzed. Since no significant differences in structural validity were found between these variants, we merged them into a unified dataset for quantitative analysis.

Each file was evaluated for structural validity, completeness with respect to schema components, and specific parser-related errors.

The evaluation metrics are defined as:

$$V = \sum \text{valid files}, \quad I = N - V \tag{1}$$

$$\text{Validity Rate } (\%) = \frac{V}{N} \times 100 \tag{2}$$

$$\text{Presence Rate } (\%) = \frac{\text{Files containing schema part}}{N} \times 100 \tag{3}$$

where N is the total number of evaluated files, V is the number of valid (correctly structured) files, and I is the number of invalid (incorrect) files, with $N = 320$, $V = 285$, and $I = 35$, yielding a validity rate of 89.1%.

5.6 Quantitative Results

Out of 320 generated MLDS files, 285 (89.1%) were structurally valid, while 35 (10.9%) exhibited parsing issues. The majority of invalid files triggered the error message `'str' object has no attribute 'get'`, indicating that a string was provided where a JSON object was expected.

As seen in Fig. 2, most schema parts were consistently included, indicating strong alignment with the meta-language definition. The significantly lower frequency of background components was expected, as their inclusion was not explicitly prompted.

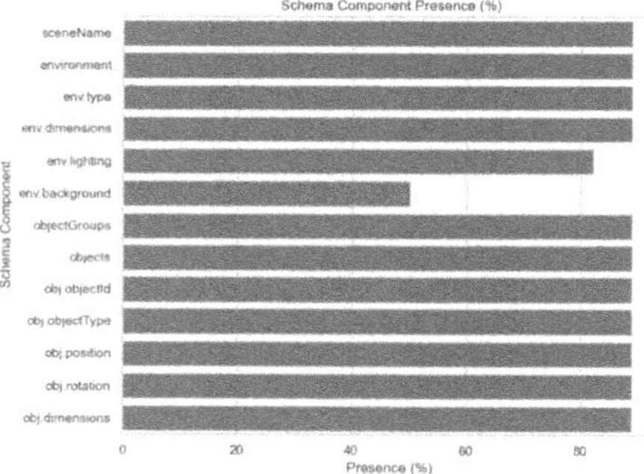

Fig. 2. Presence rates of schema parts in MLDS files.

Figure 3 provides insights into the structural complexity of the generated files. Object counts were mostly within a practical range of 20–60, and object group counts centered around 10. The nesting depth was consistent, with most files having a depth of 5, indicating good hierarchical organization.

The nesting depth was computed using the following function:

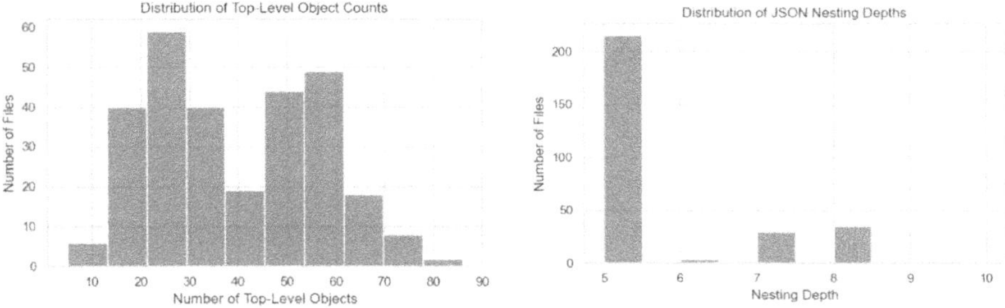

Fig. 3. Distribution of top-level object counts (left) and JSON nesting depths (right) in MLDS files.

```
1  def compute_depth(obj, depth=0):
2      if isinstance(obj, dict):
3          return max([compute_depth(v, depth+1) for v in obj.values()] or [depth])
4      if isinstance(obj, list):
5          return max([compute_depth(i, depth+1) for i in obj] or [depth])
6      return depth
```

Listing 1.3. Computing JSON nesting depth

5.7   Comparison with Traditional Approaches

We benchmarked our MLDS pipeline against a traditional structured-output setup using LangChain and Pydantic [3, 4]. While the traditional method had a slightly lower error rate, it required significantly more setup time and developer expertise. The MLDS-based pipeline produced results with only approximately 3.9% more errors, yet enabled faster prototyping and clearer prompt formulation. This makes MLDS preferable for iterative development or scenarios where deep tooling integration is not initially required.

5.8   Implications

Embedding the meta-language specification within the prompt structure demonstrably improves schema compliance and machine interpretability. Given the scalability and adaptability of our MLDS approach, it offers a viable low-barrier approach for generating structured industrial data, even at larger volumes.

6   Discussion

This section discusses the key findings of the evaluation, analyzes the contribution of the proposed MLDS approach in the context of related work, and explores implications for research and practice. Additionally, limitations of the method and threats to validity are critically assessed.

We begin by interpreting the evaluation results in Sect. 6.1. Section 6.2 compares our approach to existing methods for structured generation using LLMs.

Building on this, Sect. 6.3 highlights practical benefits. Finally, Sect. 6.4 outlines known limitations and validity threats relevant to the interpretation of our findings.

6.1   Interpretation of Evaluation Results

The evaluation confirms the high structural validity of MLDS artifacts generated by LLMs. Of the 320 generated files, 285 (89.1%) conformed to the requirements of the meta-language. This high success rate shows that MLDSI-based prompting contributes substantially to structural coherence. Even in complex scenarios, models reliably produced valid structures, indicating generalizability across domains. Invalid artifacts were mainly caused by truncated responses or incorrect parsing of JSON strings, pointing to model-specific limitations.

The quantitative analysis shows high consistency in the presence of core schema elements such as `sceneName`, `env.type`, or `objectGroups`, while optional components like `env.background` appeared less frequently, as expected. This confirms the flexibility of the meta-language and the LLMs' ability to distinguish between required and optional elements. The low variance in structural depth (typically five levels) further highlights the generation of hierarchically organized outputs.

With respect to the research questions, the following insights emerge:

Regarding R1: How can MLDSI be automatically generated from natural-language descriptions and structural examples? The results show that automatic derivation of MLDSI instructions from natural-language descriptions and tool specifications is feasible. The toolchain extracts syntactic features (e.g., blocks, placeholders) and semantic rules (e.g., data types, value ranges, dependencies), transforming them into a formal MLDSI readable by both humans and machines. The generated instructions were consistent and applicable across domains.

Regarding R2: To what extent do LLMs generate valid MLDS artifacts based on automatically derived MLDSI? The validity rate of 89.1% confirms the effectiveness of MLDSI as a structural guide. LLMs were able to generate largely error-free, machine-processable MLDS artifacts based on formal instructions. Even complex relations, such as nested structures or cardinalities, were correctly implemented. Most errors were due to model limitations or suboptimal prompts and are addressable.

Regarding R3: How usable and adaptable are the resulting MLDS artifacts in various industrial tooling environments? The use cases (VR scene generation and automotive security modeling) show that MLDS artifacts are both syntactically valid and practically usable. In both domains, outputs could be directly integrated into tools or refined with minimal effort. The structures were human-readable and machine-interpretable, enabling collaborative workflows. Modifications via editing or prompting were easily applied, indicating strong adaptability.

6.2 Comparison with Related Work

Compared to approaches like Grammar Prompting [13] or PICARD [12], our method offers greater flexibility and less intrusiveness. While such techniques require decoder-level control or extensions, our approach relies solely on declarative, human-readable instruction structures. In contrast to tool frameworks like LangChain [3] and Pydantic [4], the MLDS method reduces setup time, improves interpretability, and supports domain-specific adaptation. Although our error rate is about 3.9% higher, this is offset by faster iteration and lower entry barriers.

In addition, our method enables greater semantic control and easier adaptation to new domains. While traditional systems are bound to fixed formats like JSON or YAML, our meta-language supports fully customizable structures, crucial for hybrid, interactive toolchains (e.g., VR editors, security modeling).

6.3 Implications and Practical Benefits

MLDSI-based structuring has broad implications for integrating generative AI into industrial environments. By separating semantics, structure, and model logic, a modular architecture is established that supports both automated and manual refinement. Notably, the blank-page syndrome is effectively mitigated: users receive structured templates aligned with domain semantics as a starting point.

Moreover, the clear structure facilitates integration into existing toolchains without requiring proprietary interfaces or new formats. This opens potential use cases including automated configuration, simulation setup, or structured risk analysis. For organizations, the method offers time and cost savings during initial modeling, along with improved traceability and documentation.

6.4 Limitations and Threats to Validity

Despite promising results, several limitations must be considered. First, the method's success depends on the quality of the meta-language. Incomplete or inconsistent MLDSI definitions can result in faulty artifacts. Second, structural validity relies on the model's ability to process long prompt sequences, especially in deeply nested formats.

Another threat lies in model selection: while GPT-4o mini and DeepSeek R1 performed reliably, local models produced more frequent structural errors. Current validation focuses on syntax; semantic coherence was only checked via random sampling. Finally, the approach was tested in only two domains, VR and automotive security, so broader domain evaluations are needed to confirm generalizability.

7   Future Directions

The results of this work suggest a range of future research and development directions that could extend the proposed MLDS approach both theoretically and practically.

A central area for further work lies in the semantic validation of generated MLDS artifacts. While structural integrity can already be reliably checked, the verification of semantic coherence (e.g., plausibility of relations, value compatibility) remains only partially automated. Future work should integrate domain-specific reasoning components or hybrid validation mechanisms based on ontologies or logic rules.

Another promising development path involves the dynamic generation and adaptation of the meta-language itself. Adaptive meta-languages that extend automatically in response to newly detected use cases, object types, or contextual requirements could further enhance the generalizability of the approach in heterogeneous industrial scenarios.

Additionally, the use of Retrieval-Augmented Generation (RAG) opens new possibilities for making MLDSI generation more context-sensitive and robust. By dynamically incorporating examples, rules, or tool documentation during prompt processing, the relevance and accuracy of the generated instructions could be significantly improved.

In the long term, integration into no-code or low-code platforms appears promising. This would embed LLM-based structure generation into interactive design processes and make it accessible to non-technical users, for example, through visual interfaces, searchable component libraries, or structured prompt templates.

8   Conclusion

This work introduces a novel, modular approach to generating MLDS, enabling structured use of LLMs in industrial application scenarios. By introducing declarative MLDSI instructions as a bridge between natural-language requirements and machine-readable structures, key challenges, particularly in terms of format consistency, entry barriers, and adaptability, can be addressed effectively.

The evaluation demonstrates that the approach works across domains, produces robust results, and offers flexible extensibility. In particular, the combination of structural rules and generative AI proves to be an effective tool for the initialization and iterative development of complex artifacts.

The method has shown practical value in areas where structured modeling is essential but formal schema creation presents a bottleneck. Applications include technical education, digital twin development, and safety-critical system design, as well as immersive VR environments, where natural-language prompts were used to generate consistent, domain-specific structures without the need for specialized tooling. Across these contexts, the approach enables faster prototyping and supports collaboration between domain experts and technical stakeholders.

9   Data Availability

All relevant artifacts including two domain-specific meta-languages and MLDS-generated materials are available at: https://github.com/CoNaLaDe-MLDS/Artifacts

References

1. Bassamzadeh, N., Methani, C.: A Comparative Study of DSL Code Generation: Fine-Tuning vs. Optimized Retrieval Augmentation. arXiv preprint arXiv:2407.02742 (2024)
2. Beurer-Kellner, L., Fischer, M., Vechev, M.: Guiding LLMs the right way: fast, non-invasive constrained generation. In: Proceedings of the 41st International Conference on Machine Learning, pp. 3658–3673 (2024)
3. Chase, H.: Langchain: Building applications with large language models (2023). https://github.com/langchain-ai/langchain
4. Colvin, S.: Pydantic: data validation and settings management using python type annotations. https://pydantic.dev/
5. Fischer, A., Burk, L., Tavakoli Kolagari, R., Wienkop, U.: Conalade mlds research artifacts. https://github.com/CoNaLaDe-MLDS/Artifacts
6. Fischer, A., Tolvanen, J.P., Tavakoli Kolagari, R.: Embedded systems security co-design: modeling support for managers and developers. In: Kardas, G., et al. (eds.) Software, System, and Service Engineering. LNBIP, pp. 206–232. Springer, Cham (2025). https://doi.org/10.1007/978-3-031-84913-8_8
7. Geng, S., et al.: Generating structured outputs from language models: benchmark and studies. arXiv preprint arXiv:2501.10868 (2025)
8. Joyce, C.K.: The blank page: effects of constraint on creativity. Soc. Sci. Res. Netw. (SSRN) (2009). https://doi.org/10.2139/ssrn.1552835
9. Li, Z., Hua, W., Wang, H., Zhu, H., Zhang, Y.: Formal-LLM: integrating formal language and natural language for controllable LLM-based agents. arXiv preprint arXiv:2402.00798 (2024)
10. Netz, L., Michael, J., Rumpe, B.: From natural language to web applications: using large language models for model-driven software engineering. In: Modellierung (2024). https://doi.org/10.18420/modellierung2024_018
11. Park, K., Wang, J., Berg-Kirkpatrick, T., Polikarpova, N., D' Antoni, L.: Grammar-aligned decoding. In: Globerson, A., Mackey, L., Belgrave, D., Fan, A., Paquet, U., Tomczak, J., Zhang, C. (eds.) Advances in Neural Information Processing Systems, vol. 37, pp. 24547–24568. Curran Associates, Inc. (2024)
12. Scholak, T., Schucher, N., Bahdanau, D.: Picard: parsing incrementally for constrained auto-regressive decoding from language models. In: Proceedings of the 2021 Conference on Empirical Methods in Natural Language Processing, pp. 9895–9901 (2021). https://doi.org/10.18653/v1/2021.emnlp-main.779
13. Wang, B., Wang, Z., Wang, X., Cao, Y., A Saurous, R., Kim, Y.: Grammar prompting for domain-specific language generation with large language models. In: Advances in Neural Information Processing Systems, vol. 36, pp. 65030–65055 (2023)
14. Zhang, H., Dang, M., Peng, N., Van Den Broeck, G.: Tractable control for autoregressive language generation. In: Proceedings of the 40th International Conference on Machine Learning. ICML 2023, JMLR.org (2023)

Evaluating Architecture Refactoring Suggestions: A Study of LLMs and Retrieval-Augmented Generation Techniques on Design Review

Yi-Hui Lai[ID] and Yung-Pin Cheng[(✉)][ID]

National Central University, Taoyuan 32001, Taiwan
immensitylai@g.ncu.edu.tw, ypcheng@csie.ncu.edu.tw

Abstract. Design review is essential for ensuring software architecture quality, yet it often relies on subjective developer judgment without standardized processes. While large language models (LLMs) have shown promise in code quality analysis, prior work has largely focused on function-level code smells, with limited exploration of architecture-level review under evolving requirements. This study evaluates the effectiveness of LLMs, enhanced with Retrieval-Augmented Generation (RAG), in generating refactoring suggestions for architectural adaptation. Using three models with varying reasoning capabilities and three prompting strategies, we conduct cross-case comparisons on representative design defect scenarios. Results show that high-capacity models can produce reasonable suggestions even without retrieval support, while RAG significantly improves output quality for weaker models and enhances reasoning depth for mid-tier ones. However, RAG's effectiveness strongly depends on the semantic relevance of retrieved content. Our findings demonstrate the potential of RAG-enhanced LLMs for architecture-level design review and propose a practical pipeline for integrating LLM reasoning and retrieval. This work paves the way for future applications in CI/CD pipelines and intelligent design-assist tools.

Keywords: Design Review · Software Architecture Evaluation · Large Language Models (LLMs) · Code Refactoring · Retrieval-Augmented Generation (RAG)

1 Introduction

Software engineering is an ever-evolving discipline characterized by frequent changes in requirements. In iterative development, design review plays a key role in maintaining architectural quality by preventing degradation caused by feature expansion. However, existing review practices often rely on developer intuition and team consensus, lacking standardization and repeatability.

Recent progress in large language models (LLMs) has shown promise in automating programming tasks, particularly those involving syntax correction or repetitive logic. Yet,

T. Dohi (Ed.): ICSED 2025, CCIS 2889, pp. 184–199, 2026.
https://doi.org/10.1007/978-981-92-0202-7_13

their effectiveness diminishes in high-level design tasks such as architectural restructuring, where deeper semantic understanding and knowledge of design principles are required. This limitation stems from LLMs' reliance on internal training data, which may not sufficiently capture abstract software architecture concepts or system evolution semantics.

Retrieval-Augmented Generation (RAG) techniques, which combine external knowledge retrieval with generative reasoning, offer a potential solution. While RAG has demonstrated effectiveness in QA and summarization, its role in multi-step design review workflows remains underexplored. To bridge this gap, this study addresses two key research questions:

- RQ1: Can LLMs, guided by software requirements, generate accurate and actionable architectural refactoring suggestions?
- RQ2: Can RAG integration improve the relevance and structural quality of such suggestions?

To address these questions, six representative software defect cases were selected from textbooks, GitHub repositories, and practical industrial experience. Three prompting workflows were evaluated: (1) a direct input setup (Vanilla Prompting), (2) a task-decomposition workflow (Chain-of-Thought, CoT), and (3) a RAG-based workflow integrating HyDE and semantic retrieval. The vector database was built from object-oriented design and software engineering textbooks.

We tested three models of varying capabilities—LLaMA3.1-8B (low), GPT-4o (medium), and o4-mini (high)—using a uniform evaluation process. Results show that RAG significantly benefits low- and mid-tier models by improving accuracy and reasoning quality. High-performing models like o4-mini, however, already generate coherent and contextually rich suggestions without external retrieval.

Nevertheless, when retrieved content is semantically misaligned, RAG may introduce noise or disrupt the reasoning path. For simpler cases, CoT alone is often sufficient. These findings suggest that while RAG can enhance design reasoning, its effectiveness depends on both retrieval quality and the model's integration capacity.

2 Related Work

Software quality assessment has evolved from metric-based analysis to semantic reasoning with LLMs and retrieval-augmented techniques. This section outlines the key technologies that underpin this study.

2.1 Applications of Large Language Models in Code Correction and Architectural Analysis

Simões and Venson (2024) [1] explored the capability of LLMs to assess source code quality by comparing GPT-3.5 Turbo and GPT-4o against the industry-standard static analysis tool SonarQube. Their evaluation across two large Java open-source projects revealed that GPT-3.5 Turbo could moderately correlate with maintainability metrics, especially in aspects such as readability, naming quality, and stylistic clarity—dimensions often missed by rule-based tools. However, their findings also showed inconsistencies in newer models (e.g., GPT-4o), which tended to overestimate quality. While their work demonstrates the potential of LLMs to supplement static analysis in capturing semantic quality signals, their approach remains limited to isolated class-level analysis without architectural context or retrieval support.

B. Liu (2024) [2] reported that LLMs perform reliably on syntax-level refactoring tasks such as duplicate code elimination or variable renaming. However, their performance deteriorates significantly when handling design-level refactorings such as class decomposition, which involve system-level structural changes. These tasks often require explicit type guidance to improve output accuracy.

These findings suggest that current mainstream LLMs still exhibit limitations in understanding abstract design contexts and system evolution logic. They struggle to independently evaluate or suggest improvements to high-level architectural designs. This observation aligns with the central motivation of this study: enhancing the semantic understanding and design suggestion capabilities of LLMs in structured reasoning tasks.

2.2   Retrieval-Augmented Generation (RAG)

Lewis et al. (2020) introduced the Retrieval-Augmented Generation (RAG) architecture [3], which integrates vector-based retrieval with generative models. By enabling dynamic access to relevant external documents during inference, RAG substantially improves performance in tasks such as open-domain question answering and fact verification.

To address RAG's limitations in processing long documents and complex semantic structures, Sarthi et al. (2024) proposed RAPTOR [4], which incorporates recursive summarization and semantic clustering to build a hierarchical retrieval tree. This structure enables more contextually coherent retrieval, enhancing both reasoning accuracy and generation quality in complex tasks.

Recent work has also highlighted the value of combining retrieval with multi-step reasoning. HyDE (Hypothetical Document Embeddings) [5], for instance, generates hypothetical answers as semantic-rich queries to improve retrieval relevance. Decomposition Prompts further support complex problem-solving by dividing tasks into sub-problems, thereby improving logical coherence and consistency in model outputs [6, 7].

3   Method

Traditional Retrieval-Augmented Generation (RAG) workflows typically use the user input directly as a retrieval query to extract relevant content from a vector database.

However, in this study, the input data includes original source code, system documentation, and additional requirement descriptions. These inputs are structurally complex and semantically diverse; if used as-is for retrieval, it becomes difficult to effectively retrieve software design knowledge with high semantic relevance, thereby compromising the accuracy and usefulness of the retrieval phase.

To address this issue, we adopt a Hybrid RAG architecture, as illustrated in Fig. 1, which integrates two key techniques: HyDE (Hypothetical Document Embedding) and Decomposition Prompting. These enhancements aim to improve semantic alignment and retrieval quality during the model's reasoning process.

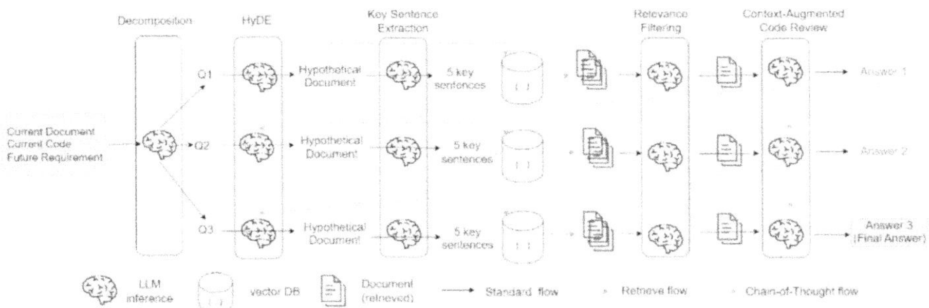

Fig. 1. Hybrid RAG-Enhanced Code Review Pipeline

The overall workflow consists of three core stages: task decomposition, hypothetical document generation, and key sentence extraction with semantic retrieval. The following sections describe each step in detail.

3.1 HyBrid RAG Design and Workflow

As shown in Fig. 2, the overall design review task is decomposed into three sub-questions: (1) understanding the current architecture, (2) identifying structural limitations for handling new requirements, and (3) proposing feasible refactoring strategies.

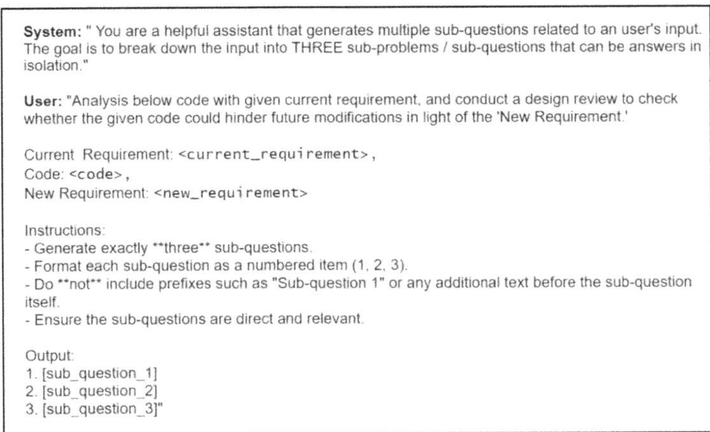

Fig. 2. Prompt template for task decomposition in the Hybrid RAG workflow

For each sub-question, a hypothetical response is first generated using a HyDE-based prompt (Fig. 3), which serves as a semantic proxy to enhance retrieval quality. From these hypothetical responses, five key sentences are extracted via a focused prompt and used as semantic queries. Retrieved results are then compared with the generated sub-question classification step filters for segments with high reasoning utility.

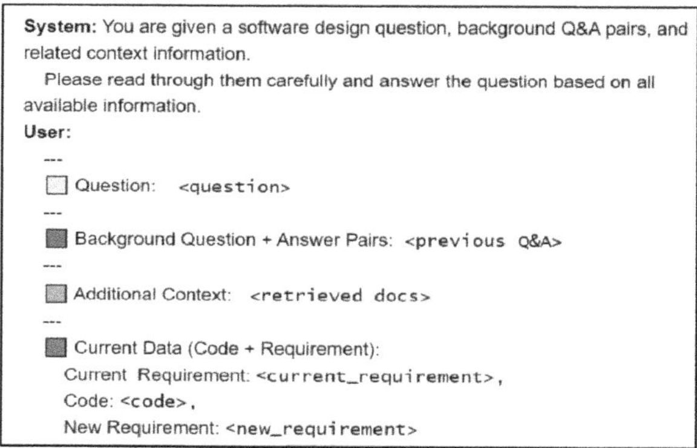

Fig. 3. Prompt template used in the HyDE step of the Hybrid RAG architecture

Finally, as shown in Fig. 4, the model synthesizes the retrieval results, original inputs, and prior intermediate answers to construct a final, step-by-step response. The output is formatted as a sequence of {question, answer} pairs, forming a coherent reasoning chain aligned with the CoT paradigm.

Fig. 4. Prompt template used in the Context-Augmented Code Review step of the Hybrid RAG architecture

This pipeline enables the Hybrid RAG framework to integrate decomposition, semantic enhancement, and selective filtering into a multi-stage, context-aware generation strategy.

3.2 Construction of the Vector Database

We constructed a vector database to support content retrieval in the RAG framework, using four representative textbooks on software engineering and object-oriented design [8–11]. These sources cover core topics such as design patterns, refactoring, responsibility-driven design, and code quality. Due to resource constraints, we limited the initial scope to these textbooks, with potential for future expansion.

To improve semantic alignment and retrieval quality, we adopted the RAPTOR system, which processes textbook content through paragraph segmentation, topic clustering, and semantic indexing to build a hierarchical retrieval structure. This enables more accurate retrieval and context-aware generation.

Additionally, we included original design case descriptions (e.g., the Movie case) from the textbooks in the database. These passages allow us to observe whether the model can retrieve relevant structural cues and improve output quality.

3.3 Baseline Architectures for Comparative Evaluation

To evaluate the effectiveness of retrieval augmentation for LLMs and compare the impact of different reasoning strategies and auxiliary mechanisms on output quality, we designed two baseline architectures as control conditions:

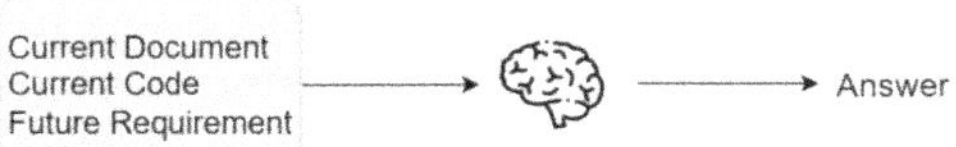

Fig. 5. Vanilla Prompting Architecture

1. Vanilla Prompting (Fig. 5):

    In this setting, the model receives only the original source code and requirement description as input. Prompts are used to elicit analysis and suggestions without incorporating any additional reasoning strategies or retrieval mechanisms.
2. LLM with CoT (Fig. 6):

    In this setting, the original task is decomposed into three subtasks using a structured prompt. This decomposition improves the structure and clarity of the model's output. The process simulates a Chain-of-Thought (CoT) reasoning strategy, enhancing the logical consistency and hierarchical organization of the model's reasoning path.

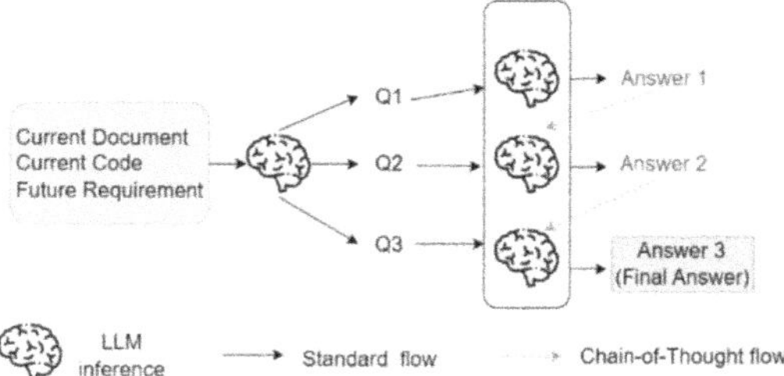

Fig. 6. Multi-Stage Reasoning Workflow with Chain-of-Thought Decomposition

3.4 Case Study Preparation

This study designs and employs six software architecture defect cases that span a variety of design issues and complexity levels. The selected cases cover common architectural challenges such as the Strategy pattern, module decoupling, data relationship optimization, command dispatching, and the Single Responsibility Principle (SRP). These cases aim to evaluate the ability of LLMs to understand and refactor diverse architectural contexts.

An overview of the six cases is provided in the Table 1. Full descriptions and source code implementations are available in the GitHub repository accompanying this work [12].

Table 1. Overview of Refactoring Case Studies Used in This Study

Case name	Source	Description
Movie	Textbook [8]	Simulates a video rental system from a software engineering textbook, illustrating refactoring from switch-case to Strategy pattern for modularity
E-book	Keyword-Rewritten from Movie	Rewritten from the Movie case to test the model's semantic and structural reasoning, avoiding memorization bias
GildedRose	GitHub [13]	Simplified store system refactored using the Strategy pattern to improve readability and support product-type extension
Wood	Keyword-Rewritten from GildedRose	Rewritten GildedRose case to prevent overlap with pretraining data
Order	Original Design	In-house order system designed to test whether the model can optimize relational structures and reduce redundancy during employee updates

(continued)

Table 1. (*continued*)

Case name	Source	Description
Scene	Real-World Unity Project	Unity module refactored from monolithic command handling to apply the Command pattern and enforce SRP for extensibility

3.5 Evaluation Mechanism and Scoring Criteria for Model Outputs

This study adopts a qualitative evaluation approach to assess the quality and practicality of refactoring suggestions generated by language models in architecture-level design review tasks.

Unlike conventional generation tasks, which can be evaluated using similarity-based metrics (e.g., BLEU, ROUGE, METEOR), this task involves multi-step reasoning over code semantics, design patterns, and evolving requirements. The output is open-ended and creative, lacking a definitive ground truth. In such cases, similarity metrics may penalize valid but novel suggestions.

We therefore analyze both the textual suggestions and corresponding code structures (supported by UML transformations), using a rubric (Table 1) that assesses flaw identification, design principle alignment, and appropriate abstraction. This approach enhances evaluation objectivity, comparability, and reproducibility (Table 2).

Table 2. Evaluation Criteria for Structural Refactoring Quality

Grade	Description
A	Accurately identifies design flaws and provides well-structured suggestions based on OOP principles
B	Identifies core issues and offers reasonable direction, but lacks detail or shows mild overengineering
C	Performs superficial structural adjustments without real decoupling or adherence to principles
D	Fails to recognize key issues or proposes unsuitable or chaotic structural changes

4 Results and Analysis

The cross-experiment results across six test cases, three language models, and three experimental configurations are summarized in Table 3. Based on the findings presented in the table, four key observations are outlined as follows.

4.1 Model Reasoning Ability as the Key to Stable Design Suggestions.

Experimental results indicate that the reasoning capability of language models has a decisive impact on the accuracy of refactoring suggestions. In scenarios without RAG assistance, models with stronger reasoning ability generally demonstrated superior performance, consistently outperforming or at least matching weaker models.

Among the three models evaluated across six cases, the o4-mini model, which exhibited the strongest reasoning ability, achieved the best overall performance with a 10/12 correctness rate. GPT-4o ranked second, while LLaMA3.1-8B showed the weakest performance. Notably, o4-mini was able to consistently generate valuable design suggestions across most cases and configurations, even without the support of RAG, and its output quality remained largely unaffected.

These results highlight that a language model's inherent understanding and reasoning capability remains the core factor determining the quality of generated design suggestions. Even without access to external knowledge, models with stronger semantic comprehension and logical reasoning can still exhibit high stability and accuracy, offering significant advantages for architecture-level refactoring tasks.

Table 3. Assessment of Refactoring Recommendation Levels Across Different Models and Case Studies

Testcase		Model		
		LLaMA3.1-8B	GPT-4o	o4-mini
Movie	Vanilla Prompting	B	C	A
	LLM with CoT	D	A	A
	Hybrid RAG	B	B	A
E-book	Vanilla Prompting	D	D	C
	LLM with CoT	B	A	A
	Hybrid RAG	A	A	A
GildedRose	Vanilla Prompting	C	B	B
	LLM with CoT	B	B	A
	Hybrid RAG	B	B	B
Wood	Vanilla Prompting	D	B	A
	LLM with CoT	C	A	A
	Hybrid RAG	B	B	A
Order	Vanilla Prompting	D	A	A
	LLM with CoT	D	A	A
	Hybrid RAG	D	A	A
Scene	Vanilla Prompting	D	C	A
	LLM with CoT	D	C	A
	Hybrid RAG	D	C	A

4.2 RAG Enhances the Refactoring Quality of Models with Limited Reasoning Ability

For models with relatively weak reasoning capabilities, the integration of Retrieval-Augmented Generation (RAG) significantly improves the correctness and completeness of their refactoring suggestions. Taking the LLaMA3.1-8B model as an example, the results across multiple test cases show clear differences among the three experimental configurations, indicating that its output quality heavily depends on external knowledge support.

In the E-book case, the original code employs a series of if-else statements to determine book categories and calculate prices and reward points (as shown in Fig. 7).

```java
public String printHistory() {
  double OrderSum = ;
  int OrderPoint = ;
  String content = "Order Record for " + getName() + "\n";

  Enumeration Orders = _Orders.elements();

  while(Orders.hasMoreElements()){
    double total = ;
    Order thisOrder = (Order) Orders.nextElement();

    if(thisOrder.geteBook().getTypeIndex() == eBook.TECH){
      OrderPoint+= ;
      total += ;
      if(thisOrder.getDays()> )
        total += (thisOrder.getDays()- )* ;
    }
    else if(thisOrder.geteBook().getTypeIndex() == eBook.TOP_10){
      total += ;
      OrderPoint+= ;
      if(thisOrder.getDays()> )
        total += (thisOrder.getDays()- )* ;
    }
    else if(thisOrder.geteBook().getTypeIndex() == eBook.MIND) {
      total += ;
      OrderPoint+= ;
      if(thisOrder.getDays()> )
        total += (thisOrder.getDays()- )* ;

    }

    content += "\t" + thisOrder.geteBook().getbookName() + "\t" +
        String.valueOf(total) + "\n";
    OrderSum += total;
  }
```

Fig. 7. Partial Source Code of the E-book Test Case

The performance under different prompting strategies is summarized as follows:

- Vanilla Prompting: Extracts update logic into separate functions, called via a `switch` statement (Fig. 8). However, type-based control flow remains, limiting extensibility.
- LLM with CoT: Introduces separate classes for each eBook type and delegates logic accordingly. Still relies on `if-else` type checks, violating the Open-Closed Principle (Fig. 9).
- Hybrid RAG: Applies the Strategy Pattern by integrating the eBookCategory interface, fully removing type checks. Refactoring is influenced by a retrieved Movie case, improving structural clarity and reasoning accuracy.

```java
private double calculateRentalFee(Order order) {
    eBook book = order.geteBook();

    switch (book.getCategory()) {
        case MIND:
            return 15 + (order.getDays() - 7) * 1.5;
        case TECH:
            return 25 + (order.getDays() - 10) * 3;
        case TOP_10:
            return 30 + (order.getDays() - 7) * 5;
        case HEALTH:
            return order.getDays();
        default:
            throw new UnsupportedOperationException("Unsupported book category");
    }
}
```

Fig. 8. Partial refactoring code suggestions for the E-book case under the LLaMA3.1-8B × Vanilla Prompting architecture

```java
private BookCategory getBookCategory(eBook eBook){
    if(Ebook.HEALTH == eBook.getTypeIndex()){
        return new HealthBookCategory();
    }else if(Ebook.TOP_10 == eBook.getTypeIndex()){
        return new Top10BookCategory();
    }else if(Ebook.TECH == eBook.getTypeIndex()){
        return new TechBookCategory();
    }else if(Ebook.MIND == eBook.getTypeIndex()){
        return new MindBookCategory();
    }
    return null;
}


while(Orders.hasMoreElements()){
    double total = 0;
    Order thisOrder = (Order) Orders.nextElement();

    BookCategory category = getBookCategory(thisOrder.geteBook());
    if(category != null){
        Total += thisOrder.calculateRentalFee(category);
        OrderPoint+=thisOrder.getRewardPoints(category);
        //..
    }
}
```

Fig. 9. Partial refactoring code suggestions for the E-book case under the LLaMA3.1-8B × LLM with CoT architecture

Another example is the Wood case, in which the original code uses deeply nested if-else statements to determine object types and perform corresponding update operations (see Fig. 10). The comparison across the three architectures is summarized as follows:

- Vanilla Prompting: Handles objects using a switch statement and extracts the update logic into functions (Fig. 11), but retains the original control flow structure.
- LLM with CoT: Abstracts the `update` behavior into separate classes but maps object types to their update logic using an `enum` and `HashMap`. This lacks extensibility and violates key design principles.
- Hybrid RAG: Initially uses `enum` and conditionals in the HyDE stage. However, the text explicitly mentions "polymorphism to handle different behaviors," prompting the model to retrieve textbook content on polymorphism. As a result, it suggests using inheritance to separate wood type behaviors. Although `instanceof` checks remain

in the main function, the design better aligns with object-oriented principles than the other two approaches.

```java
public void updateGrade() {
    for (int i = ; i < logs.length; i++) {
        if (!logs[i].species.equals("Seasoned Oak")
            && !logs[i].species.equals("Event Cedar")) {
            if (logs[i].grade > ) {
                if (!logs[i].species.equals("Ancient Redwood")) {
                    logs[i].grade = logs[i].grade - ;
                }
            }
        } else {
            if (logs[i].grade < ) {
                logs[i].grade = logs[i].grade + ;

                if (logs[i].species.equals("Event Cedar")) {
                    if (logs[i].storageDays < ) {
                        if (logs[i].grade < ) {
                            logs[i].grade = logs[i].grade + ;
                        }
                    }

                    if (logs[i].storageDays < ) {
                        if (logs[i].grade < ) {
                            logs[i].grade = logs[i].grade + ;
                        }
                    }
                }
            }
        }
    }
```

Fig. 10. Partial source code of the Wood case

```java
public void updateGrade() {
    for (WoodLog log : logs) {
        switch (log.species) {
            case SEASONED_OAK:
                updateGradeForSpecies(log.species, );
                break;
            case EVENT_CEDAR:
                updateGradeForSpecies(log.species, );
                updateGradeForSpecies(log.species, );
                break;
            case ANCIENT_REDWOOD:
                // No grade update for Ancient Redwood
                break;
            case CONJURED_PINE:
                // Update Conjured Pine logic here
                break;
    }
```

Fig. 11. Partial refactoring code suggestions for the Wood case under the LLaMA3.1-8B × Vanilla Prompting architecture

In summary, even without direct case matches in the database, RAG can guide low-capacity models toward more accurate design suggestions through semantic retrieval of relevant keywords. This result further confirms that, when intrinsic reasoning capability is limited, semantic retrieval can effectively compensate for knowledge gaps and enhance the logical coherence and practical value of refactoring outputs.

4.3 The Dual Impact of RAG on Generation Quality in Medium-To-High Reasoning Models

In medium-to-high reasoning capability models, Retrieval-Augmented Generation (RAG) presents a double-edged effect. On one hand, appropriate retrieved content can expand the model's design perspective, leading to deeper and more forward-looking recommendations. On the other hand, if the retrieved content is misaligned with the problem context, it may misguide the model's reasoning, resulting in output that deviates from sound design principles.

Taking the GildedRose case as an example, the o4-mini model performed slightly better under the CoT architecture compared to the Hybrid RAG setup. Under CoT, o4-mini correctly recognized the deeply nested if-else control structure and recommended a refactoring using the Strategy pattern (see Fig. 12). When an additional requirement was introduced—"add a Conjured item that updates twice as fast as a Normal item"—the CoT-based o4-mini was able to treat Conjured as a distinct object and assign it an independent strategy.

In contrast, under the Hybrid RAG architecture (Fig. 13), o4-mini misinterpreted Conjured as a subclass of Normal and handled it through inheritance. A closer inspection of the HyDE stage reveals that although the model initially attempted to implement a new object, the retrieved documents included instructional material featuring Strategy pattern examples implemented via abstract class and extends. This external influence ultimately diverted the generation process from a previously more appropriate design direction. This case demonstrates that when retrieved content does not semantically align with the problem scenario, it may disrupt the model's correct reasoning trajectory.

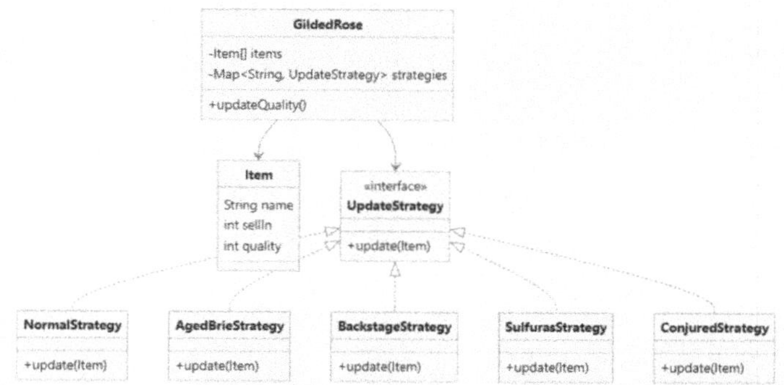

Fig. 12. Refactoring Suggestion for the GildedRose Case under o4-mini × LLM with CoT

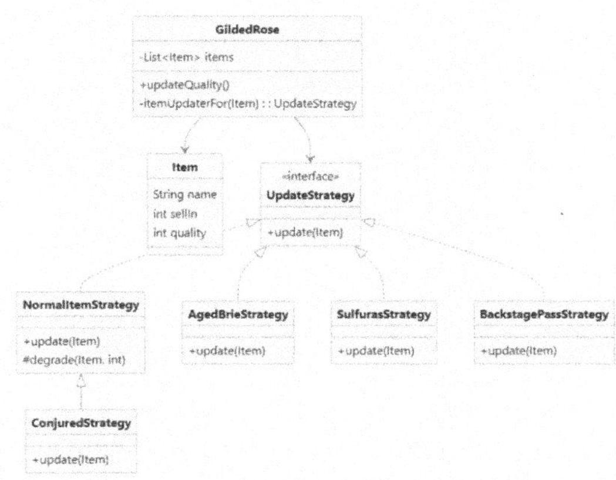

Fig. 13. Refactoring Suggestion for the GildedRose Case under o4-mini × Hybrid RAGzz

Conversely, in the Order test case, Hybrid RAG enhanced GPT-4o's performance beyond standard refactoring. While Vanilla and CoT setups suggested typical class-level changes, RAG enabled the model to propose an Observer Pattern to notify customers when employees leave—demonstrating deeper design adaptability.

This improvement was driven by semantically aligned HyDE prompts like "Adapting software to business changes" and "Observer Pattern for contact updates," which guided the model toward broader architectural insights.

Overall, these cases show that RAG can significantly aid or hinder performance in mid-to-high reasoning models, depending on retrieval quality and alignment. Effective retriever design and domain-relevant corpora are crucial to RAG's success in software design tasks.

4.4   Limitations of RAG in Specific Tasks

While RAG generally enhances LLM performance, its effectiveness is constrained in tasks requiring domain-specific knowledge or deeper structural reasoning.

In the Order case, none of the LLaMA3.1-8B workflows correctly identified the many-to-many relationship issue. Retrieved content focused on general OOP and design patterns, lacking relevant database modeling concepts. Thus, the model's output remained limited by its own reasoning capacity.

In the Scene case, involving a large Unity-based project, all models failed to generate meaningful suggestions—even with Hybrid RAG. Retrieved content, mostly from Java/OOP contexts, was semantically misaligned with the target domain, offering little value.

These cases highlight that RAG's effectiveness depends on high-quality, context-aligned retrieval. Without it, even strong models show limited improvement, and RAG may offer minimal or no benefit.

5 Conclusion

This study evaluates the effectiveness of Large Language Models (LLMs) in architecture-level design review tasks driven by evolving requirements, with a focus on how Retrieval-Augmented Generation (RAG) impacts the quality and structural soundness of refactoring suggestions. Using representative defect cases, three LLMs of varying reasoning ability were tested across three prompting strategies, including a Hybrid RAG setup combining HyDE and task decomposition.

Results show that stronger models (e.g., o4-mini) can generate coherent suggestions independently, while RAG significantly improves output quality for weaker models—especially when retrieved content aligns semantically with the task. However, irrelevant or noisy retrieval can mislead reasoning, highlighting the importance of retrieval precision and integration quality. Overall, RAG shows strong potential for enhancing LLM-driven design reviews when paired with well-curated vector databases and context-aware prompting.

6 Limitations and Future Work

This study is limited by the small number of test cases and may not fully capture the complexity of real-world software architectures. LLM performance also degrades with large or context-rich inputs, such as multi-file Unity projects. Additionally, the evaluation relies solely on source code and requirement descriptions, excluding other artifacts like design specs or change logs. Future work may expand the dataset, incorporate richer contextual inputs, and enhance transparency by linking generated suggestions to their source content, improving traceability and user trust.

References

1. Da Silva Simões, I.R., Venson, E.: Evaluating source code quality with large language models: a comparative study. arXiv preprint arXiv:2408.07082 (2024). https://doi.org/10.48550/arXiv.2408.07082
2. Liu, B., Jiang, Y., Zhang, Y., Niu, N., Li, G., Liu, H.: An empirical study on the potential of LLMs in automated software refactoring. arXiv preprint arXiv:2411.04444 (2024). https://doi.org/10.48550/arXiv.2411.04444
3. Lewis, P., et al.: Retrieval-augmented generation for knowledge-intensive NLP tasks. arXiv preprint arXiv:2005.11401 (2021). https://doi.org/10.48550/arXiv.2005.11401
4. Sarthi, P., Abdullah, S., Tuli, A., Khanna, S., Goldie, A., Manning, C.D.: RAPTOR: re-cursive abstractive processing for tree-organized retrieval. arXiv preprint arXiv:2401.18059 (2024). https://doi.org/10.48550/arXiv.2401.18059
5. Gao, L., Ma, X., Lin, J., Callan, J.: Precise zero-shot dense retrieval without relevance labels. arXiv preprint arXiv:2212.10496 (2022).https://doi.org/10.48550/arXiv.2212.10496
6. Zhou, D., et al.: Least-to-most prompting enables complex reasoning in large language models. arXiv preprint arXiv:2205.10625 (2023). https://doi.org/10.48550/arXiv.2205.10625
7. Trivedi, H., Balasubramanian, N., Khot, T., Sabharwal, A.: Interleaving retrieval with chain-of-thought reasoning for knowledge-intensive multi-step questions. arXiv pre-print arXiv:2212.10509 (2023). https://doi.org/10.48550/arXiv.2212.10509

8. Fowler, M.: Refactoring: Improving the Design of Existing Code. Addison-Wesley, Boston (1999)
9. Wirfs-Brock, R., McKean, A., Jacobson, I., Vlissides, J.: Object Design: Roles, Responsibilities, and Collaborations. Pearson Education, Upper Saddle River (2002)
10. Gamma, E., Helm, R., Johnson, R., Vlissides, J.: Design Patterns: Elements of Reusable Object-Oriented Software. Addison-Wesley, Boston (1995)
11. Freeman, E., Freeman, E., Bates, B., Sierra, K.: Head First Design Patterns. O'Reilly, Sebastopol (2004)
12. Lai, Y.H.: LLM-RefactorTestSet. https://github.com/yihui2001/LLM-RefactorTestSet. Accessed 04 Aug 2025
13. Bache, E.: GildedRose-refactoring-kata. https://github.com/emilybache/GildedRose-Refactoring-Kata. Accessed 04 Aug 2025

A Study on Cross-Language Static Defect Analysis with Fine-Tuned Large Language Models

Junyi He, Shiyu Yan[✉], Xiaohua Yang, Meng Li, and Jie Liu

University of South China, Hengyang, Hunan, China
junyihe@stu.usc.edu.cn, {yanshiyu,mlemon,jieliu}@usc.edu.cn,
xiaohua1963@foxmail.com

Abstract. Static analysis is a crucial component of software testing. The realization of static analysis across languages is crucial for enhancing the efficiency of automated software testing. However, existing static analysis tools are limited in terms of supported programming languages, rely on language-specific rules, involve complex configurations, and lack a deep understanding of program context, semantics, and syntax. As a result, they are incapable of performing cross-language static analysis for general coding rules or common defects. As a result, they fail to perform cross-language static analysis based on general rules and common errors. This paper conducts research on the application of fine-tuning LLM to assist in cross-language static defect analysis. We conduct experiments and analyses on six widely used programming languages, evaluating two common types of static errors: array out-of-bounds and defined but unused variables/functions. The experimental results show that fine-tuning effectively improves the efficiency of static analysis and provides a new method for cross-language static error detection.

Keywords: static-analysis · cross-language · large language mode · defect detection

1 Introduction

As a technique for detecting potential defects without executing a program, static analysis plays an essential role in ensuring code quality. With the increasing complexity and scale of software systems, multi-language programming has become increasingly common, introducing new challenges for cross-language static code analysis. Cross-language static analysis refers to the process of detecting errors across programs written in multiple programming languages simultaneously. Existing static analysis tools primarily rely on predefined rules and employ techniques such as abstract syntax trees (AST) and pattern matching to analyze code. While these tools can effectively identify certain common programming errors, their performance significantly deteriorates in cross-language scenarios. The root cause lies in the fact that most existing tools are restricted to a single or limited set of languages and cannot analyze multiple languages simultaneously. They require separate rule sets and parsers for each language, leading

T. Dohi (Ed.): ICSED 2025, CCIS 2889, pp. 200–214, 2026.
https://doi.org/10.1007/978-981-92-0202-7_14

to high configuration complexity. Moreover, they generally lack support for general rule sets—rules derived from common and recurring errors across different programming languages in real-world development. In addition, these tools fall short in understanding program context and semantics, limiting their ability to interpret rule violations and perform efficient cross-language static analysis.

Recently, Large Language Models (LLMs) such as ChatGPT have demonstrated significant potential in various reasoning and decision making roles, serving as intelligent agents, especially in Software Engineering (SE) tasks such as code generation and understanding [1–3]. This has prompted researchers to explore their potential applications in cross-language static analysis. Notably, the superior performance of LLMs in code comprehension and generation suggests their potential to overcome the limitations faced by traditional tools when handling multi-language code. However, numerous investigations leverage prompt engineering in their utilization of LLMs [4–6] rather than fundamentally enhancing the model's ability to enforce specific programming rules.

We conducted experiments to address these issues, using LLM fine-tuning to assist in cross-language analysis. First, we analyzed the common rules of six commonly used programming languages (C, C++, Java, Python, C#, PHP). Based on this analysis, the method constructs a fine-tuning dataset through tailored data collection, preprocessing, and structured data formatting.

We adopt Qwen2.5-coder-7B as the base model and apply the LoRA fine-tuning strategy. By employing the LORA fine-tuning strategy, it is possible to reduce the memory requirements and data volume demands, while also increasing the training speed and enhancing the cross-language static checking performance.

Experimental results demonstrate that LORA fine-tuning strategy significantly enhances the performance of the base model in cross-language static error detection. The experimental data used to evaluate the performance of the fine-tuned model is based on defect of two general rules.

LORA strategy achieves 90% accuracy in detecting "array out-of-bounds" errors and 89% accuracy in identifying "defined but unused variables/functions". These results validate the effectiveness of LORA in cross-language static analysis and provide valuable practical insights for future research in this field.

2 Background

Static bug detection is an automated technique for inspecting and analyzing a program's source code, object code, or binaries, all without executing the program [7, 8]. This process identifies potential bugs by examining how the code's control and data flow align with specific bug patterns and rules [9]. Multiple tools and methods have been developed in both research and industry for static bug detection [10], such as Infer and C++ Test. These tools typically rely on predefined heuristic rules to scan and analyze the codebases or binaries of software projects [11–13].

Although existing static analysis tools such as Infer and PMD support code checking for different languages, most are limited to a single or a small set of programming languages and cannot perform static analysis across multiple languages using a unified parser.

These tools require language-specific parsers and rule sets, resulting in high configuration complexity and significant human and resource costs. Moreover, existing static analysis tools are unable to check for generalizable rules across languages. They lack consideration for commonalities and universal coding rules shared among different programming languages—rules that are often overlooked but frequently lead to recurring errors.

Additionally, these tools have limited capabilities in deep program context analysis, which can lead to misinterpretation of erroneous statements and a high number of false positives—alerts that do not genuinely indicate actual bugs [14–20]—thereby making efficient cross-language static analysis challenging. The motivation of this study is to leverage the powerful code understanding and reasoning capabilities of LLMs to perform static analysis across different programming languages based on generalizable coding rules.

LLMs have gained significant popularity in recent research and industrial applications. Numerous recent studies are investigating the utilization of LLMs in the field of SE, driven by the significant progress and advancements achieved by LLMs [21–24]. Studies have shown that LLMs have been deeply integrated into static analysis and vulnerability detection in complex scenarios. For example, Microsoft's CodeQL framework utilizes LLMs for cross-module vulnerability reasoning, while the DeepSeek-R1 framework employs multi-granularity code representation techniques to accurately locate logical defects. By introducing lightweight fine-tuning techniques (such as LoRA) and hybrid analysis architectures, LLMs have significantly enhanced efficiency in practical engineering scenarios.

Fine-tuning, as a key technical approach in modern machine learning, currently includes mainstream strategies such as Adapter Tuning, Prefix Tuning, Prompt Tuning, and LoRA. Among them, the LoRA strategy achieves dynamic adjustment of model weights by introducing two learnable low-rank matrices A and B in parallel while freezing the original parameters of LLMs. By reducing the number of training parameters, LoRA reduces memory usage and computational costs, and demonstrates performance in multiple natural language processing tasks that is close to or even reaches the level of full fine-tuning.

This study employs an innovative approach by training a large language model (LLM) using the rules of a single programming language (e.g.C) to enable cross-language static analysis. This method overcomes the syntax constraints of different programming languages by extracting commonalities and semantics from the rules across various languages. By leveraging the LLM's code comprehension abilities, the approach deeply analyzes the semantics and context of the program. Therefore, the method only requires rule set data from one programming language for model training, enabling it to perform cross-language static error detection across multiple languages.

3 Data Preparation and Processing

The objective of this study is to use LLMs and fine-tuning techniques to achieve automated, cross-language static analysis based on general coding rules. However, pretrained LLMs lack a deep understanding of specific rule items, and directly applying them to cross-language static analysis tasks may lead to hallucinations. To address this limitation, We employ the LORA fine-tuning strategy to assist in cross-language static defect analysis.

The details of data preparation and processing are shown in Fig. 1. This figure mainly illustrates the process of training an LLM using fine-tuning techniques to enable it to have cross-language static checking capabilities. The main steps include data collection and processing, and fine-tuning strategies.

The key to data processing lies in extracting the common features and semantic information expressed by multiple languages in the general rules. By constructing fine-tuned data using a single programming language, the aim is to break through the syntactic limitations between different programming languages, enabling the model to deeply analyze the semantic connotations and contextual information of the programs.

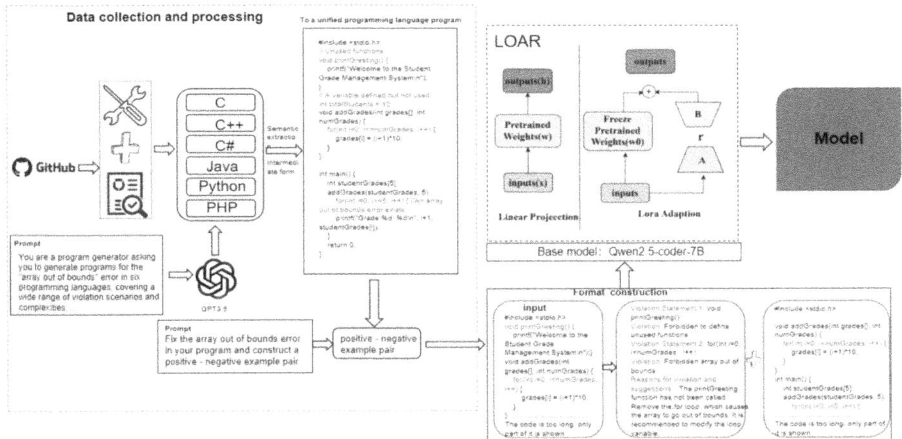

Fig. 1. The Fine-Tuning-Based Workflow for assisted Cross-Language Static Analysis

3.1 Data Collection

This study mainly focuses on analyzing the programming languages that are frequently used in enterprise development, have a large user base, and are the most common among static tools. We systematically reviewed the coding standards of six mainstream programming languages (C, C++, C#, Python, Java, PHP), and selected two common general defects, "array out-of-bounds" and "defining unused variables or functions", for experiments.

Most existing tools implement cross-language checking functions by integrating multi-language interpreters with coding standards, lacking targeted support for general rules. It is worth noting that different programming languages have significant differences in the specific implementation details and violation scenarios of the same coding rule, and this language characteristic-level difference is a technical difficulty that existing tools cannot fully cover.

Data quality is a key factor affecting the performance of LLMs, and data diversity significantly influences the generalization ability of the model. Data collection and processing were carried out for two common general defects, namely "array out-of-bounds" and "undefined use of variables or functions".

By performing preprocessing and data augmentation on the raw data, we constructed a fine-tuning dataset to enhance the LLM's generalization ability and detection accuracy in cross-language static error checking tasks. The data sources primarily consist of the following two components:

The first portion of the data is sourced from open-source projects on GitHub, which include programs written in various programming languages. On one hand, we performed static analysis using a combination of manual inspection and automated tools to identify programs containing the two types of errors: array out-of-bounds and unused variable or function definitions. On the other hand, for programs that did not originally contain these errors, we manually injected the corresponding violations to create the required faulty examples.

The second portion of the data is generated through data augmentation using ChatGPT. By designing prompt engineering strategies, we instructed ChatGPT to generate multilingual code snippets containing the two targeted errors—array out-of-bounds and unused variable or function definitions.

3.2 Data Processing

Due to the considerable diversity in how different programming languages express the same type of violation, we first leverage language-specific static analysis tools and ChatGPT-assisted techniques to abstract the syntactic and semantic features of code fragments containing violations. This abstraction aims to eliminate language-specific syntactic discrepancies while preserving the essential semantic information of the violations. The extracted information is then encoded into a unified, cross-language representation in JSON format(as shown in Fig. 2).Next, the JSON representation is systematically converted into violation examples written in C, serving as the standardized input for subsequent model processing. To further enhance the model's understanding of program semantics beyond language-specific syntax, ChatGPT is employed to perform fine-grained semantic interpretation of these code fragments. This facilitates the LLM's ability to capture deeper program logic and contextual dependencies. Finally, violation statements within the code are explicitly marked and annotated, resulting in a labeled dataset tailored for fine-tuning and optimized for cross-language static error detection tasks.

Building upon the previous steps, we utilize prompt engineering techniques to correct violation-containing C code examples, thereby constructing positive-negative example pairs.

In total, this study collects 200 pairs of positive and negative examples, each containing violations. Each negative example may contain multiple violations. The advantage of using positive-negative pairs lies in their ability to help the model understand the relationship between erroneous and correct code, thus enhancing the model's ability to perform code correction.

```json
1 ▾ {
2     "defect_type": "array out-of-bounds",
3     "description": "Accessing or modifying an index position that exceeds the declared range of the array may lead to undefined behavior.",
4     "language": "c",
5 ▾   "array_details": {
6       "array_name": "numbers",
7       "declared_length": 5,
8 ▾     "valid_index_range": {
9         "min": 0,
10        "max": 4
11      }
12    },
13 ▾  "violation_instances": [
14 ▾    {
15        "operation_type": "Access",
16        "code_snippet": "printf(\"numbers[5] = %d\\n\", numbers[5]);"
17      }
18    ]
19 }
```

Fig. 2. The intermediate representation in JSON format

3.3 Fine-Tuning

In cross-lingual static analysis tasks, the diversity of error types and rule sets—combined with the scarcity of task-specific datasets—necessitates manual data collection and processing. Therefore, selecting a fine-tuning strategy that is both data-efficient and computationally lightweight is critical. For this reason, we adopt the LoRA (Low-Rank Adaptation) fine-tuning strategy, which enables efficient model customization by introducing a small number of trainable low-rank parameters on top of a pre-trained model. Following our pipeline, we find that fine-tuning the model with as few as 200 structured samples is sufficient to significantly enhance the model's capability in cross-lingual static error detection.

First, after setting the necessary parameters, the fine-tuning data is parsed into three components: (1) Instruction—a description of the static code analysis task, (2) Input—a C code snippet containing an array out-of-bounds error, and (3) Output—the corresponding violation statement, its cause and recommendation, and the corrected code. Through the mapping between input and output, the model learns how to perform static checks and generate actionable suggestions based on the defined rules.

To enhance the model's cross-lingual static analysis capability, LoRA is applied to key layers of the model, such as fully connected layers or attention mechanisms. Instead of retraining all model parameters, LoRA adjusts the pre-trained model weights through the optimization of low-rank matrices.

During training, the model updates the LoRA-specific matrices A and B to align the generated outputs with the target outputs in the dataset. Through this fine-tuning process, the model learns to identify violation statements in erroneous programs and generate corresponding recommendations and fixes.

The loss function guides the optimization of matrices A and B, enabling the model to incrementally reduce the gap between predicted and expected outputs.

Our fine-tuning data format is built upon a three-part structure: instruction, input, and output. The details are shown in the format construction section in Fig. 1.

- The instruction section specifies the static analysis task, clearly defining the model's expected output and the associated requirements.

- The input section contains one or more violation-related statements extracted from the program, along with their semantic context.
- The output section includes detailed information such as the violating statements, the violated rules, the cause of the violation, recommendations for correction, and the repaired version of the program.

This structured data format facilitates the model's understanding of violation segments within a program and enables it to accurately identify specific offending statements. It helps the model map these violations to the corresponding rules, while also providing explanations for the violations and suggestions for remediation—further enhancing the model's comprehension of the problematic code. Finally, by providing the correct program, the model can understand the relevance between the violation program and the correct program.

4 Experiment Setup

The objective of this experiment is to evaluate the effectiveness of the proposed approach in enhancing the cross-language static error detection capabilities of LLMs using the constructed dataset. As illustrated in Fig. 3, the overall workflow consists of two main components:

(1) Data collection and processing for the experimental dataset.
(2) Evaluation of the effectiveness of the proposed fine-tuning method in improving cross-language static error detection performance.

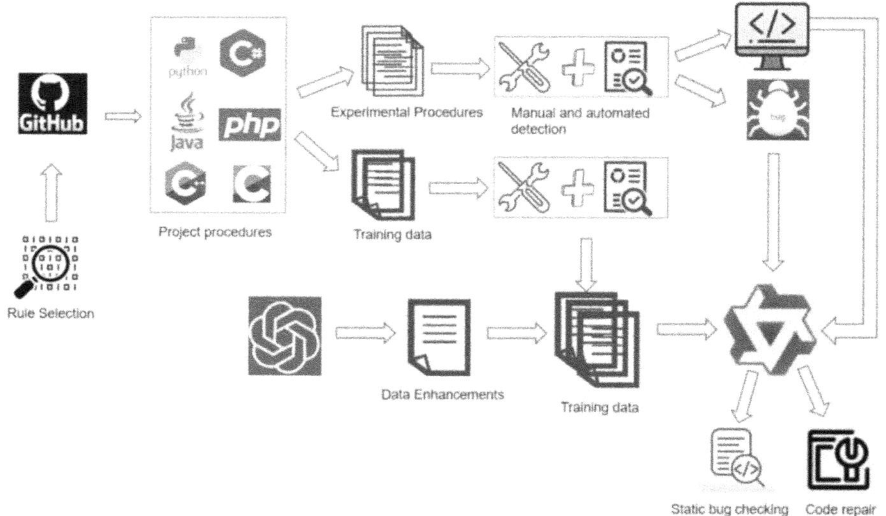

Fig. 3. Experimental Framework for Evaluating

To evaluate the effectiveness of the fine-tuning method, we design experiments to answer the following research questions:

RQ1: How effective is fine-tuning in detecting array out-of-bounds errors in cross-language static analysis?
RQ2: How effective is fine-tuning in detecting unused variable or function definitions in cross-language static analysis?
RQ3: How do the effects of static analysis tools and fine-tuned models compare at the level of a single language?

4.1 Validation Dataset Preparation

To rigorously assess the effectiveness of the proposed fine-tuning in cross-language static error detection, we constructed a dedicated dataset, as no publicly available benchmark currently addresses this task. Ensuring the credibility and representativeness of the dataset is critical for reflecting the model's true capability. Therefore, we adopted a systematic data preparation strategy combining domain expert knowledge with automated static analysis tools. We select two typical and widely-studied bugs [25–31]. Specifically, we selected two representative and high-impact general coding rules for this study: (1) array bounds must not be exceeded, and (2) unused variables and functions must be avoided. These rules are frequently violated in industrial software development and are known to cause severe issues. Array out-of-bounds errors can lead to runtime crashes, memory corruption, or even critical security vulnerabilities. Similarly, unused variables and functions compromise code readability, maintainability, and, under certain conditions, may introduce security threats such as data leakage or buffer overflows. The constructed dataset, therefore, captures both the prevalence and practical relevance of these two categories of errors.

To construct the experimental dataset, we collected 120 program samples from GitHub, covering the two targeted error types across six programming languages. We first performed preprocessing on the collected programs, including the removal of comments and other redundant information. Then, leveraging a combination of expert knowledge and automated tools, we identified and annotated instances of the two error types within the programs. For those samples that did not originally contain these errors, we applied fault injection techniques to deliberately introduce the corresponding violations.

As a result, the final dataset comprises 245 annotated error instances, including 121 cases of array out-of-bounds access and 124 cases involving unused variable or function definitions.

4.2 Parameter Design

In Low-Rank Adaptation (LoRA) fine-tuning, parameter design plays a crucial role. The key parameters include rank (r), learning rate, and training epochs. The choice of rank should be based on the task's complexity and the dataset size. A lower rank can reduce the number of parameters in the model, thereby lowering computational costs, but it may sacrifice the model's expressive power. On the other hand, a higher rank can better capture complex patterns in the data but may lead to overfitting. In our experiments on cross-language static checking, the results indicated that a rank of 32 yielded the best performance across multiple datasets. The learning rate controls the speed of parameter updates. Since LoRA only updates a small number of parameters, a relatively higher learning rate (e.g., $1e-4$ or $5e-4$) is typically suitable. Regarding training epochs, LoRA fine-tuning usually achieves good results with fewer epochs, typically between 3 and 10 rounds. By optimizing these parameters, we can significantly reduce computational and storage costs while maintaining model performance, thereby achieving efficient fine-tuning.

4.3 Evaluation Indicators

To assess the usability and accuracy of the cross-language static error checking system, this study uses Accuracy, Precision, and Recall as the core evaluation metrics. These metrics are evaluated based on the ground truth (true labels) we constructed for the experimental dataset. During the experiment, the fine-tuned model systematically analyzes 120 experimental programs, collecting data on the correct warnings and false positives for each program. Based on this, the following evaluation metrics are calculated:

- Accuracy: Measures the overall correctness of the model's predictions across all classes.
- Precision: Assesses how many of the identified errors are actually true errors (i.e., how many of the predicted violations are correct).
- Recall: Evaluates how many of the true errors were correctly identified by the model (i.e., how many of the actual violations were detected).

Finally, we calculate and present the F1 score, which is the harmonic mean of precision and recall.

5 Evaluation

RQ1: How effective is fine-tuning in detecting array out-of-bounds errors in cross-language static analysis?

To evaluate the impact of LORA on enhancing the static error detection capabilities of LLMs, this study strictly controls experimental variables by excluding potential confounding factors such as prompt engineering, chain-of-thought, and retrieval-Augmented. The evaluation is specifically focused on measuring the performance gains attributable to the LORA method itself. The rationale is that techniques like prompt engineering may influence the model's output during the evaluation process, thereby obscuring the actual contribution of LORA and hindering an accurate assessment of its effectiveness.

Currently, there is no prior work in the research community that applies fine-tuning techniques to the task of cross-lingual static analysis. As a result, no existing benchmark dataset is available for evaluation. To address this gap, we constructed our evaluation dataset using a combination of expert domain knowledge and automated tooling. Finally, we constructed a dataset containing 121 array out-of-bounds defects and 125 defined-but-unused variable/function defects.

We categorized the programs by programming language and fed them—without any prompt engineering—into the fine-tuned model for cross-lingual static analysis. For each input, the model was expected to identify and output the violating statement(s), the violated rule, the reason for the violation, suggested fixes, and the corrected version of the code.

To ensure the accuracy and reliability of the evaluation results, we engaged four experienced software testing researchers to manually review all outputs.

The experimental results demonstrate that the fine-tuned model performs excellently in detecting "array out-of-bounds" violations. The average accuracy reaches 90%, while the precision, recall, and F1-Score are 95%, 93%, and 94%, respectively. Specifically, the model performs particularly well in C language projects, with an accuracy of 95%, precision of 100%, recall of 95%, and an F1-Score of 97%. In C + + projects, the model's performance slightly declines, with an accuracy of 80%, precision of 94%, recall of 85%, and an F1-Score of 89%.

The detailed evaluation metrics for other programming languages are shown in Table 1, which further validate the improvement of the model's static error detection capability across different programming language environments using the fine-tuning technique.

Table 1. Evaluation Results of the Fine-Tuned Model for "Array Out-of-Bounds" Violations in Different Programming Languages

Programming Language	Error types	Accuracy (%)	Precision (%)	Recall (%)	F1-Score (%)
C	Array out of bounds	95%	100%	95%	97%
C++	Array out of bounds	86%	94%	85%	89%
Java	Array out of bounds	90%	91%	95%	93%
Python	Array out of bounds	90%	91%	100%	95%
C#	Array out of bounds	86%	91%	95%	93%
PHP	Array out of bounds	95%	100%	90%	95%
average		90%	95%	93%	94%

RQ2: How effective is fine-tuning in detecting unused variable or function definitions in cross-language static analysis?

The experimental process for RQ2 follows the same steps as RQ1, with the specific implementation steps as follows: First, we deployed the fine-tuned Qwen2.5-coder-7B model and input program samples from six programming languages (including C, C++, Java, Python, C#, and PHP) into the fine-tuned model for evaluation, in order to test the model's cross-language static error checking ability. These samples contained a total of 124 "unused variable or function definition" violations, covering typical error scenarios in different programming languages. Then, we sequentially input these program samples into the model for static error detection and thoroughly recorded the model's output detection results, including accuracy, precision, recall, and F1-Score.

The experimental results show that for the typical violation of "unused variable or function definition," the model's average detection accuracy is 89%, with precision reaching 95%, recall at 93%, and F1-Score at 94%, demonstrating the model's overall stable performance in cross-language scenarios. Specifically, in C language projects, the fine-tuned Qwen2.5-coder-7B model exhibited excellent violation detection performance, with an accuracy of 95%, precision at 100%, recall at 95%, and an F1 score of 97%, indicating the model's high ability to recognize C language syntax rules and error patterns. For C++ programs, the model's detection accuracy was 80%, with precision at 94%, recall at 85%, and F1 score at 89%. Although slightly lower than the performance in C language, it still shows strong detection capability. For other programming languages, such as Java, Python, C#, and PHP, the model's detection performance also exhibited some variation, with specific evaluation metrics shown in the Table 2.

Table 2. Evaluation Results of the Fine-Tuned Model for "Unused Variable or Function Definition" Violation Across Different Programming Languages

Programming Language	Error types	Accuracy (%)	Precision (%)	Recall (%)	F1-Score (%)
C	defined but unused variables/functions	95%	95%	100%	97%
C++	defined but unused variables/functions	91%	96%	96%	96%
Java	defined but unused variables/functions	91%	100%	91%	95%
Python	defined but unused variables/functions	83%	95%	86%	90%
C#	defined but unused variables/functions	91%	91%	100%	95%
PHP	defined but unused variables/functions	83%	95%	86%	90%
average		89%	95%	93%	94%

Overall, the experimental results suggest that the fine-tuned model has high applicability and robustness in cross-language static error detection tasks, effectively identifying typical error patterns across multiple programming languages. The fine-tuned model demonstrates good generalization ability in static error analysis tasks. However, its performance in languages like C++/PHP is not as good as that of other programming languages. This is because the syntax of C++ is much more complex than that of languages like C and Java, which causes the model not to learn these complex structures, resulting in slightly poorer performance. Moreover, PHP has a significant difference in syntax from general programming languages, which leads to slightly poorer performance of the model on certain datasets.

RQ3: How do the effects of static analysis tools and fine-tuned models compare at the level of a single language?

We used the evaluation dataset constructed by ourselves and the public Juliet dataset as the benchmark datasets.

This dataset contains a total of 497 samples, among which 267 are samples with array out-of-bounds defects, and 230 are samples with unused variable/function defects.

The experimental results are listed in Table 3 and Table 4. We applied the dataset to the one-shot strategy, the commercial static analysis tool C++ Test, and the fine-tuned Qwen2.5-coder-7B.

For the one-shot strategy, we adopted the form of "one sample code plus a prompt". For example: "You are a static analysis expert. Please learn from the above 'array out-of-bounds' defective code, then analyze the code I provide, identify the violating statements and rules, and give suggestions along with the modified code."

The results show that our fine-tuned large language model outperforms other methods in terms of precision. For the one-shot method, due to the insufficient number of given examples, the defect scenarios learned by the model are limited, making it unable to accurately identify the corresponding defects—thus resulting in low precision and recall of this method. C++ Test, on the other hand, analyzes programs based on rules and Abstract Syntax Trees (ASTs). Although it achieves good precision and recall on most programs, it generates some false positives and false negatives for complex structures involving large data volumes and control flows.

By comparing the overall experimental data, we can conclude that our method is superior to other methods, and fine-tuning technology can enhance the model's static analysis capability and cross-language capability.

Table 3. Comparison of the effectiveness of the prompt engineering, C++ Test, and the fine-tuned Qwen2.5 model in addressing array out-of-bounds defects

Method	Array out of bounds			
	Accuracy	Precision	Recall	F1-Score
One-shot	65%	60%	70%	65%
C++ Test	88%	86%	90%	88%
Qwen2.5-coder (Fine-tuned)	95%	100%	95%	97%

Table 4. Comparison of the effectiveness of the prompt engineering, C++ Test, and the fine-tuned Qwen2.5 model in addressing "Unused Variable or Function Definition" defects

Method	Unused Variable or Function Definition			
	Accuracy	Precision	Recall	F1-Score
One-shot	62%	65%	68%	67%
C++ Test	84%	86%	88%	87%
Qwen2.5-coder (Fine-tuned)	95%	95%	100%	97%

6 Conclusion

This paper conducts the first study on cross-language static defect analysis assisted by LLM fine-tuning. We focusing on two common programming errors: array out-of-bounds and defined-but-unused variables/functions. We performed rigorous cleaning and preprocessing of the fine-tuning dataset and systematically evaluated the effectiveness of our method on these two representative cross-language static analysis tasks.

This study places a strong emphasis on optimizing two key components: data construction and processing. To further enhance the model's cross-language comprehension, we applied syntactic and semantic abstraction and generalization to multilingual programs within the dataset. Specifically, we extracted semantic information from violation statements across different programming languages and used this information to annotate the training data. This approach enables the LLM to move beyond surface-level syntax and develop a deeper understanding of the underlying characteristics of code violations.

Experimental results demonstrate that the fine-tuned large language model achieves significant performance improvements in cross-language static error detection tasks. Moreover, the proposed method offers clear advantages in reducing analysis cost and complexity, highlighting its practical value.

We plan to broaden the scope of our research to include a wider range of LLMs, such as Meta's LLaMA, Google's Bard, and PaLM2. In addition, we aim to further explore alternative LLM fine-tuning techniques and model distillation strategies. We are also committed to developing efficient prompt engineering methods tailored to specific tasks, with the goal of identifying cost-effective approaches to enhance the model's performance on domain-specific static analysis tasks.

Acknowledgment. Thank you for the support from the research group and the teachers. Project number: Hunan Provincial Natural Science Foundation (Regional Joint) Project, (Project Number: 2025JJ70193).

References

1. Hou, X.: Large language models for soft- ware engineering: a systematic literature review. arXiv preprint arXiv:2308.10620 (2023)

2. Song, C.H., Wu, J., Washington, C., Sadler, B.M., Chao, W.-L., Su, Y.: LLM-planner: few-shot grounded planning for embodied agents with large language models. In: Proceedings of the IEEE/CVF International Conference on Computer Vision, pp. 2998–3009 (2023)
3. Wang, G., et al.: Voyager: an open-ended embodied agent with large language models. arXiv preprint arXiv:2305.16291 (2023)
4. Cao, J., Li, M., Wen, M., Cheung, S.-C.: A study on prompt design, advantages and limitations of chatgpt for deep learning program repair. arXiv preprint arXiv:2304.08191 (2023)
5. Kang, S., Yoon, J., Yoo, S.: Large language models are few-shot testers: exploring LLM-based general bug reproduction. In: ICSE 2023, pp. 2312–2323. IEEE (2023)
6. Min, B., et al.: Recent Advances in natural language processing via large pre-trained language models: a survey. ACM Comput. Surv. **56**(2), Article 30, 40 p. (2023)
7. Ashfaq, Q., Khan, R., Farooq, S.: A comparative analysis of static code analysis tools that check java code adherence to java coding standards. In: 2019 2nd International Conference on Communication, Computing and Digital systems (C-CODE). IEEE, pp. 98–103 (2019)
8. Li, L., et al.: Static analysis of android apps: a systematic literature review. Inf. Softw. Technol. **88**(2017), 67–95 (2017)
9. Vassallo, C., Panichella, S., Palomba, F., Proksch, S., Gall, H.C., Zaidman, A.: How developers engage with static analysis tools in different contexts. Empirical Softw. Eng. **25**(2020), 1419–1457 (2020)
10. Harzevili, N.S., et al.: Automatic static bug detection for machine learning libraries: are we there yet? ArXiv (2023). https://arxiv.org/abs/2307.04080. Accessed 18 Oct 2023
11. Carvalho, A., Luz, W., Marcílio, D., Bonifácio, R., Pinto, G., Canedo, E.D.: C-3PR: a bot for fixing static analysis violations via pull requests. In: SANER 2020, pp. 161–171 (2020). https://doi.org/10.1109/SANER48275.2020.9054842
12. Liu, K., Koyuncu, A., Kim, D., Bissyandè, T.F.: AVATAR: fixing semantic bugs with fix patterns of static analysis violations. In: SANER2019, pp. 1–12 (2019). https://doi.org/10.1109/SANER.2019.8667970
13. Marcilio, D., Bonifácio, R., Monteiro, E., Canedo, E., Luz, W., Pinto, G.: Are static analysis violations really fixed? A closer look at realistic usage of SonarQube (ICPC'19), pp. 209–219 (2019)
14. Hanam, Q., Tan, L., Holmes, R., Lam, P.: Finding patterns in static analysis alerts: improving actionable alert ranking. In: Proceedings of the 11th Working Conference on Mining Software Repositories (Hyderabad, India) (MSR 2014), pp. 152–161. Association for Computing Machinery, New York (2014). https://doi.org/10.1145/2597073.2597100
15. Heckman, S., Williams, L.: A systematic literature review of actionable alert identification techniques for automated static code analysis. Inf. Softw. Technol. **53**(4), 363–387 (2011)
16. Kang, H.J., Aw, K.L., Lo, D.: Detecting false alarms from automatic static analysis tools: how far are we? (ICSE '22), pp. 698–709. Association for Computing Machinery, New York (2022)
17. Kharkar, A., et al.: Learning to reduce false positives in analytic bug detectors. In: Proceedings of the 44th International Conference on Software Engineering, pp. 1307–1316 (2022)
18. Muske, T., Serebrenik, A.: Techniques for efficient automated elimination of false positives. In: SCAM, pp. 259–263 (2020)
19. Reynolds, Z.P., Jayanth, A.B., Koc, U., Porter, A.A., Raje, R.R., Hill, J.H.: Identifying and documenting false positive patterns generated by static code analysis tools. In: SER&IP 2017, pp. 55–61 (2017)
20. Shen, H., Fang, J., Zhao, J.: EFindBugs: effective error ranking for findbugs. In: ICST 2011, pp. 299–308 (2011)
21. Fan, Z., Gao, X., Roychoudhury, A., Tan, S.H.: Improving automatically generated code from codex via automated program repair. arXiv preprint arXiv:2205.10583 (2022)

22. Shin, J., Tang, C., Mohati, T., Nayebi, M., Wang, S., Hemmati, H.: Prompt engineering or fine tuning: an empirical assessment of large language models in automated software engineering tasks. arXiv preprint arXiv:2310.10508 (2023)
23. Xia, C.S., Wei, Y., Zhang, L.: Automated program repair in the era of large pre-trained language models (ICSE '23), pp. 1482–1494. IEEE Press (2023). https://doi.org/10.1109/ICSE48619.2023.00129
24. Zeng, Z., Tan, H., Zhang, H., Li, J., Zhang, Y., Zhang, L.M.: An extensive study on pre-trained models for program understanding and generation. In: ISSTA, pp. 39–51 (2022)
25. Bhatt, B.N., Furia, C.A.: Automated repair of resource leaks in android applications. J. Syst. Softw. **192**(2022), 111417 (2022). https://doi.org/10.1016/j.jss.2022.111417
26. Cui, M., Chen, C., Xu, H., Zhou. Y.: SafeDrop: detecting memory deallocation bugs of rust programs via static data-flow analysis. ACM Trans. Softw. Eng. Methodol. **32**(4), Article 82, 21 p. (2023). https://doi.org/10.1145/3542948
27. Ghanavati, M., Costa, D., Seboek, J., Lo, D., Andrzejak, A.: Memory and resource leak defects and their repairs in Java projects. Empirical Softw. Eng. **25**(1), 678–718 (2020). https://doi.org/10.1007/s10664-019-09731-8
28. Kellogg, M., Shadab, N., Sridharan, M., Ernst, M.D.: Lightweight and modular resource leak verification (ESEC/FSE 2021), pp. 181–192. Association for Computing Machinery, New York (2021)
29. Lee, J., Hong, S., Oh, H.: NPEX: repairing Java null pointer exceptions without tests. In: Proceedings of the 44th International Conference on Software Engineering (Pittsburgh, Pennsylvania) (ICSE '22), pp. 1532–1544. Association for Computing Machinery, New York (2022). https://doi.org/10.1145/3510003.3510186
30. Li, W., Cai, H., Sui, Y., Manz, D.: PCA: memory leak detection using partial call-path analysis (ESEC/FSE 2020), pp. 1621–1625 (2020)
31. Tomassi, D.A., Rubio-González, C.: On the real-world effectiveness of static bug detectors at finding null pointer exceptions, pp. 292–303 (2021)

A Systematic Literature Review on SQL Injection Attack Detection Using Deep Learning and Large Language Models

Kunmin Zhang[1], Dongcheng Li[2](✉), and Yuanni Wang[1]

[1] School of Computer Science, China University of Geosciences, Wuhan, China
[2] Department of Computer Science, California State Polytechnic University - Humboldt, Arcata, USA
dl313@humboldt.edu

Abstract. SQL injection remains a major threat to web application security, compromising data integrity and service availability. Leveraging advanced feature extraction and semantic modeling capabilities, deep learning and large language models have emerged as pivotal approaches for SQL injection detection. This paper systematically reviews recent advances in this field, with a focus on architectural designs, detection performance, and application contexts of deep neural networks and hybrid models. The review also examines datasets, evaluation metrics, and the relationship between architectural choices and detection efficacy, highlighting the benefits and deployment challenges of large language models, and concludes by identifying key issues and future research directions.

Keywords: SQL Injection · Deep Learning · Large Language Models · Vulnerability Detection

1 Introduction

With the proliferation of web applications, SQL injection (SQLi) attacks have become a pervasive and severe security threat [1]. By embedding malicious SQL into legitimate requests, such as altering a login query to username = "admin" OR "1" = "1", attackers can bypass authentication and gain unauthorized database access, compromising data integrity, confidentiality, and availability. Consistently ranked among the OWASP Top 10 security risks [2], SQLi affects critical sectors including government, finance, and e-commerce, highlighting the need for advanced detection mechanisms.

Existing detection techniques, including static analysis, dynamic analysis, hybrid approaches, and machine learning-based methods, have shown success in specific scenarios [3]. However, they often exhibit limited feature representation, heavy reliance on handcrafted rules, and poor generalization to complex nested structures, multilingual variations, or context-dependent attacks [4]. Obfuscated payloads, such as those using comment delimiters or irregular whitespace, further hinder semantic interpretation and contextual modeling. To overcome these challenges, recent research has increasingly

T. Dohi (Ed.): ICSED 2025, CCIS 2889, pp. 215–230, 2026.
https://doi.org/10.1007/978-981-92-0202-7_15

adopted deep learning (DL) [5], leveraging automated feature extraction and structural modeling to enhance the recognition of ambiguous semantics and polymorphic attack patterns [6]. Building on these advances, pretrained language models such as BERT and GPT [7] have shifted SQLi detection from rigid pattern matching toward semantic reasoning [8], enabling more effective handling of complex, natural-language-like injection statements. Nevertheless, the high computational cost, inference latency, and limited interpretability of large language models (LLMs) remain significant barriers to practical deployment [9].

This review systematically examines DL- and LLM-based SQLi detection, analyzing model architectures, detection performance, datasets, and evaluation metrics, and assessing how architectural design influences efficacy. It further identifies challenges in scalability, engineering applicability, and trustworthiness, and outlines directions for future research.

2 Research Methods

This study follows three phases: planning, execution, and reporting. The planning phase involves defining research questions and formulating the strategy. The execution phase comprises reviewing relevant literature and systematically analyzing selected works. The reporting phase is dedicated to presenting and discussing the findings.

2.1 Research Questions

Q1: How do DL architectures impact accuracy, generalization, and efficiency in SQLi detection?
Q2: How do LLMs improve complex injection detection, and what are their strengths and limitations?
Q3: Do current datasets and metrics adequately assess capability and adaptability?

2.2 Research Strategy

To ensure systematicity and rigor, this review adopts a standardized literature review methodology. Relevant studies were retrieved from Google Scholar, IEEE Xplore, and ScienceDirect, with a focus on publications between 2017 and 2025. The search employed representative strings including ("SQL injection") AND ("detection methods" OR "survey" OR "review"), and ("SQL injection") AND ("deep learning" OR "large language model"). The initial search yielded approximately 690 records. After removing duplicates and irrelevant works, 180 studies remained. To enhance the precision and validity of the literature selection process, the following inclusion and exclusion criteria were established:

Inclusion Criteria

- The study explicitly investigates SQLi detection using DL or LLMs.
- The title, abstract, or keywords contain relevant technical terms.
- The publication is sourced from reputable journals or conferences.

Exclusion Criteria

- Studies that do not involve SQLi detection or do not utilize DL- and LLM-based methods.
- Research with insufficient methodological detail or lacking empirical validation.
- Purely commentary, review-oriented, or non-technical papers lacking implementation details.

Based on the aforementioned screening strategy, 46 eligible studies were ultimately included in the systematic review. Figure 1 illustrates the annual distribution of the selected publications, showing a clear upward trend in research output from 2017 to 2024, with a projected continuation into 2025, reflecting the growing academic interest in DL- and LLM-based approaches for SQLi attack detection.

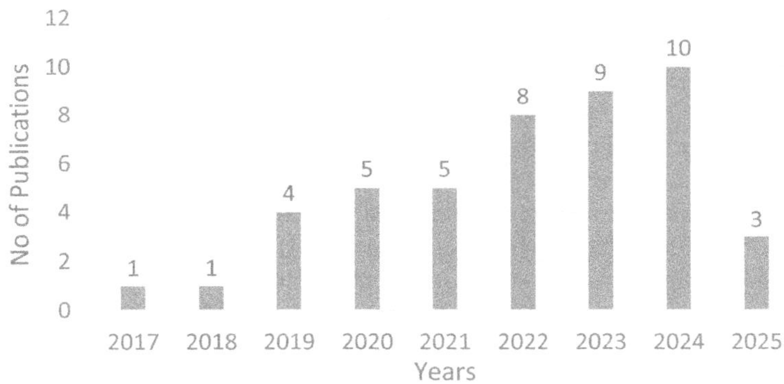

Fig. 1. Distribution of Papers Published by Year

To contextualize this review, prior surveys either provided broad DL overviews with limited treatment of SQLi [10] or focused on feature engineering while overlooking DL advances and LLM-based methods [11]. In contrast, this review examines architectural distinctions, modeling strengths, and deployment challenges, addressing persistent gaps in semantic modeling, practical applicability, and evaluation diversity.

3 Deep Learning Detection Methods

Deep learning, with its capability for automatic feature extraction and complex pattern modeling, has been widely applied to SQL statement analysis. Studies employ CNNs, RNNs, FNNs, and their variants, leveraging CNNs for local syntactic patterns, RNNs for contextual dependencies, and FNNs for lightweight real-time detection, as summarized in Fig. 2. The following subsections examine the core strategies and performance of these models.

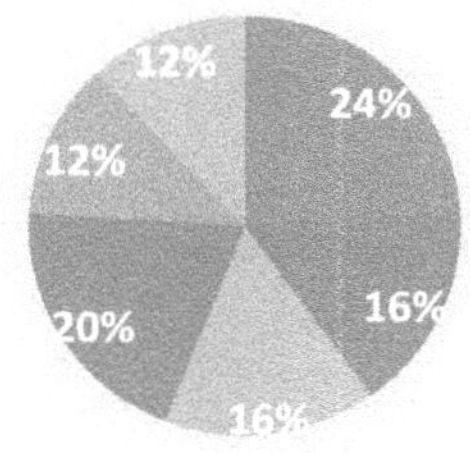

Fig. 2. Distribution of DL Technologies in SQLi Detection

3.1 Convolutional Neural Networks

Convolutional Neural Networks (CNNs), known for local feature extraction and pattern recognition [12], have shown strong potential in SQLi detection. Studies have applied CNNs to model web traffic, browser requests, and textual inputs, achieving high accuracy and robustness. Luo et al. [13] reported that CNNs outperform rule-based methods in precision and false positive rate. Falor et al. [14] highlighted their strength in capturing local syntactic patterns, while Natarajan et al. [15] combined CNNs with natural language processing to improve contextual modeling of malicious keywords. Sangeeta et al. [16] incorporated a ResNet structure to mitigate vanishing gradients, enabling deeper representation learning and higher detection accuracy. Table 1 summarizes the applicability, advantages, and limitations of these CNN-based approaches.

Table 1. Applications of CNNs in SQLi Detection

Ref	Method	Applicable scenarios	Advantages	Limitations	Suggestions for improvement
[13]	CNN	Network traffic detection	Robust and accurate	Data-dependent	Diversify data
[14]	CNN	Web attack detection	Broad coverage	Time-consuming	Reduce feature dimensions
[15]	NLP + CNN	Browser request injection	Context-aware	High overhead	Design lightweight models
[16]	ResNet	Deep injection detection	Reliable performance	Slow training, sparse samples	Refine architecture

While CNNs effectively detect typical SQLi patterns, their limited receptive fields hinder modeling of long-range dependencies and complex semantics. They perform well on short-range keyword combinations but struggle with obfuscated payloads that disrupt keyword positions, and their insensitivity to input order can obscure query distinctions. Consequently, CNNs are better suited for local syntactic feature extraction than standalone detection. Integrating CNNs with sequential models or attention mechanisms can balance local and global context modeling, improving accuracy, robustness, and generalization to diverse attack variants.

3.2 Recurrent Neural Networks

Recurrent Neural Networks (RNNs) and variants such as LSTM and GRU are employed in SQLi detection to capture long-range contextual dependencies. By preserving sequential semantics, they detect complex attacks involving nested structures, logical obfuscation, and word order perturbations, as illustrated in Table 2.

Table 2. Applications of RNNs and Its Variants in SQLi Detection

Ref	Method	Applicable scenarios	Advantages	Limitations	Suggestions for improvement
[18]	RNN-LSTM/GRU	SQLi detection in web applications	Capable of automatic modeling	Complex architecture	Introduce multi-source features
[19]	RNN Autoencoder	SQL structure reconstruction	High detection accuracy	Generalizability unproven	Enrich data diversity
[20]	AST + LSTM	Syntax attack detection	Structure-aware	High false positive rate	Grammar optimization
[21]	BERT + LSTM	Semantic detection	Rich semantics	Parameter sensitivity	Streamline model

RNNs process input sequentially, retaining historical information through internal states. LSTM mitigates gradient vanishing via gating mechanisms [17], while GRU offers a more efficient design. Sherstinsky et al. [18] combined LSTM and GRU in the DSQLIS system for multi-layer sequential modeling, achieving high performance in detecting diverse injection behaviors. Alghawazi et al. [19] developed an RNN-based autoencoder for structural reconstruction and anomaly detection with limited data. Zhuo et al. [20] integrated Abstract Syntax Trees with LSTM to detect nested and obfuscated attacks, and Liu et al. [21] incorporated BERT-generated contextual representations into LSTM to jointly capture semantic and structural cues. Overall, RNN-based models enhance SQLi detection by capturing sequential and contextual relationships, making them effective for order-sensitive and structurally complex attacks. Future work should consider integration with graph structures, pre-trained language models, and lightweight architectures to balance accuracy with deployment efficiency.

3.3 Feedforward Neural Networks

Feedforward Neural Networks (FNNs), valued for simplicity, training efficiency, and low deployment cost, are widely used in SQLi detection. The Multi-Layer Perceptron (MLP), as a representative FNN, classifies SQL statements via multi-layer nonlinear mappings [22] and is frequently adopted in lightweight intrusion detection systems. Table 3 summarizes representative studies.

Table 3. Applications of FNNs in SQLi Detection

Ref	Method	Applicable scenarios	Advantages	Limitations	Suggestions for improvement
[23]	FNN	Web SQLi detection	Customizable features	Limited feature scope	Auto feature extraction
[24]	CNN + MLP + Word2Vec	HTTP request SQLi detection	Fully automated modeling	Limited to first-order attacks	Expand attack coverage
[25]	MLP + LSTM	Traffic SQLi detection	Semantic-structural	Traffic SQLi detection	Feature optimization
[26]	MLP	Real-world SQL traffic	Real-data validated	No targeted improvements	Add syntactic features
[27]	PatternMLP	Structural SQL detection	High accuracy	Small dataset	Data expansion

Hassan et al. [23] developed an FNN-based model with 19 handcrafted features, outperforming traditional machine learning on small datasets and demonstrating suitability for lightweight classification. Chen et al. [24] introduced a hybrid Word2Vec-CNN-MLP model for hierarchical HTTP request modeling, where MLP achieved superior accuracy, training efficiency, and resource utilization but was less effective for complex patterns. Tang et al. [25] integrated MLP with LSTM for joint feature modeling, achieving over 99% accuracy, and later applied ANNs to real SQL traffic [26] to balance accuracy with deployment efficiency. Arock et al. [27] proposed a pattern-driven MLP focusing on the WHERE clause to detect localized malicious patterns. Overall, FNNs combine architectural simplicity with efficient inference, making them suitable for detecting SQLi with clear semantics and regular patterns, yet their limited contextual and structural modeling constrains effectiveness against complex or obfuscated attacks. Integration with pretrained language models, sequential architectures, or syntactic features could improve robustness and generalization.

3.4 Other Deep Learning Models

Beyond CNNs and RNNs, recent SQLi detection research has employed diverse DL models to overcome limitations in feature representation, data sparsity, and structural perception. These include fully connected networks, probabilistic learning, Deep Belief Networks (DBN), and pretrained language models such as BERT and synBERT, which enhance feature extraction, semantic modeling, and multimodal integration. Table 4 summarizes representative studies.

Table 4. Applications of Other DL Models in SQLi Detection

Ref	Method	Applicable scenarios	Advantages	Limitations	Suggestions for improvement
[28]	SQLNN	Network SQLi detection	Mitigates overfitting	Limited diversity	Diverse training data
[29]	DBN	Real-time pattern detection	Unsupervised pretraining	Imbalanced samples	Balanced supervision
[30]	PNN+ BAT	Traffic injection detection	Strong generalization	Sensitive to noise	Rule-guided features
[31]	BERT + MLP	Web app classification	Deep semantic capture	Unstable for advanced attacks	Multitask attack detection
[32]	synBERT	SQL syntax-semantics fusion	Tree-BERT integration	Advanced attack vulnerable	Enhanced attack corpus
[33]	ADF	Low-resource detection	Resource-efficient	Scalability issues	Depth optimization

These models reflect a shift from structure-driven learning to semantic perception and feature adaptivity. Zhang et al. [28] proposed SQLNN with sparse matrices and Dropout to mitigate overfitting but without evaluation on diverse attacks. Zhang et al. [29] applied a DBN-based unsupervised framework with layer-wise pretraining, improving anomaly detection but reducing robustness on imbalanced datasets. Alarfaj et al. [30] integrated a Probabilistic Neural Network with BAT optimization, achieving high accuracy on small samples but remaining vulnerable to perturbations. Pan et al. [31] combined BERT embeddings with MLP, CNN, and LSTM, with BERT-MLP achieving the highest accuracy; Lu et al. [32] proposed synBERT to detect privilege escalation and obfuscated payloads; and Li et al. [33] introduced Adaptive Deep Forest with AdaBoost to address data imbalance but with reduced stability at scale. Although these DL models achieve high accuracy, efficiency, and feature modeling, they are limited by poor generalizability, reliance on labeled data, and low robustness to complex injections. Future research should focus on unified semantic representations, lightweight architectures, and multi-source data augmentation to improve scalability and practical deployment.

3.5 Hybrid Deep Learning Models

With increasingly sophisticated SQLi techniques, single-model DL is limited in feature extraction, contextual awareness, and training stability. Recent work uses hybrid models combining CNNs, RNNs, attention mechanisms, and FNNs to capture local patterns, temporal dependencies, and semantic features, improving accuracy and adaptability to complex attacks. Table 5 summarizes representative studies.

Table 5. Applications of Hybrid DL Models in SQLi Detection

Ref	Method	Applicable scenarios	Advantages	Limitations	Suggestions for improvement
[34]	CNN + LSTM	Web SQLi detection	Local-sequential fusion	Unverified generalization	Extend to other security tasks
[35]	MVC-BiCNN	Multi-view detection	Expressive	No dynamic detection	Add dynamic perception
[36]	TextCNN + LSTM + Attention	Semantics-enhanced detection	High accuracy, scalable to large datasets	Limited adversarial robustness	Adversarial defense for advanced attacks
[37]	CNN + BiLSTM	Database injection	Local-global modeling	Small dataset	Optimize input encoding
[38]	LSTM + MLP	General web detection	Simple and efficient	Limited scalability	Add syntax or attention
[39]	Feature fusion	General detection	Complementary features	Single-source limitation	Scalable fusion framework

SQLi payloads often blend syntactic obfuscation with logical transformations. Tautology-based injections suit CNN-based local pattern recognition, whereas blind injections require LSTMs for long-range semantic modeling. Tadhani et al. [34] showed that CNN-LSTM architectures combine lexical and sequential modeling, outperforming single structures but risking overfitting on unseen attacks. Kakisim et al. [35] proposed MVC-BiCNN with multi-view encoding and bidirectional CNNs for improved interpretability, though reliant on hand-crafted features. Sun et al. [36] integrated TextCNN, BiLSTM, and attention for scalability but struggled with second-order attacks. Gandhi et al. [37] extended bidirectional semantic modeling with CNN-BiLSTM, effective on small datasets yet variable with multilingual or noisy data. Sharma et al. [38] combined LSTM with MLP for lightweight deployment, and Zhao et al. [39] fused deep and hand-crafted features for better cross-dataset generalization. While hybrid models enhance accuracy and structural modeling, robustness against evasive attacks remains limited. Future work should combine structural augmentation, semantic modeling, and adversarial training to improve practicality and resilience.

4 Large Language Model Detection Methods

With advances in pretrained language models for NLP and program understanding, LLMs have emerged as a complement to pattern matching and shallow semantic modeling in SQLi detection. Leveraging strong semantic comprehension, contextual reasoning, and code generation, LLMs can identify complex attack patterns, detect obfuscated statements, and emulate expert analysis. Table 6 summarizes representative LLM-based approaches and their performance.

Table 6. Applications of LLMs in SQLi Detection

Ref	Method	Applicable scenarios	Advantages	Limitations	Suggestions for improvement
[40]	LLMSQLi	Expert reasoning	Multi-agent collaboration	Hallucination issues	Knowledge generation
[41]	SqliGPT + RAG	Attack evasion	Prompt learning and RAG	Complex integration	Architecture simplification
[42]	LLM + WAF	Traffic monitoring	High scalability	Lacks interpretability	Enhance representation consistency
[43]	Multi-LLM	Software vulnerability	Strong pattern learning	High false positives	Hybrid static analysis

Yang et al. [40] proposed LLMSQLi, integrating LLMs with a multi-agent collaborative inference framework that simulates expert testing. Prompt-guided agents explored injection paths, outperforming tools like SQLmap on novel or contextually altered attacks but suffered from hallucination and unstable reasoning, underscoring the need for structural priors. Gui et al. [41] developed SqliGPT, a Retrieval-Augmented Generation (RAG) model that classifies requests and generates context-aware payloads for bypass detection, offering adaptability under semantic perturbations but incurring high computational cost. Rezanejad et al. [42] combined LLMs with Web Application Firewalls for edge-node traffic analysis, improving multi-source detection but limited by weak interpretability and generalization. Purba et al. [43] evaluated open-source LLMs for vulnerability detection, showing strong code semantic generalization but high dependence on preprocessing and a tendency toward redundancy and false alarms.

In summary, LLMs support SQLi detection through semantic modeling, contextual reasoning, fuzzy pattern recognition, and expert behavior simulation. Challenges include high deployment cost, limited interpretability, adversarial sensitivity, and reliance on large labeled datasets. Mitigation strategies include structured prompts, retrieval-augmented generation, attention-guided visualization, symbolic reasoning, and adversarial training. Large model size and inference latency hinder real-time use but can be reduced through distillation, pruning, quantization, or hybrid integration. Future work should focus on structure-guided semantic enhancement, transparent prompting, and integration into multi-module frameworks to improve robustness and deployability.

5 Transferable Methods for SQL Injection Detection

Previous sections have systematically reviewed detection methods tailored to SQLi; however, broader research in cybersecurity also provides important methodological insights for SQLi detection. Terawi et al. [44] introduced intrusion detection by incorporating inter-arrival time features with recurrent neural networks, highlighting the role of temporal dependencies in identifying attack patterns. This approach is relevant to SQLi, which often spans multiple requests and relies on session context, making sequence modeling effective for capturing its dynamic characteristics. Alshattnawi et al. [45], through studies on social media spam detection, demonstrated that contextual embedding models can effectively identify obfuscation and adversarial patterns in short texts. Such capabilities align closely with the characteristics of SQLi payloads, enabling more accurate modeling of syntactic anomalies and latent attack semantics. Alsobeh et al. [46] proposed a runtime monitoring framework that integrates Aspect-Oriented Programming, statistical model checking, and LLMs, illustrating the feasibility of combining LLMs with traditional statistical methods. This direction is equally applicable to SQLi defense, particularly in Web Application Firewall and Intrusion Detection System contexts, where adaptive and interpretable mechanisms are crucial.

6 Analysis and Discussion

6.1 Dataset and Evaluation Metric Analysis

In DL- and LLM-based SQLi detection, the source, scale, and diversity of datasets significantly influence model performance. Common benchmarks include UNSW-NB15, KDD99, HTTP-CSIC [13], Kaggle [15, 17, 18, 28, 38], GitHub [26], and SQLiMicroBenchmark [34, 35], which provide good accessibility but often lack the complexity necessary to represent real-world threats. Some studies incorporate data from internet platforms or operational systems to improve practical relevance, though this increases collection costs, sampling bias, and reduces diversity. Dataset sizes vary considerably; small datasets raise overfitting risk, while large ones increase computational demands. Selection should therefore balance representativeness, attack diversity, and processing feasibility to enhance generalizability and practical utility.

For performance evaluation, accuracy, precision, recall, and F1-score are most common, with some studies adding AUC [14, 18, 27], false acceptance rate [25, 26, 31], true positive rate [20], and false negative rate to address different data distributions and security needs. Training time and inference latency are also critical, with high-risk domains prioritizing low false negatives and resource-constrained settings emphasizing efficiency. Some reported high accuracy stems from datasets with strong structural regularity and salient semantic features, leading to pattern memorization rather than true semantic learning. This overfitting reduces robustness to complex or unseen attacks, producing overly optimistic results. Realistic benchmarks with semantic diversity, cross-language structures, and adversarial characteristics, combined with context-specific, multi-metric evaluation, are essential for reliable and generalizable assessment.

6.2 Quantitative Comparative Analysis of Model Performance

SQLi detection studies use datasets that differ in size, source, and attack type coverage, limiting performance comparability. The lack of a standardized benchmarking platform further impedes objective evaluation. To address this, this paper compiles key performance metrics of representative methods on public datasets, as shown in Table 7, to support more systematic and comparable assessments.

Table 7. Quantitative Comparison of Models for SQLi Detection

Model Type	Ref	Dataset	Acc	F1-score	FAR	AUC
CNN	[13]	UNSW-NB15 + KDD99	0.98	0.88	0.03	0.96
CNN + NLP	[15]	Kaggle	0.97	0.87	0.02	-
ResNet	[16]	Custom Dataset	0.98	0.89	0.02	-
RNN-LSTM	[18]	Kaggle	0.98	0.88	0.02	-
AST + LSTM	[20]	SQL-A + SQL-B	0.99	0.91	-	0.97
BERT + LSTM	[21]	HttpParams	0.99	0.92	0.01	-
FNN	[23]	Kaggle	0.97	0.86	-	-
CNN + LSTM	[34]	SQLiMicroBenchmark	0.98	0.90	0.02	0.95
MLP + LSTM	[38]	Kaggle	0.99	0.91	-	-
LLMSQLi	[40]	Real-world	0.99	0.93	-	-

Table 7 shows consistent performance patterns on public SQLi detection datasets. Overall accuracy ranges from 0.97 to 0.99, with hybrid architectures such as CNN-LSTM and BERT-LSTM outperforming single models by jointly capturing structural and semantic features. LLM-based methods achieve the highest F1-score, indicating strong precision-recall balance, but often rely on proprietary or synthetic datasets lacking standardized benchmarks. Traditional models such as FNN and CNN, though slightly less accurate, are advantageous for deployment in resource-constrained settings due to smaller size and lower computational cost. Several studies report AUC values above 0.95, confirming strong discriminative capability, yet deployment metrics such as inference latency and parameter count are rarely reported, limiting evaluation of real-time applicability and engineering feasibility.

6.3 Correlation Analysis Between Model Architecture and Detection Performance

Performance differences among DL models for SQLi detection depend on both training conditions and architectural design. CNNs excel at extracting local features for syntactic and parameter pattern recognition but struggle with long-range semantic dependencies. RNNs capture sequential context more effectively, offering higher robustness for dynamically constructed or nested attacks, and perform better when integrated with Abstract

Syntax Trees. FNNs and MLPs, with low computational overhead, are practical for resource-constrained or small-scale deployments. Hybrid models combining local feature extraction and global semantic understanding improve accuracy and false positive control, while LLMs provide strong semantic comprehension for natural language-based injection patterns but face deployment challenges due to high computational demands. Overall, architectural design determines both detection performance and applicability, and future work should focus on structural integration, semantic enhancement, and lightweight optimization to balance accuracy with feasibility.

6.4 Deployment and Practicality Analysis of Detection Models

Despite promising results, DL- and LLM-based SQLi detection methods face significant deployment challenges. Architectures such as Transformer and LLMs often incur high inference latency, substantial resource demands, limited generalization across database platforms and novel attack types, and insufficient interpretability for security auditing. Large model size and computational cost restrict use in edge or low-power environments, and integration with existing security infrastructures remains limited.

Recent work has explored hybrid strategies, embedding LLMs as semantic feature generators within lightweight models such as CNNs or LSTMs, or employing them as pre-detection modules in Web Application Firewalls with subsequent rule-based verification. Retrieval-Augmented Generation has been applied to enhance contextual modeling, reduce hallucinations, and stabilize inference. These approaches integrate the semantic strengths of LLMs with the efficiency of traditional architectures, enabling more practical and controllable solutions. Future research should prioritize lightweight designs for real-time use, improve cross-platform and multilingual adaptability, incorporate explainability for auditability, and develop end-to-end integration frameworks for seamless deployment in operational environments.

6.5 Research Challenges and Future Directions

DL- and LLM-based SQLi detection methods have improved feature representation, semantic understanding, and generalization but still face challenges in accuracy, interpretability, cross-scenario adaptability, and deployment efficiency. Many models perform poorly on structurally complex or semantically diverse attacks and rely heavily on specific training data, causing performance degradation across platforms and languages. The lack of unified, large-scale, and structurally diverse benchmarks limits fair evaluation and reproducibility. High computational costs hinder real-time or edge deployment of DL models, while LLMs, despite strong representational capacity, exhibit hallucination, false alarms, and unstable inference.

Future research should focus on standardized multilingual benchmarks, hybrid frameworks integrating static analysis with deep semantic modeling, few-shot detection via prompt engineering, model lightweighting for constrained environments, and enhanced interpretability and causal reasoning. Progress in multimodal feature fusion, efficient deployment, and trustworthy assurance is essential to address increasingly sophisticated SQLi attacks.

7 Conclusion

This paper reviews DL- and LLM-based SQLi detection methods, analyzing representative architectures for accuracy, semantic modeling, and deployment adaptability. By comparing datasets, evaluation metrics, and results, it outlines the strengths and limitations of current approaches in generalization, interpretability, and practicality. The findings highlight structural integration and semantic enhancement as essential for improved detection, while lightweight design and controllable reasoning remain key deployment challenges. Future research should emphasize multimodal feature fusion, standardized evaluation, and end-to-end deployable systems to achieve high performance, reliability, and practical applicability.

References

1. Jemal, I., Cheikhrouhou, O., Hamam, H., Mahfoudhi, A.: SQL injection attack detection and prevention techniques using machine learning. Int. J. Appl. Eng. Res. **15**, 569–580 (2020)
2. OWASP Top Ten | OWASP Foundation. https://owasp.org/www-project-top-ten/. Accessed 13 May 2025
3. Roy, P., Kumar, R., Rani, P.: SQL injection attack detection by machine learning classifier. In: 2022 International Conference on Applied Artificial Intelligence and Computing (ICAAIC), pp. 394–400 (2022). https://doi.org/10.1109/ICAAIC53929.2022.9792964
4. Demilie, W.B., Deriba, F.G.: Detection and prevention of SQLI attacks and developing compressive framework using machine learning and hybrid techniques. J Big Data. **9**, 124 (2022). https://doi.org/10.1186/s40537-022-00678-0
5. Zeng, P., Lin, G., Pan, L., Tai, Y., Zhang, J.: Software vulnerability analysis and discovery using deep learning techniques: a survey. IEEE Access. **8**, 197158–197172 (2020). https://doi.org/10.1109/ACCESS.2020.3034766
6. Muslihi, M.T., Alghazzawi, D.: Detecting SQL injection on web application using deep learning techniques: a systematic literature review. In: 2020 Third International Conference on Vocational Education and Electrical Engineering (ICVEE), pp. 1–6 (2020). https://doi.org/10.1109/ICVEE50212.2020.9243198
7. Xu, H., et al.: Large language models for cyber security: a systematic literature review (2024). https://doi.org/10.48550/arXiv.2405.04760. http://arxiv.org/abs/2405.04760
8. Basic, E., Giaretta, A.: Large language models and code security: a systematic literature review (2025). https://doi.org/10.48550/arXiv.2412.15004. http://arxiv.org/abs/2412.15004
9. Song, Y., Liu, R., Chen, S., Ren, Q., Zhang, Y., Yu, Y.: SecureSQL: evaluating data leakage of large language models as natural language interfaces to databases. In: Findings of the Association for Computational Linguistics: EMNLP 2024, pp. 5975–5990 (2024)
10. Alaoui, R.L., Nfaoui, E.H.: Deep learning for vulnerability and attack detection on web applications: a systematic literature review. Future Internet **14**, 118 (2022)
11. Alghawazi, M., Alghazzawi, D., Alarifi, S.: Detection of SQL injection attack using machine learning techniques: a systematic literature review. J. Cybersec. Priv. **2**, 764–777 (2022). https://doi.org/10.3390/jcp2040039
12. Li, Z., Liu, F., Yang, W., Peng, S., Zhou, J.: A survey of convolutional neural networks: analysis, applications, and prospects. IEEE Trans. Neural Netw. Learn. Syst. **33**, 6999–7019 (2022). https://doi.org/10.1109/TNNLS.2021.3084827
13. Luo, A., Huang, W., Fan, W.: A CNN-based approach to the detection of SQL Injection attacks. In: 2019 IEEE/ACIS 18th International Conference on Computer and Information Science (ICIS), pp. 320–324 (2019). https://doi.org/10.1109/ICIS46139.2019.8940196

14. Falor, A., Hirani, M., Vedant, H., Mehta, P., Krishnan, D.: A deep learning approach for detection of SQL injection attacks using convolutional neural networks. In: Gupta, D., Polkowski, Z., Khanna, A., Bhattacharyya, S., Castillo, O. (eds.) Proceedings of Data Analytics and Management. LNDECT, vol. 91, pp. 293–304. Springer, Singapore (2022). https://doi.org/10.1007/978-981-16-6285-0_24

15. Natarajan, Y., Karthikeyan, B., Wadhwa, G., Srinivasan, S.A., Akilesh, A.S.P.: A deep learning based natural language processing approach for detecting SQL injection attack. In: Abraham, A., Pllana, S., Casalino, G., Ma, K., Bajaj, A. (eds.) Intelligent Systems Design and Applications, pp. 396–406. Springer, Cham (2023). https://doi.org/10.1007/978-3-031-35507-3_38

16. Sangeeta, Nagasundari, S., Honnavali, P.B.: SQL injection attack detection using ResNet. In: 2019 10th International Conference on Computing, Communication and Networking Technologies (ICCCNT), pp. 1–7 (2019). https://doi.org/10.1109/ICCCNT45670.2019.8944874

17. ALAzzawi, A.: SQL injection detection using RNN deep learning model. J. Appl. Eng. Technol. Sci. (JAETS) **5**, 531–541 (2023). https://doi.org/10.37385/jaets.v5i1.2864

18. Sherstinsky, A.: Fundamentals of Recurrent Neural Network (RNN) and Long Short-Term Memory (LSTM) network. Physica D **404**, 132306 (2020). https://doi.org/10.1016/j.physd.2019.132306

19. Alghawazi, M., Alghazzawi, D., Alarifi, S.: Deep learning architecture for detecting SQL injection attacks based on RNN autoencoder model. Mathematics **11**, 3286 (2023). https://doi.org/10.3390/math11153286

20. Zhuo, Z., Cai, T., Zhang, X., Lv, F.: Long short-term memory on abstract syntax tree for SQL injection detection. IET Softw. **15**, 188–197 (2021). https://doi.org/10.1049/sfw2.12018

21. Liu, Y., Dai, Y.: Deep learning in cybersecurity: a hybrid BERT–LSTM network for SQL injection attack detection. IET Inf. Secur. **2024**, 5565950 (2024). https://doi.org/10.1049/2024/5565950

22. Ojha, V.K., Abraham, A., Snášel, V.: Metaheuristic design of feedforward neural networks: a review of two decades of research. Eng. Appl. Artif. Intell. **60**, 97–116 (2017). https://doi.org/10.1016/j.engappai.2017.01.013

23. Hassan, M.M., Ahmad, R.B., Ghosh, T.: SQL injection vulnerability detection using deep learning: a feature-based approach. Indonesian J. Electr. Eng. Inform. (IJEEI) **9**, 702–718 (2021). https://doi.org/10.52549/.v9i3.3131

24. Chen, D., Yan, Q., Wu, C., Zhao, J.: SQL injection attack detection and prevention techniques using deep learning. J. Phys.: Conf. Ser. **1757**, 012055 (2021). https://doi.org/10.1088/1742-6596/1757/1/012055

25. Tang, P., Qiu, W., Huang, Z., Lian, H., Liu, G.: SQL injection behavior mining based deep learning. In: Gan, G., Li, B., Li, X., Wang, S. (eds.) ADMA 2018. LNCS (LNAI), vol. 11323, pp. 445–454. Springer, Cham (2018). https://doi.org/10.1007/978-3-030-05090-0_38

26. Tang, P., Qiu, W., Huang, Z., Lian, H., Liu, G.: Detection of SQL injection based on artificial neural network. Knowl.-Based Syst. **190**, 105528 (2020). https://doi.org/10.1016/j.knosys.2020.105528

27. A, M.B., Arock, M.: Efficient detection of SQL injection attack (SQLIA) using pattern-based neural network model. In: 2021 International Conference on Computing, Communication, and Intelligent Systems (ICCCIS), pp. 343–347 (2021). https://doi.org/10.1109/ICCCIS51004.2021.9397066

28. Zhang, W., et al.: Deep neural network-based SQL injection detection method. Secur. Commun. Netw. **2022**, 4836289 (2022). https://doi.org/10.1155/2022/4836289

29. Zhang, H., Zhao, B., Yuan, H., Zhao, J., Yan, X., Li, F.: SQL injection detection based on deep belief network. In: Proceedings of the 3rd International Conference on Computer Science and

Application Engineering, pp. 1–6. Association for Computing Machinery, New York (2019). https://doi.org/10.1145/3331453.3361280

30. Alarfaj, F.K., Khan, N.A.: Enhancing the performance of SQL injection attack detection through probabilistic neural networks. Appl. Sci. **13**, 4365 (2023). https://doi.org/10.3390/app13074365

31. Pan, Z., et al.: Deep learning based SQL injection attack detection. In: Jin, H., Pan, Y., Lu, J. (eds.) Artificial Intelligence and Machine Learning, pp. 127–141. Springer Nature, Singapore (2024). https://doi.org/10.1007/978-981-97-1277-9_10

32. Lu, D., Fei, J., Liu, L.: A semantic learning-based SQL injection attack detection technology. Electronics **12**, 1344 (2023). https://doi.org/10.3390/electronics12061344

33. Li, Q., Li, W., Wang, J., Cheng, M.: A SQL injection detection method based on adaptive deep forest. IEEE Access **7**, 145385–145394 (2019). https://doi.org/10.1109/ACCESS.2019.2944951

34. Tadhani, J.R., Vekariya, V., Sorathiya, V., Alshathri, S., El-Shafai, W.: Securing web applications against XSS and SQLi attacks using a novel deep learning approach. Sci. Rep. **14**, 1803 (2024). https://doi.org/10.1038/s41598-023-48845-4

35. Kakisim, A.G.: A deep learning approach based on multi-view consensus for SQL injection detection. Int. J. Inf. Secur. **23**, 1541–1556 (2024). https://doi.org/10.1007/s10207-023-00791-y

36. Sun, H., Du, Y., Li, Q.: Deep learning-based detection technology for SQL injection research and implementation. Appl. Sci. **13**, 9466 (2023). https://doi.org/10.3390/app13169466

37. Gandhi, N., Patel, J., Sisodiya, R., Doshi, N., Mishra, S.: A CNN-BiLSTM based approach for detection of SQL injection attacks. In: 2021 International Conference on Computational Intelligence and Knowledge Economy (ICCIKE), pp. 378–383 (2021). https://doi.org/10.1109/ICCIKE51210.2021.9410675

38. Sharma, V., Kumar, S.: Multi-input MLP and LSTM-based neural network model for SQL injection detection. In: Shukla, P.K., Singh, K.P., Tripathi, A.K., Engelbrecht, A. (eds.) Computer Vision and Robotics, pp. 443–453. Springer Nature, Singapore (2023). https://doi.org/10.1007/978-981-19-7892-0_35

39. Zhao, C., Si, S., Tu, T., Shi, Y., Qin, S.: Deep-learning based injection attacks detection method for HTTP. Mathematics **10**, 2914 (2022). https://doi.org/10.3390/math10162914

40. Yang, T., Jiang, Z., Wang, Y.: LLMSQLi: a black-box web SQLi detection tool based on large language model. In: 2024 5th International Conference on Big Data & Artificial Intelligence & Software Engineering (ICBASE), pp. 629–633 (2024). https://doi.org/10.1109/ICBASE63199.2024.10762654

41. Gui, Z., et al.: SqliGPT: evaluating and utilizing large language models for automated SQL injection black-box detection. Appl. Sci. **14**, 6929 (2024). https://doi.org/10.3390/app14166929

42. Rezanejad, A., Danesh, A.S., Feyzi, F.: A new approach in diagnosing and preventing SQLIA with Large Language Models (LLMs). Commun. Combinatorics, Cryptogr. Comput. Sci. **2023**, 120–126 (2023)

43. Purba, M.D., Ghosh, A., Radford, B.J., Chu, B.: Software vulnerability detection using large language models. In: 2023 IEEE 34th International Symposium on Software Reliability Engineering Workshops (ISSREW), pp. 112–119 (2023). https://doi.org/10.1109/ISSREW60843.2023.00058

44. Terawi, N., Ashqar, H.I., Darwish, O., Alsobeh, A., Zahariev, P., Tashtoush, Y.: Enhanced detection of intrusion detection system in cloud networks using time-aware and deep learning techniques. Computers **14**, 282 (2025). https://doi.org/10.3390/computers14070282

45. Alshattnawi, S., Shatnawi, A., AlSobeh, A.M.R., Magableh, A.A.: Beyond word-based model embeddings: contextualized representations for enhanced social media spam detection. Appl. Sci. **14**, 2254 (2024). https://doi.org/10.3390/app14062254
46. AlSobeh, A., Shatnawi, A., Al-Ahmad, B., Aljmal, A., Khamaiseh, S.: AI-powered AOP: enhancing runtime monitoring with large language models and statistical learning. IJACSA **15** (2024). https://doi.org/10.14569/IJACSA.2024.0151113

Design and Assessment of an IoT-Enabling Nursing Assistant Robot for Remote Patient Care

Luisito Lolong Lacatan^(✉) and Carlo N. Romero

Polytechnic University of the Philippines, Metro Manila, Philippines
{lllacatan,cnromero}@pup.edu.ph

Abstract. This study aimed to develop and evaluate an IoT-based nurse assistant system for real-time vital signs monitoring. The system integrated a smart headband with sensors for heart rate, blood pressure, and temperature, along with a mobile application for data visualization and remote monitoring. Data collection involved continuous monitoring of vital signs and system performance metrics. Statistical analysis compared measurements from the prototype with standard medical devices. Results indicated a strong correlation between the prototype's measurements and traditional methods, demonstrating its potential for accurate and reliable vital signs monitoring. User feedback highlighted the system's usability and potential to improve patient care. Future research should focus on expanding the system's capabilities and conducting larger-scale clinical trials.

Keywords: Internet of Things · Nurse Assistant Robot · Remote Patient Monitoring · Real Time Vital Signs

1 Introduction

The increasing demand for efficient and accessible healthcare services indicates the need for innovative solutions. The Internet of Things (IoT) has emerged as a promising technology to revolutionize patient care by enabling remote monitoring and timely interventions [1]. However, existing remote care systems often fall short in providing continuous, comprehensive, and actionable patient data [2].

Studies have also highlighted that various health conditions can significantly impair individuals' ability to perform daily activities, emphasizing the importance of continuous health monitoring and assistance [7].

This research addresses this critical gap by developing an IoT-based nurse assistant system capable of real-time vital signs monitoring. The proposed system aims to enhance patient outcomes by enabling early detection of health deteriorations, facilitating timely interventions, and reducing the burden on healthcare providers. By integrating advanced sensors, robust data analytics, and secure communication protocols, the system seeks to transform remote patient care delivery.

T. Dohi (Ed.): ICSED 2025, CCIS 2889, pp. 231–244, 2026.
https://doi.org/10.1007/978-981-92-0202-7_16

A key innovation of this research lies in the development of a nurse assistant robot equipped with a comprehensive suite of vital signs monitoring sensors. Unlike traditional remote monitoring systems that rely solely on patient self-reporting, this system offers continuous and objective data collection. Additionally, the integration of two-way communication empowers healthcare professionals to remotely assess patients, provide guidance, and intervene as needed.

This study contributes to the growing body of knowledge on IoT applications in healthcare by demonstrating the feasibility and effectiveness of an IoT-based nurse assistant system. By addressing the limitations of current remote care solutions, this research has the potential to significantly improve patient care, particularly for those with chronic conditions or recovering from surgery.

2 Review of Related Literature

2.1 Hardware and Software Requirements

The proposed nurse assistant robot incorporates a mobile platform equipped with four-wheel drive to navigate patient environments effectively. A Holistic Health Monitoring and Autonomous Care System outlines a comprehensive system integrating various sensors, microcontrollers, and communication technologies to monitor health parameters and provide assistance [3]. This configuration enables live video consultations between patients and healthcare providers.

For remote operation, an IoT-based interface allows medical professionals to wirelessly control the robot. The system employs Wi-Fi communication to transmit commands to the onboard controller, enabling real-time maneuverability [4]. To ensure uninterrupted operation, the robot includes a battery status monitoring system and charging mechanism.

Fig. 1. MLX90614 Infrared Thermometer Sensor

The MLX90614 Infrared Thermometer Sensor as shown in Fig. 1 is a non-contact infrared temperature sensor with high precision. This sensor, unlike most sensing devices, measures temperature without being physically touched. The MLX90614 measures two temperatures: the object temperature and the ambient temperature. It can sense a broader range of temperatures than most digital sensors because it does not need to touch the object being measured [5].

The main feature of the MLX90614 is that it is a high-accuracy non-contact IR temperature sensor. As a result, it can be used in industries to determine the temperature of moving objects such as a rotating motor shaft. It is also utilized in various applications including advertising, medical services, and household use due to its high precision and accuracy, such as room temperature monitoring and body temperature monitoring [6].

2.2 Conceptual Framework

Figure 2 illustrates the data flow from sensors to the cloud, emphasizing secure data transmission and storage. The user interface facilitates remote monitoring, control, and patient interaction.

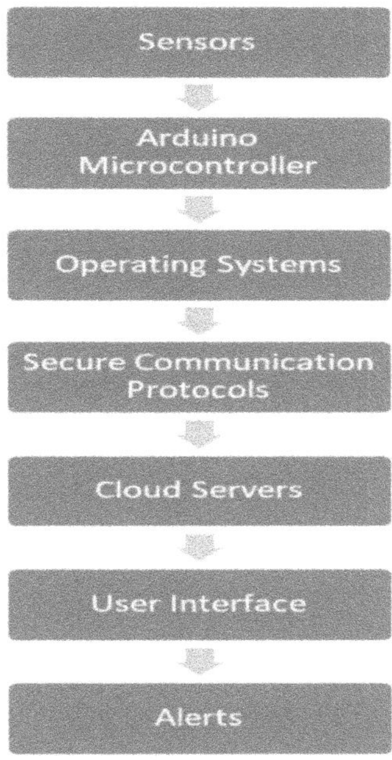

Fig. 2. Conceptual Framework

3 Methodology

3.1 Project Design

This study employs a mixed-methods approach to comprehensively evaluate the effectiveness of an IoT-based nurse assistant robot in remote patient care. The research design consists of two interconnected phases:

1. **Quantitative Phase:** Focuses on the development and testing of the robot's hardware and software components. this phase involves:

a) *Hardware Development:* Designing and constructing the robot's physical structure, including sensors, actuators, and power systems.

b) *Software Development:* Developing the underlying algorithms, user interface, and communication protocols for the robot's operation.

c) *System Testing:* Rigorous evaluation of the robot's performance under controlled conditions to assess its functionality and reliability.

2. **2. Qualitative Phase:** Explores the user experience and usability of the robot through in-depth user studies. This phase involves:

a) *Participant recruitment:* Selecting a diverse group of nurses and patients to represent the target population.

b) *Data collection:* Conducting semi-structured interviews, observations, and surveys to gather qualitative data on user perceptions, experiences, and suggestions.

C) *Data analysis:* Thematic analysis of qualitative data to identify patterns, themes, and insights.

Additionally, the integration of two-way communication empowers healthcare professionals to remotely assess patients, provide guidance, and intervene as needed. This aligns with recent findings that AI-driven conversational systems can enhance user engagement and critical reasoning through interactive dialogue [8].

3.2 Data Collection

Data collection for this study involved both quantitative and qualitative methods. Quantitative data included continuous monitoring of vital signs (e.g., heart rate, blood pressure, temperature) through integrated sensors, as well as system performance metrics such as response time, accuracy, and battery life. Qualitative data was gathered through semi-structured interviews with nurses and patients, direct observations of robot-user interactions in real-world settings, and surveys assessing user satisfaction, acceptance, and perceived benefits.

3.3 Project Development

The project development phase focuses on building and implementing the hardware and software components:

1. *Hardware Implementation:*

- *Sensors and Components:* Various sensors, such as the MLX90614 for temperature and GPS for location tracking, are initialized. The system activates when a medical professional powers it on. Nurses can then utilize this prototype as a remote patient monitoring assistant.

2. *Robot Operation:*

- *Continuous Monitoring: The Virtual Nurse Assistant Robot roams a designated area, continuously monitoring patients' vital signs. These readings are then transmitted to a database.*

- *Alert Generation: Based on temperature and heart rate data, the system generates automatic alerts.*

The Virtual Nurse Assistant Robot roams a designated area, continuously monitoring patients' vital signs. These readings are then transmitted to a database. Based on the temperature and heart rate data, the system generates automatic alerts. For example, an alert will appear if a patient's temperature indicates a fever or hypothermia.

3. *System Layout:*

The virtual nurse assistant robot utilizes a four-wheel drive robotic vehicle for smooth navigation within a patient's environment. This mobile platform houses a controller box for essential circuitry. Additionally, a mounting bracket allows for the secure attachment of a mobile phone or tablet, facilitating live video calls between doctors and patients.

In Fig. 3, it shows the Design Layout of the prototype on its front view section.

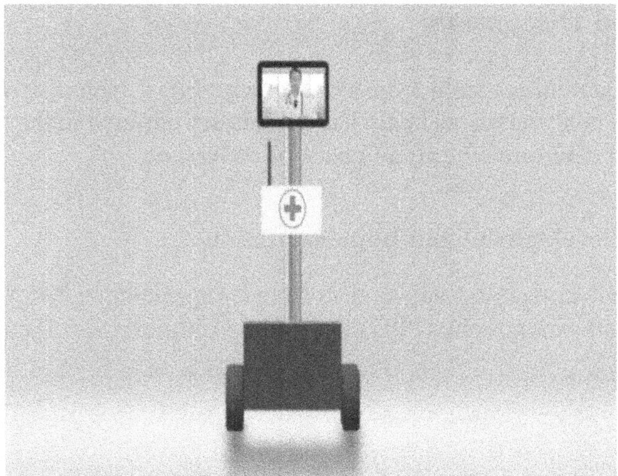

Fig. 3. Front view of the Virtual IoT Nurse Assistant Robot

For remote control, doctors can also use an IoT-based panel. The control commands transmitted online are seamlessly received by the robot controller operating over Wi-Fi. These commands are processed in real-time, and the robot motors are actuated accordingly to achieve the desired movement. Notably, the robot boasts additional functionalities, including a battery status alert system that provides timely reminders for charging.

The proposed system will also utilize the Arduino IDE for coding the Arduino microcontroller. The Arduino IDE is essential for programming the Arduino board, allowing for the processing of inputs and outputs within the system. This software was selected specifically because the system's microcontroller is an Arduino.

The data gathered from the Arduino, specifically temperature and blood pressure readings, will be presented in the mobile application. Figure 4 shows the integration of hardware and software.

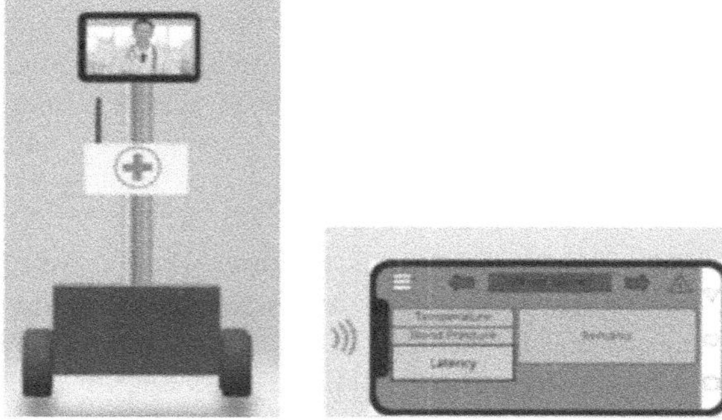

Fig. 4. Integration of hardware (IoT module of a Virtual Doctor Robot) and software (mobile application).

4   Results and Discussion

In this chapter, the data gathered from testing procedures, including measurements, is listed. The data is analyzed using statistical techniques outlined in the testing procedure and interpreted to determine the significance of the results.

4.1   Prototype Development and Implementation

The prototype will utilize and apply an Infrared Thermometer MLX90614 Breakout Board, a Photoplethysmography (PPG) Unit, and a Lithium LiPo Battery.

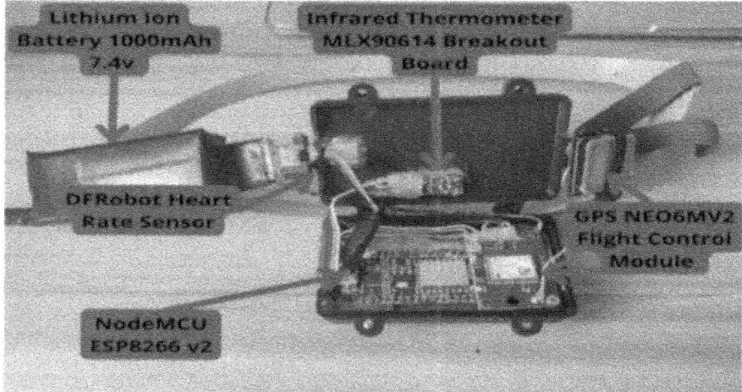

Fig. 5. Components of the Actual Prototype

The actual design of the prototype is shown in Fig. 5. The main prototype is divided into two cases: the battery case and the main case, where most components are placed.

The hardware interface of the actual prototype of the IoT Nurse Assistant Robot is shown in Fig. 6. It includes a tablet device used for virtual consultation and remote assistance to patients.

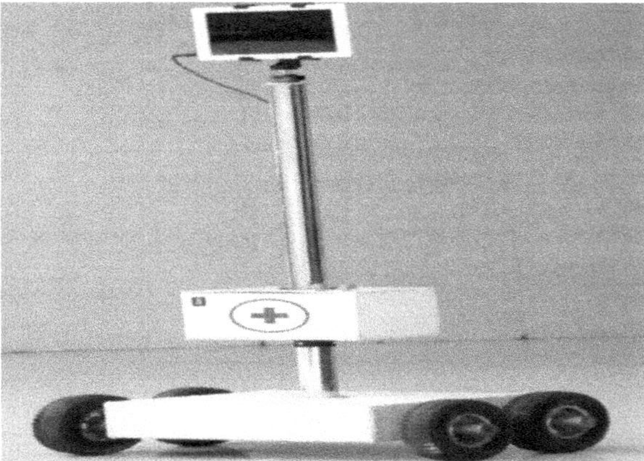

Fig. 6. Actual Prototype of an IoT Nurse Assistant Robot

The smart headband wearable device as shown in Fig. 7, is located in a box panel, contains the vital signs monitoring device. The patient can wear the headband, and through remote instructions from a doctor, medical professionals can start checking blood pressure and heart rate using a Photoplethysmography (PPG) sensor.

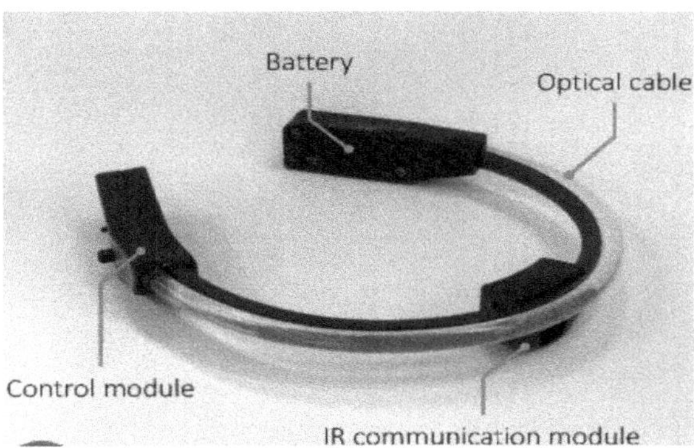

Fig. 7. Forehead/headband PPG Device

4.2 Data Accuracy and Blood Pressure Data Collection

Using the IoT Virtual Nurse Assistant Robot, blood pressure and temperature data of patients were collected. A digital sphygmomanometer was attached to the user's arm, and the smart headband was attached to the forehead. Data were recorded after the digital sphygmomanometer completed the blood pressure measurement. The data gathered is divided into four columns: two columns for systolic and two for diastolic values, with one for each method. Table 1 below shows the blood pressure levels.

Table 1. Blood Pressure Level

Trial	Systolic (SPBM)	Systolic (Smart Headband)	Diastolic (SPBM)	Diastolic (Smart Headband)
1	122	125	72	74
2	115	120	70	74
3	126	127	72	74
4	118	122	73	73
5	129	125	82	80
6	132	133	80	76
7	116	111	71	74
8	110	116	71	69
9	118	117	67	62
10	134	134	79	78
11	135	136	80	85
12	132	132	78	73
13	116	116	76	78
14	113	112	73	74
15	122	125	84	80
16	125	128	84	87
17	121	124	74	74
18	118	116	64	62
19	124	125	72	74
20	132	130	75	76
21	123	122	70	74
22	117	116	72	69
23	132	131	79	76
24	128	128	81	78
25	113	114	73	76
26	121	118	76	78
27	138	132	82	85
28	142	150	83	85
29	117	117	75	76
30	148	149	100	105

Values taken are recorded in Table 2 wherein the Orthodox Method of taking temperature is located at the first column aside from the trial number and second is where the data gathered using the Smart Headband.

Table 2. Temperature Level Reading

Trial	Temperature Gun	Smart Headband
1	34.6	34
2	34.5	34
3	36	35
4	36	35
5	35.3	35
6	35.4	35
7	36.2	36
8	35.8	36
9	36.2	36
10	36.2	36
11	35.1	35
12	35	35
13	33.7	34
14	33.8	34
15	35.3	35
16	35.2	35
17	35	35
18	35.1	35
19	35.4	35
20	35.2	35
21	35.1	35
22	35.2	35
23	35.2	35
24	35.1	35
25	36.1	36
26	36.2	36
27	36.3	36
28	36.2	36
29	35.9	36
30	35.9	35

4.3 Statistical Analysis

The statistical test used in analyzing the data is t-Test Two-Tail Assuming Unequal Variances. The data is processed using the Data Analysis toolkit of Microsoft Excel with the setting shown in Table 3 for the Systolic and Table 4 for the Diastolic.

Table 3. T-Test Two Tail Assuming Unequal Variances Settings for Systolic Values

Systolic (ORTHODOX)	Systolic (SMART HEADBAND)	Diastolic (ORTHODOX)	Diastolic (SMART HEADBAND)
122	125	72	74
115	120	70	74
126	127	72	74
118	122	73	73
129	125	82	80
132	133	80	76
116	111	71	74
110	116	71	69
118	117	67	62
134	134	79	78
135	136	80	85
132	132	78	73
116	116	76	78
113	112	73	74
122	125	84	80
125	128	84	87
121	124	74	74
118	116	64	62
124	125	72	74
132	130	75	76
123	122	70	74
117	116	72	69
132	131	79	76
128	128	81	78
113	114	73	76
121	118	76	78
138	132	82	85
142	150	83	85
117	117	75	76
148	149	100	105

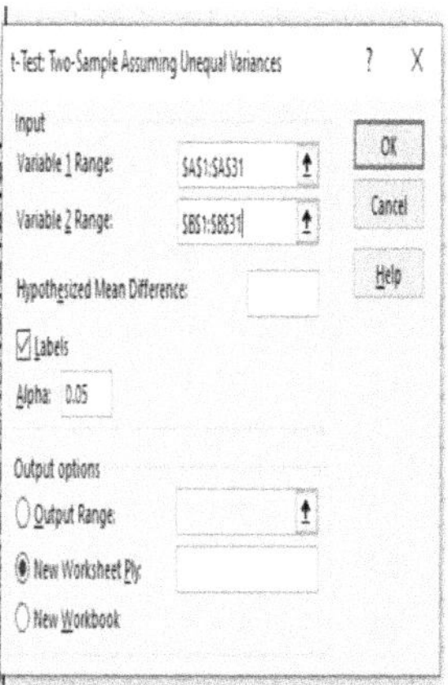

Table 4. T-Test Two Tail Assuming Unequal Variances Settings for Diastolic Values

Systolic (ORTHODOX)	Systolic (SMART HEADBAND)	Diastolic (ORTHODOX)	Diastolic (SMART HEADBAND)
122	125	72	74
115	120	70	74
126	127	72	74
118	122	73	73
129	125	82	80
132	133	80	76
116	111	71	74
110	116	71	69
118	117	67	62
134	134	79	78
135	136	80	85
132	132	78	73
116	116	76	78
113	112	73	74
122	125	84	80
125	128	84	87
121	124	74	74
118	116	64	62
124	125	72	74
132	130	75	76
123	122	70	74
117	116	72	69
132	131	79	76
128	128	81	78
113	114	73	76
121	118	76	78
138	132	82	85
142	150	83	85
117	117	75	76
148	149	100	105

t-Test: Two-Sample Assuming Unequal Variances   ?   X

Input
Variable 1 Range: $CS1:$CS31
Variable 2 Range: $DS1:$DS31

Hypothesized Mean Difference:

☑ Labels

Alpha: 0.05

Output options
◯ Output Range:
◉ New Worksheet Ply:
◯ New Workbook

OK   Cancel   Help

A Two-tailed Test using T-Test is used for evaluation of data in relation with the Systolic Values. T-Test is done to know if there is a significant difference between the two groups namely the Orthodox Method or Using a Digital Sphygmomanometer and the Smart Headband. The null hypothesis in this t-test is that there is no significant difference between the two groups. If the t-stat is outside the range of the t critical two-tail, the null hypothesis is rejected. Furthermore, if the p-value of the two tails is less than the significance level which is 0.05, the null hypothesis is rejected.

The output of using the t-Test Two of the Systolic and Diastolic Values is shown in Table 5 and Table 6 respectively.

Table 5. T-Test Two Tail Assuming Unequal Variances Settings for Diastolic Values

	ORTHODOX	SMART HEADBAND
Mean	124.666667	125.0333333
Variance	85.84022989	92.37816092
Observation	30	30
Hypothesized Mean Difference	0	
Degrees of freedom	58	
t stat	-0.191465773	
P(T<=t) one-tail	0.424414701	
t critical one-tail	1.671552762	
P(T<=t) two-tail	0.848829403	
t critical two-tail	2.001717484	

Based on the Table 5, t stat of -0.191 is within the range of t Critical two-tail which is 2.002 and the p-value of 0.849 is greater than the significance level of 0.05. When the test statistic is greater than the critical value, the null hypothesis is rejected. Therefore, null hypothesis is accepted. Since the null hypothesis is accepted then, there was no significant difference in the values between the Orthodox Method (M = 124.57, SD = 9.27) and Smart Headband (M = 125.03, SD = 9.61); t (58) = −0.191, p = 0.849).

Table 6. T-Test of Diastolic using Data Analysis toolkit

	ORTHODOX	SMART HEADBAND
Mean	76.26666667	76.6333333
Variance	46.4091954	61.41264368
Observation	30	30
Hypothesized Mean Difference	0	-
Degrees of freedom	57	-
t stat	-0.193409895	-
P(T<=t) one-tail	0.423662763	-
t critical one-tail	1.672028888	-
P(T<=t) two-tail	0.847325527	-
t critical two-tail	2.002465459	-

Based on the Table 6, t stat of -0.193 is within the range of t Critical two-tail which is 2.002 and the p-value of 0.847 is greater than the significance level of 0.05. When the test statistic is greater than the critical value, the null hypothesis is rejected. Therefore, null hypothesis is accepted. Since the null hypothesis is accepted then, there was no significant difference in the values between the Orthodox Method (M = 76.27, SD = 6.81) and Smart Headband (M = 76.63, SD = 7.84); t (57) = -0.193, p = .847).

For systolic blood pressure, a p-value lower than 0.05 (e.g., p-value <0.05) in Table 5 would indicate a significant difference between the readings from the two methods. The t-statistic direction (positive or negative) from this table would also tell us if the smart headband readings tend to be higher or lower than the traditional method on average. Conversely, a p-value greater than 0.05 (e.g., p-value >0.05) suggests no statistically significant difference between the systolic blood pressure readings from the two devices. Proponents can repeat this approach for diastolic blood pressure using the p-value and t-statistic from Table 6. Here, a p-value less than 0.05 indicates a significant difference, while a value greater than 0.05 suggests no significant difference between the diastolic readings from the two methods.

Similar to systolic blood pressure, the t-statistic direction from Table 6 would tell us if the smart headband readings tend to be higher or lower than the traditional method for diastolic blood pressure.

For the temperature analysis, the average temperature taken by the temperature gun (35.41°) is slightly higher than the average temperature taken by the smart headband (35.17°). There is a noticeable difference between the average temperatures (means) between the two methods.

The standard deviation of the temperature gun readings (0.6°) is larger than the standard deviation of the smart headband readings (0.64°).

This indicates that the temperature gun data has a larger spread than the smart headband data. In other words, the temperatures measured by the temperature gun are more varied than the temperatures measured by the smart headband (Table 7).

Table 7. Summary of Temperature Data for both the Temperature Gun and Smart Headband

Method	Mean Value	Standard Deviation
Temperature Gun	35.41 °C	0.67 °C
Smart Headband	35.17 °C	0.64 °C

References

1. Abdulmalek, S., et al.: IoT-based healthcare-monitoring system towards improving quality of life: a review. Healthcare (Basel) **10**(10), 1993 (2022). https://doi.org/10.3390/healthcare10 101993

2. Khan, M.M., Alanazi, T.M., Albraikan, A.A., Almalki, F.A.: [Retracted] IoT-based health monitoring system development and analysis. Secur. Commun. Netw. (2022). https://doi.org/10.1155/2022/9639195
3. Deepthi, J., Dharani, N.P., Aswini, S., Priya, D.G., Harsha, K.M., Bhargav, Y.S.S.S.: Care guard: holistic health monitoring and autonomous care system. In: 2024 3rd International Conference on Applied Artificial Intelligence and Computing (ICAAIC), Salem, India, pp. 1325–1331 (2024). https://doi.org/10.1109/ICAAIC60222.2024.10574934
4. Rahman, N., Sadi, M.S., Saeed, M.A.: VIoT: a voice and IoT controlled unmanned automated vehicle. In: 2024 3rd International Conference on Advancement in Electrical and Electronic Engineering (ICAEEE), Gazipur, Bangladesh, pp. 1–6 (2024). https://doi.org/10.1109/ICAEEE62219.2024.10561882
5. Last Minute Engineers: In-depth: Interface MLX90614 IR temperature sensor with Arduino. Last Minute Engineers (2022). https://lastminuteengineers.com/mlx90614-ir-temperature-sensor-arduino-tutorial/
6. Components101: MLX90614 non-contact IR temperature sensor. Components101. https://components101.com/sensors/melexis-mlx90614-contact-less-ir-temperature-sensor. Accessed 21 Oct 2022
7. Esteban, C., Alonso, F., San Martin, J., Useche, S., Lee, A.: Reported prevalence of health conditions that affect drivers. Cogent Medicine (2017). https://doi.org/10.1080/2331205X.2017.1303920
8. Obiwuru, O.M.: Impacts of AI-chatbots usage on the knowledge construction and critical reasoning of university students: a mixed methods approach in a Nigerian University (2024)
9. García, M., Requesens, J., Cano, S.: User experience evaluation methods in mixed reality environments. In: International Conference on Human-Computer Interaction, pp. 179–193. Springer Nature Switzerland, Cham (2024). https://doi.org/10.1007/978-3-031-61281-7_12

Verification of Linear Temporal Properties over Timed Events

Hosna Habibi Baghi[(✉)][iD], Ali Jannatpour[iD],
and Constantinos Constantinides[iD]

Department of Computer Science and Software Engineering, Concordia University,
Montreal, QC, Canada
ho_hab@live.concordia.ca,
{ali.jannatpour,constantinos.constantinides}@concordia.ca

Abstract. Temporal properties specify how systems must evolve over time, requiring events to occur, conditions to persist, or responses to follow triggers within given intervals. Their verification is essential in safety-critical and reactive domains where behavior is expressed as sequences of timed events, such as UML state machines and activity diagrams. To address this limitation, we introduce a framework centered on a Common Declarative Language (CDL), which encodes execution traces as Prolog facts and provides a reusable foundation for analysis. On top of CDL, a Python engine, called Timed Event Logic Analyzer (TELA), evaluates Linear Temporal Logic (LTL) queries through recursive finite-trace semantics. Supporting both Prolog queries and LTL property checks, the framework enables interactive, on-demand reasoning directly over recorded traces without regenerating models or exploring full state spaces. The key contribution of this work is the integration of CDL as a unifying declarative layer with TELA as an interactive analysis engine, providing flexibility, portability, and iterative "what-if" reasoning across diverse modeling notations and application domains.

Keywords: Temporal Logic · Common Declarative Language · UML State Machine · Declarative Modeling

1 Introduction

Verifying temporal properties is critical for ensuring that reactive systems behave as intended, especially in safety-critical domains such as aerospace, automotive, and industrial automation. Unified Modeling Language (UML) state machines and activity diagrams are widely used in model-driven engineering to describe system responses as discrete state changes over time, making them valuable for early-stage design and analysis. However, verifying that such models meet temporal requirements involving ordering of events, timing bounds, or causal responses remains challenging.

Traditional model checking translates models and properties into automata and explores the resulting state space. While powerful, these methods are computationally expensive and not ideal when engineers want to validate specific

T. Dohi (Ed.): ICSED 2025, CCIS 2889, pp. 245–262, 2026.
https://doi.org/10.1007/978-981-92-0202-7_17

execution scenarios rather than full models. Toolchains are often tightly coupled to particular modeling environments or pipelines, which limits portability and hinders exploratory, on-demand queries. Runtime verification offers a lighter alternative by checking partial executions during simulation or deployment, but it is usually bound to a specific simulator and lacks a reusable, general-purpose backend.

These limitations highlight the need for an approach that can analyze recorded traces directly, without automata or solver encodings, while still supporting expressive temporal reasoning. To meet this need, we introduce a framework with two components: a Common Declarative Language (CDL) that encodes traces as Prolog facts, and a Python engine, the Timed Event Logic Analyzer (TELA), that evaluates Linear Temporal Logic (LTL) queries using recursive finite-trace semantics. By separating event capture from analysis, the framework supports reusable traces, scenario-specific queries, and interactive "what-if" reasoning, bridging simulation and formal analysis in a notation-agnostic way.

Unlike automata-based model checking and SMT/BMC encodings, which require translating each model and property into an exploration or solving artifact, our approach evaluates properties directly on recorded traces represented once in a unifying declarative layer (CDL). This design enables: (i) a reusable, notation-agnostic trace backbone that decouples modeling/simulation from analysis; (ii) interactive, on-demand LTL checking via recursive finite-trace semantics without automata construction or solver invocations; and (iii) a dual query surface (Prolog and LTL) over the same facts for structural and temporal reasoning in one place. This combination targets early design and debugging workflows where rapid iteration, portability of traces, and scenario-specific reasoning are paramount.

2 Related Work

The verification of temporal properties has long been central to formal methods, ensuring reliability in domains such as aerospace, automation, and model-driven engineering. Pnueli's introduction of Temporal Logic [1] established the foundation for reasoning about event orderings, inspiring a range of verification techniques. Havelund and Peled [2] classified LTL properties by their verifiability over finite traces, while Goodloe and Havelund [3] demonstrated runtime verification in safety-critical workflows.

Automata-theoretic methods remain the backbone of LTL verification, translating formulas into automata for systematic exploration. On-the-fly algorithms by Couvreur [4] and Gerth et al. [5] reduced the need for full state-space construction, while Somenzi and Bloem [6] advanced symbolic Büchi automata, and Daniele et al. [7] refined construction templates. Diekert and Gastin [8] characterized first-order definable languages, and Chatterjee et al. [9] introduced witness-based reasoning for verifying LTL properties on polynomial programs.

Satisfiability Modulo Theories (SMT) [10] and bounded model checking (BMC) [11] replaced explicit automata traversal with constraint solving, offering scalability at the cost of model translation. Tools such as SPIN [12], ProB [13], and SMT-based bounded checkers embody this paradigm.

Runtime verification complements model checking by monitoring finite executions. Besnard et al. [14] integrated UML simulation with verification, Schützenmeier et al. [15] explored scenario-based checking for declarative processes, and Maggi et al. [16] applied runtime verification to declarative models. André et al. [17] surveyed the translation of UML state machines into analyzable models, highlighting challenges in preserving executable semantics. Such approaches are effective but often tied to specific simulators or modeling environments.

Recent efforts extend verification infrastructure with hybrid symbolicâĂŞsimulation frameworks and data-driven analysis. Deep-learning or anomaly-detection methods, while effective for behavioral prediction, focus on statistical regularities rather than formal property satisfaction. These approaches remain complementary to our goal of enabling reusable declarative traces and interactive temporal reasoning within a logical framework. In contrast to online monitoring or predictive anomaly detection, our objective is offline, declarative verification over recorded executions with a unified query surface (`Prolog+LTL`).

Compared with automata-, solver-, and runtime-based methods, our framework: (i) operates directly on recorded traces instead of reconstructed models, (ii) unifies declarative querying and temporal verification in one environment, and (iii) emphasizes portability and interactivity over exhaustive exploration. This positions it as a lightweight, scenario-specific complement to traditional model checking for early design analysis.

3   Framework Overview

The framework provides a trace-driven approach to verifying temporal properties in reactive system models. Its architecture centers on two components: a *Common Declarative Language* (CDL) for encoding execution traces, and the *Timed Event Logic Analyzer* (TELA), which evaluates temporal properties through direct Prolog queries and recursive Linear Temporal Logic (LTL) semantics. Together, they enable reasoning directly over recorded traces without automata translations or exhaustive state-space exploration.

The verification pipeline begins with a *scenario-based simulator* that executes a Unified Modeling Language (UML) state machine under user-defined scenarios. The simulator records timed events as structured, human-readable descriptions of observable behaviors; for instance, `execute(Configuring.Entry)` denotes execution of the `Entry` action for the `Configuring` state. These events form a precise, time-indexed account of system behavior and are transformed into CDL, which represents states, variable valuations, and events as Prolog facts in a uniform, queryable structure. CDL thus provides the declarative backbone of the framework, ensuring explicit and reusable representations of execution. On top of CDL, TELA performs verification by parsing user queries, applying finite-trace semantics to LTL formulas, and consulting the Prolog knowledge base to return Boolean results with supporting or counterexample traces. Separating

CDL as the declarative representation from TELA as the analysis engine enables trace reuse, iterative "what-if" exploration, and extension beyond UML-specific models to any system capable of generating timed events. The following subsections present a detailed case study and describe the workflow of CDL and TELA in practice.

3.1 Case Study

To illustrate the framework, we use a *temperature and carbon monoxide detector* modeled as a Unified Modeling Language (UML) state machine (Fig. 1). This example represents a class of reactive safety-critical systems where environmental and internal conditions must be coordinated over time. The detector serves as a benchmark for evaluating how the proposed Common Declarative Language (CDL) and Timed Event Logic Analyzer (TELA) handle nested states, concurrency, and time-dependent transitions.

The model captures the behavioral complexity typical of reactive systems, combining sensor inputs, guarded transitions, asynchronous triggers, and interruptible actions. These interactions yield structurally rich traces with nested activations and concurrent event streams, providing a meaningful testbed for assessing the expressiveness of CDL and the finite-trace reasoning of TELA.

The UML state machine includes composite and concurrent states, explicit entry and exit actions, pseudostates, and interruptible behaviors. During operation, the detector monitors temperature and gas levels, activating alarms and light indicators when thresholds are exceeded. Figure 1 depicts, from top to bottom, the hierarchical structure, concurrent monitoring and configuration regions, and interruptible routines such as the siren and LED blinking. The main modeling features and their corresponding implications for CDL and TELA are summarized in Table 1. These constructs generate execution traces involving hierarchical activations, guarded updates, and asynchronous events.

Table 1. Key modeling elements in the detector and their implications for CDL and TELA.

Element	Description
Nested composite states	Multiple substate hierarchies; CDL represents nested activations, and TELA verifies properties spanning hierarchical transitions.
Entry/exit actions	**Entry/Exit** behaviors recorded as timed events; CDL encodes them for ordering and causality checks.
Pseudostates	Initial states and choice points captured as conditional branches; properties are checked across all paths.
Guarded transitions	Boolean guards (e.g., temperature thresholds) recorded with valuations; TELA verifies guard-dependent properties.
Signals	External triggers and alerts encoded as events; temporal properties can reference asynchronous communication.
Concurrent regions	Parallel regions generate simultaneous events; CDL records concurrency, and TELA supports interleaved reasoning.
Interruptible behaviors	Aborted **do** actions produce explicit **abort** events; CDL encodes them, and TELA handles incomplete executions.

Recorded execution data are transformed into CDL facts representing variables, states, and events. TELA then verifies temporal properties, such as safety ("the siren never sounds unless an emergency state is active") and liveness ("every configuration completion eventually activates the green LED"), directly on these encoded traces. This demonstrates how the framework reasons over realistic, concurrent behaviors without model translation or exhaustive exploration.

Although based on a single model, the same encoding and analysis pipeline applies to other UML or non-UML systems that emit timed events, such as workflow engines or industrial controllers. The detector thus acts as a representative instance illustrating the general applicability of the approach.

This case study establishes the foundation for the following subsections, which detail the scenario language, event encoding, and declarative clause signatures used for temporal analysis.

3.2   Scenario and Commands

A *scenario* is a structured sequence of commands defining how the system executes over time. Commands include variable initializations, function calls, or

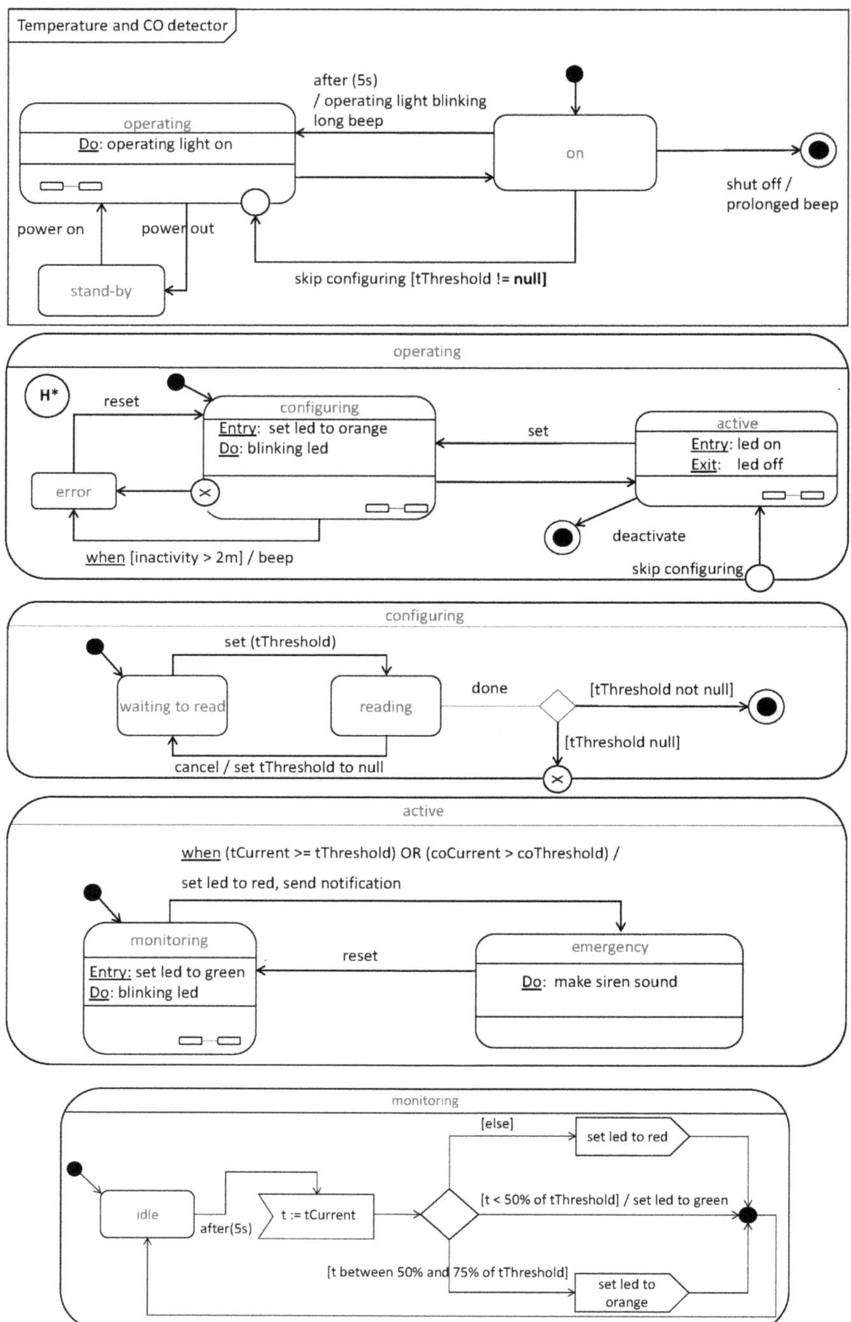

Fig. 1. Case study: Top-level and composite states.

timing directives. Each is processed by the simulator in the context of the UML state machine, producing timed events that are later encoded in CDL for temporal analysis with TELA.

Table 2. Scenario commands and their encoding in CDL.

Command	Type	Description
`start`	command	Marks the start of execution; CDL records it as the initial trace marker for query evaluation.
`init <var> <val>`	command	Initializes a variable before simulation, stored as a `var/3` fact.
`call <event>`	command	Triggers a call event encoded as `event/3` with a `call` signature.
`change <var> <val>`	command	Updates a variable silently; may trigger an implicit `change` event if a guard holds.
`set <var> <val>`	command	Updates a variable and explicitly emits a `set` event, distinguished from implicit changes.
`at <time>`	hint	Executes the next command at an absolute timestamp; stored as a `time/3` fact.
`after <time>`	hint	Executes the next command relative to the previous event; encoded as relative timing metadata.
`noop`	command	Idle step; index is preserved.
`end`	command	Marks termination; CDL records the final index as the finite trace bound.

As presented in Table 2, *commands* (e.g., `init`, `call`, `change`, `set`) update the system configuration or trigger observable events, while *hints* (`at`, `after`) only affect scheduling. A key distinction is that `change` may implicitly generate a `change/1` event if a guard is satisfied, whereas `set` always emits an explicit `set/1` event. Executing a scenario yields *timed events* that are encoded in CDL as facts of the form `event(?T, ?Index, ?EItem)`, where `?T` is the time identifier, `?Index` is the event index in the trace, and `?EItem` is an event item whose procedure is one of the clause signatures listed in Table 5 (e.g., `set/1`, `change/1`, `call/1`, `execute/1`, `abort/1`, `completion/1`). Variables fall into two disjoint categories: environment variables (V_e), such as `tCurrent`, which represent the operating context and are read-only during execution but can be altered in simulation; and controlled variables (V_c), such as `tThreshold`, which represent internal system quantities that can be updated. Thus

$$V_e \cap V_c = \emptyset, \quad V_e \cup V_c = V.$$

The sample scenario in Table 3 illustrates initialization, updates, event triggers, and timing directives. Its execution trace (Table 4) records, for each logical

Table 3. Sample scenario.

Line	Command	Line	Command
1	`init tCurrent 5`	8	`after 5 s`
2	`at 10h00`	9	`change tCurrent 55`
3	`start`	10	`call reset`
4	`after 10 s`	11	`call deactivate`
5	`set tThreshold 40`	12	`call shutoff`
6	`call done`	13	`end`
7	`change tCurrent 35`		

instant, timestamps, variable values, active states, and triggered events. State transitions are inferred by comparing successive configurations of active states, e.g., a move from s_1 to s_2 is captured as $s_1 \wedge \mathbf{X} s_2$. The trace also records complex behaviors: aborted `do` activities via explicit `abort` events, concurrent execution where regions generate simultaneous events, and the distinction between implicit triggers (`set` with guards) and explicit triggers (`set`). This timestamped, queryable representation forms the backbone of CDL and directly supports temporal reasoning in TELA. Table 4 presents the concrete execution trace produced by the sample scenario. This trace is encoded in the Common Declarative Language (CDL) as Prolog facts, forming the basis for all subsequent temporal analysis. Figure 2 shows an excerpt of the corresponding CDL representation, illustrating how variables, states, and observable events are recorded uniformly using the `event/3` predicate.

3.3 Declarative Model and Clause Signatures

To enable systematic verification, timed events from scenarios are encoded in a *Common Declarative Language* (CDL). CDL captures states, variable valuations, and behavioral events as *Prolog facts*, giving traces a precise and queryable structure. This encoding serves as the basis for both logical queries in Prolog and temporal reasoning with LTL formulas, ensuring consistency of results across analyses. For example, updating the threshold at time index 3 is encoded as `event(3, 1, set("tThreshold"))`, and the concurrent activation of a state is captured by `state(3, 'reading')`.

Table 5 summarizes the clause signatures used to encode all categories of timed behavior. Variable valuations are expressed with `var/3`, while `time/3` associates each time identifier with absolute and relative temporal metadata. Observable behaviors are unified under `event/3`, where the third argument encodes an event item whose procedure corresponds to one of the clause signatures listed in Table 5 (e.g., `call/1`, `set/1`, `change/1`, `execute/1`, `abort/1`, `completion/1`). State activity is recorded using `state/2`, while asynchronous interactions are captured through `signal/1` and timeout-triggered `time/1` events.

Table 4. Trace of execution of the sample scenario. CDL encodes these events as facts; temporal properties are evaluated directly over them using TELA.

Time			tThreshold	tCurrent	State	Event(s)	Xref
Ordinal	Absolute	Relative					
-	-	-	-	5	-	-	1
1	10h00:00	-	-	5	on	-	2,3
2	10h00:05	+5 s	-	5	operating, configuring, waiting to read	exec operating light blinking, exec long beep, exec operating light on, exec set led to orange, exec blinking led	-
3	10h00:10	+5 s	40	5	operating, configuring, reading	set tThreshold, exec blinking led	4,5
4	?	?	40	5	operating, active, monitoring, idle	call done, abort blinking led, completion configuring, exec led on, exec set led to green, exec blinking led	6
5	?	?	40	35	operating, active, monitoring, idle	exec blinking led	7
6	?	?	40	35	operating, active, monitoring, idle	exec set led to red, exec blinking led	-
7	?	+5 s	40	55	operating, active, emergency	change tCurrent$\geq$tThreshold, exec set led to red, exec send notification, exec make siren sound	8,9
8	?	?	40	55	operating, active, monitoring, idle	call reset, abort make siren sound, exec set led to green, exec blinking led	10
9	?	?	40	55	on	call deactivate, abort blinking led, exec led off, completed operating, abort operating light on	11
10	?	?	40	55	on	call shutoff, exec prolonged beep, completion {system}	12

This representation ensures that every piece of simulation evidence is explicitly recorded. By combining structural predicates (e.g., **state/2**) with behavioral event markers embedded within **event/3**, CDL supports expressive and unambiguous temporal queries. These clause signatures constitute the atomic predicates over which LTL semantics are evaluated in TELA.

```
% Init
var(0, 'tCurrent', 5).

% Time ID 1
time(1, '10h00:00', nil).
state(1, 'on').

% Time ID 2
event(2, 1, completion('on')).
event(2, 2, execute("operating light blinking")).
event(2, 3, execute("long beep")).
event(2, 4, execute("operating light on")).
...

% Time ID 3
event(3, 1, call('set')).
event(3, 2, set('tThreshold')).
event(3, 3, change('tThreshold')).
...

% Time ID 4
event(4, 1, call('done')).
event(4, 2, completion('configuring')).
...
```

Fig. 2. Excerpt of CDL facts corresponding to the execution trace in Table 4, illustrating how timed observations are encoded using the unified **event/3** representation.

3.4   Framework Workflow

Figure 3 shows the workflow, which separates the *system under verification* (a UML state machine and user-defined scenario) from the *verification framework* (simulation, CDL encoding, and query-based analysis).

The process unfolds in five stages. **Stage 1** takes the UML model and scenario as input. **Stage 2** simulates the scenario line by line, producing a trace of timed events. **Stage 3** converts this trace into CDL facts, forming a declarative, queryable knowledge base. Analysis then proceeds in two complementary paths: **Stage 4.1** supports direct Prolog queries over CDL facts and derived rules (e.g., state/2, transition/3), while **Stage 4.2** evaluates LTL formulas by parsing them into an abstract syntax tree (AST) and applying recursive finite-trace semantics. An interactive REPL interface returns Boolean outcomes with supporting traces or counterexamples. This workflow enables interactive verification: users can build scenarios, inspect traces, pose queries, and refine models. Since CDL is notation-independent, the framework applies to any system capable of generating timed event traces.

Table 5. Clause signatures in CDL - queryable structure for temporal reasoning.

Clause Signature	Description
`var/3`	`var(?T, ?VarName, ?Value)` – variable `?VarName` holds value `?Value` at time `?T`.
`time/3`	`time(?T, ?Absolute, ?After)` – associates time `?T` with absolute and relative metadata.
`event/3`	`event(?T, ?Index, ?EItem)` – unified representation of timed events; `?EItem` indicates type.
`state/2`	`state(?T, ?State)` – records that `?State` is active at time `?T`.
`execute/1`	`execute(?Action)` – execution of an action or entry/exit behavior.
`abort/1`	`abort(?Behavior)` – interrupted execution of a `do` behavior. `nil` implies system abort (execution error).
`completion/1`	`completion(?StateOrDo)` – completion of a state or behavior. `nil` implies the system completion.
`call/1`	`call(?Event)` – call event triggering a transition.
`set/1`	`set(?Var)` – explicit set event changing a variable value.
`change/1`	`change(?Guard)` – implicit change caused by a satisfied guard.
`signal/1`	`signal(?Name)` – external signal reception event.
`time/1`	`time(?Timeout)` – timeout-triggered event.

4 Query-Based Analysis of Temporal Behavior

The verification of temporal properties in the framework is performed through a query-based analysis pipeline. CDL provides a declarative base in Prolog, while two complementary forms of reasoning are supported: logical querying over CDL facts and rules, and temporal verification via recursive evaluation of LTL formulas. This hybrid design integrates declarative modeling with imperative evaluation, giving users the ability to inspect system behavior at different levels of abstraction.

4.1 Grammar and LTL Query Evaluator

The formal analysis of temporal properties in the framework is guided by a satisfaction relation that connects the grammar of formulas to their interpretation over finite traces. User-provided LTL queries are parsed into an abstract syntax tree (AST), and recursive semantics are applied to determine truth values against the CDL facts. The evaluation process unfolds in four phases. First, the user submits an LTL formula, optionally together with a starting time index. Next, the formula is parsed according to the grammar and transformed into an AST. In the third phase, the AST is traversed and the semantics of Boolean and

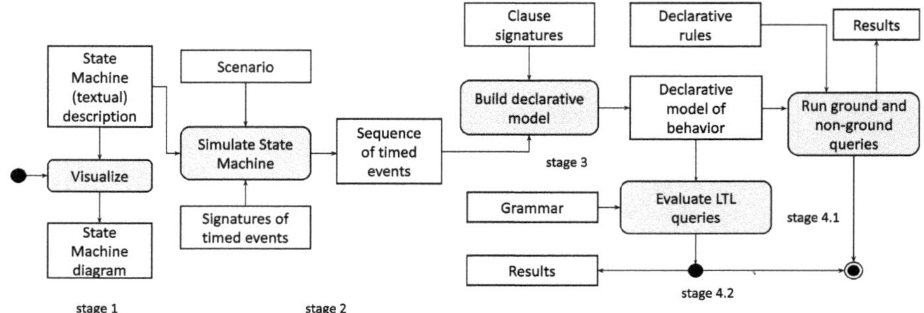

Fig. 3. Verification framework workflow. The upper half depicts the UML model and scenario, the lower half the framework. Simulation produces a trace of timed events, encoded in CDL for analysis via Prolog queries or LTL evaluation in TELA.

temporal operators are applied, with CDL facts consulted whenever atomic predicates are encountered. Finally, the evaluator produces a Boolean outcome: if the property holds, a supporting trace is reported, whereas if the property is violated, a counterexample trace is generated. This design ensures that LTL formulas are checked directly on recorded traces without automata construction or model translation, providing an intuitive interface for property verification (Fig. 4).

4.2   Declarative Rules and REPL Interface

Alongside the evaluator, the framework provides a declarative platform for analyzing system behavior. CDL facts form the base layer, while additional Prolog rules enrich reasoning by inferring transitions, state activations, or variable dependencies. For example:

```prolog
% Define state as most recent transition before or at T
state(T, State) :-
    event(TT, _, _, transition, State),  TT =< T,
    \+ (event(TO, _, _, transition, _), TO > TT, TO =< T).

% Define transition based on current and previous state
transition(T, From, To) :-
    event(T, _, _, transition, To), previous_state(T, From).

previous_state(T, From) :-
    T1 is T - 1, state(T1, From).
```

Fig. 4. Example Prolog rules extending CDL facts.

Users interact with this hybrid environment through a Read–Evaluate–Print Loop (REPL) whose commands are summarized in Table 6. The interface supports two complementary types of queries. The first type consists of direct

Prolog queries, which operate over the CDL database to extract structural or variable-related information. The second type involves LTL queries, which are parsed according to the grammar and evaluated through recursive semantics as described in Sect. 4.1.

Table 6. Supported REPL Commands for Query Execution.

Command	Description
`Load «CDL».`	Loads the CDL file and initializes the query database.
`TIME «TID».`	Sets the current evaluation index to `TID`. The default is 1.
`«query».`	Evaluates the query in either LTL or Prolog syntax.

This dual querying capability supports interactive exploration: structural assumptions can be tested through Prolog queries, while temporal requirements are verified with LTL formulas. Results are returned as Boolean values together with supporting traces or counterexamples, making the analysis both rigorous and transparent.

4.3   LTL Evaluation and Semantics

The meaning of LTL queries in the framework is defined through a recursive satisfaction relation evaluated over finite traces. Let a trace be $\Sigma = (\sigma_0, \sigma_1, \ldots, \sigma_n)$, where each σ_t is the set of atomic facts true at time t (states, variable values, and events). We define a semantic function

$$[\![\varphi]\!]_t \in \{\text{true}, \text{false}\}$$

that evaluates whether a formula φ holds at position t in Σ.

Boolean and conditional expressions.

$$[\![\text{var}[x] = v]\!]_t = \begin{cases} \text{true} & \text{if variable } x \text{ has value } v \text{ in } \sigma_t \\ \text{false} & \text{otherwise} \end{cases}$$

$$[\![\text{state}[s]]\!]_t = \begin{cases} \text{true} & \text{if } s \in \sigma_t \\ \text{false} & \text{otherwise} \end{cases}$$

$$[\![\text{exec}[a]]\!]_t = \begin{cases} \text{true} & \text{if action } a \text{ executes at } t \\ \text{false} & \text{otherwise} \end{cases}$$

Boolean connectives follow standard logic:

$$[\![\text{not } \varphi]\!]_t = \neg[\![\varphi]\!]_t, \quad [\![\varphi_1 \text{ and } \varphi_2]\!]_t = [\![\varphi_1]\!]_t \wedge [\![\varphi_2]\!]_t,$$

and similarly for `or`, `xor`, `iff`, and `implies`.

$$[\![X\,\varphi]\!]_t = \begin{cases} [\![\varphi]\!]_{t+1} & t < n \\ \texttt{false} & t = n \end{cases}$$

$$[\![F\,\varphi]\!]_t = \exists t' \geq t : [\![\varphi]\!]_{t'}$$

$$[\![G\,\varphi]\!]_t = \forall t' \geq t : [\![\varphi]\!]_{t'}$$

$$[\![\varphi_1\,U\,\varphi_2]\!]_t = \exists t' \geq \ t : [\![\varphi_2]\!]_{t'} \wedge \forall t'' \in [t, t'-1], [\![\varphi_1]\!]_{t''}$$

$$[\![\varphi_1\,W\,\varphi_2]\!]_t = [\![\varphi_1\,U\,\varphi_2]\!]_t \vee \forall t' \geq t : [\![\varphi_1]\!]_{t'}$$

$$[\![\varphi_1\,M\,\varphi_2]\!]_t = [\![\varphi_1\,U\,\varphi_2]\!]_t \quad \text{with the side condition that } \varphi_2 \text{ eventually holds.}$$

Past operators.

$$[\![P\,\varphi]\!]_t = \exists t' \leq t : [\![\varphi]\!]_{t'}.$$

These semantics are implemented directly in Python. An abstract syntax tree (AST) is constructed by the parser, and recursive traversal applies the semantics while resolving atomic predicates against CDL facts.

The expressiveness of the framework is demonstrated through representative properties formulated on the detector case study. Table 7 summarizes each property: the natural-language intent, the corresponding LTL query, and the evaluation result. Boolean outcomes are returned together with supporting traces or counterexamples, making the analysis interpretable and verifiable. These examples span safety, causality, persistence, stability, response, ordering, liveness, and fairness, confirming that CDL and the evaluation pipeline can capture a broad range of correctness requirements, from safety invariants to progress guarantees, directly on recorded execution traces.

5   Conclusion and Recommendations

This paper presented a framework for verifying temporal properties of reactive systems by combining a Common Declarative Language (CDL) with a Python-based LTL evaluator. CDL encodes execution traces as Prolog facts, while temporal reasoning is performed through recursive finite-trace semantics. This separation of event capture from analysis enables both declarative queries and direct property checking on recorded traces. The approach was demonstrated on a non-trivial case study of a temperature and carbon monoxide detector, whose nested states, guarded transitions, concurrent regions, and interruptible behaviors generated complex traces. CDL captured these behaviors in a structured form, and analysis proceeded in two modes: Prolog rules for reasoning about states, transitions, and variables, and LTL queries evaluated interactively through a REPL interface. Properties spanning safety, causality, persistence, stability, response, ordering, liveness, and fairness confirmed the framework's expressiveness. Unlike conventional methods requiring automata translations or constraint solving, our approach operates directly on traces, making it lightweight, reusable, and

Table 7. Representative temporal properties evaluated on the detector trace.

Category	Intent	LTL Formula (Result)
Safety	No emergency if temperature < 50.	`G(var[tCurrent] < 50 implies not state[emergency])` (True)
Causality	Exceeding 50 in `idle` eventually triggers `emergency` and siren.	`G(var[tCurrent] > 50 and state[idle] implies X(state[emergency]) and X(exec["Make Siren Sound"]))` (True)
Persistence	Emergency persists until reset occurs.	`G(state[emergency] implies (state[emergency] W call[reset]))` (True)
Stability	Once in `exit`, the system remains there.	`G(X state[exit] implies state[exit])` (True)
Response	Completing configuration eventually activates green LED.	`G(completion[configuring] implies F exec["set led to green"])` (True)
Ordering	Siren may only sound after emergency.	`G(exec["Make Siren Sound"] implies (P state[emergency]))` (True)
Liveness	Eventually the green LED turns on.	`F exec["set led to green"]` (True)
Fairness	Each return to `idle` eventually activates the green LED.	`G(state[idle] implies F exec["set led to green"])` (True)

domain-agnostic. Its novelty lies in unifying a declarative representation with an interactive analysis engine, bridging simulation-based exploration with formal verification.

Future work will focus on extending the grammar with event calculus and interval-based semantics, and applying the framework to a broader range of UML and non-UML models. Another direction is to conduct empirical benchmarking and runtime evaluation against existing verification tools such as ProB and SMT-based approaches. We also plan to enhance the REPL environment with counterexample-guided diagnostics and trace visualization, positioning CDL and its evaluator as a flexible platform for scenario-driven temporal property verification.

A Appendix: LTL Formula Grammar

```
<expr>          ::= <expr> «iff» <iexpr> | <iexpr>
<iexpr>         ::= <bexpr> «implies» <iexpr> | <bexpr>
<bexpr>         ::= <bexpr> («or» | «xor» | «xnor») <bterm> | <bterm>
<bterm>         ::= <bterm> «and» <bfactor> | <bfactor>
<bfactor>       ::= <texpr> <binop> <bfactor> | <texpr>
<texpr>         ::= «not» <texpr> | <unop> <texpr>
                  | «(» <expr> «)» | <cexpr> | <bvalue>
<cexpr>         ::= <aexpr> <comp_op> <aexpr>
                  | <bexpr> («=» | «!=») <bexpr>
<aexpr>         ::= <aexpr> «+» <aterm>
                  | <aexpr> «-» <aterm> | <aterm>
<aterm>         ::= <aterm> «*» <afactor>
                  | <aterm> «/» <afactor> | <afactor>
<afactor>       ::= «(» <aexpr> «)» | <value>
<unop>          ::= «G» | «F» | «X» | «P»
<binop>         ::= «U» | «R» | «W» | «S» | «M»
<comp_op>       ::= «=» | «!=» | «<» | «<=» | «>» | «>=»
<bvalue>        ::= <boolean> | <bsysvar>
<value>         ::= <number> | <string> | <var>
<bsysvar>       ::= <state> | <event> | <action>
<var>           ::= «var» «[» ( <string> | <atom> ) «]»
<state>         ::= «state» «[» ( <string> | <atom> ) «]»
<event>         ::= «call» «[» ( <string> | <atom> ) «]»
                  | «change» «[» <string> «]»
                  | «at» «[» <string> «]»
                  | «time» «[» <string> «]»
                  | «signal»
                  | «completion» «[» ( <string> | <atom> ) «]»
<action>        ::= («exec» | «execute») «[» ( <string> | <atom> ) «]»
                  | («exec» | «execute») «[» <behav> «]»
                  | «abort» «[» ( <string> | <atom> ) «]»
                  | «abort» «[» <do-behav> «]»
<behav>         ::= <atom> «.» ( «entry» | «do» | «exit» )
<do-behav>      ::= <atom> «.do»
<number>        ::= <integer> | <float>
<integer>       ::= [ <sign-opt> ] <digit>+
<float>         ::= [ <sign-opt> ] <digit>+ «.» <digit>+
<sign-opt>      ::= «+» | «-»
<boolean>       ::= «true» | «false»
<atom>          ::= <alpha> { <alphanum> }*
                  | «'» { <alpha-ch> }* «'»
<string>        ::= «"» { <string-ch> }* «"»
<alphanum>      ::= <alpha> | <digit>
<digit>         ::= «0» | «1» |...| «9»
<alpha>         ::= «A» |...| «Z» | «a» |...| «z»
<alpha-ch>      ::= any character except «'», and control chars
<string-ch>     ::= any character except «"», and control chars
```

References

1. Pnueli, A.: The temporal logic of programs. In: Proceedings of of the 18th Annual Symposium on Foundations of Computer Science, SFCS 1977, pp. 46–57. IEEE Computer Society. USA (1977)
2. Havelund, K., Peled, D.: On monitoring linear temporal properties. Formal Methods Syst. Des. **60**, 1–21 (2023)
3. Goodloe, A., Havelund, K.: High-integrity runtime verification. Computer **57**, 37–45 (2024)
4. Couvreur, J.-M.: On-the-fly verification of linear temporal logic. In: Wing, J.M., Woodcock, J., Davies, J. (eds.) FM 1999. LNCS, vol. 1708, pp. 253–271. Springer, Heidelberg (1999). https://doi.org/10.1007/3-540-48119-2_16
5. Gerth, R., Peled, D., Vardi, M.Y., Wolper, P.: Simple on-the-fly automatic verification of linear temporal logic. In: PSTV 1995. IAICT, pp. 3–18. Springer, Boston, MA (1996). https://doi.org/10.1007/978-0-387-34892-6_1
6. Somenzi, F., Bloem, R.: Efficient Büchi automata from LTL formulae. In: Emerson, E.A., Sistla, A.P. (eds.) CAV 2000. LNCS, vol. 1855, pp. 248–263. Springer, Heidelberg (2000). https://doi.org/10.1007/10722167_21
7. Daniele, M., Giunchiglia, F., Vardi, M.Y.: Improved automata generation for linear temporal logic. In: Halbwachs, N., Peled, D. (eds.) CAV 1999. LNCS, vol. 1633, pp. 249–260. Springer, Heidelberg (1999). https://doi.org/10.1007/3-540-48683-6_23
8. Diekert, V., Gastin, P.: First-order definable languages. In: Flum, J., Grädel, E., Wilke, T., (eds.), Logic and Automata: History and Perspectives. Texts in Logic and Games, vol. 2, pp. 261–306 (2008)
9. Chatterjee, K., Goharshady, A.K., Goharshady, E.K., Karrabi, M., Žikelić, Đ.: Sound and complete witnesses for template-based verification of LTL properties on polynomial programs (2024)
10. Barrett, C., Sebastiani, R., Seshia, S.A., Tinelli, C.: Satisfiability modulo theories. Handbook of Satisfiability, pp. 825–885 (2009)
11. Biere, A., Cimatti, A., Clarke, E., Zhu, Y.: Symbolic model checking without BDDs. In: Cleaveland, W.R. (ed.) TACAS 1999. LNCS, vol. 1579, pp. 193–207. Springer, Heidelberg (1999). https://doi.org/10.1007/3-540-49059-0_14
12. Holzmann, G.J.: The model checker SPIN. IEEE Trans. Software Eng. **23**(5), 279–295 (1997)
13. Leuschel, M., Butler, M.: ProB: a model checker for B. In: Araki, K., Gnesi, S., Mandrioli, D. (eds.) FME 2003. LNCS, vol. 2805, pp. 855–874. Springer, Heidelberg (2003). https://doi.org/10.1007/978-3-540-45236-2_46
14. Besnard, V., Brun, M., Jouault, F., Teodorov, C., Dhaussy, P.: Unified LTL verification and embedded execution of UML models. In: Proceedings of the 21st ACM/IEEE International Conference on Model Driven Engineering Languages and Systems, pp. 112–122. ACM (2018)
15. Schützenmeier, N., Käppel, M., Fichtner, M., Jablonski, S.: Scenario-based model checking of declarative process models. In: Proceedings of the 25th International Conference on Enterprise Information Systems (ICEIS 2023), pp. 406–417. SciTePress, Lisbon (2023)

16. Maggi, F.M., Westergaard, M., Montali, M., van der Aalst, W.M.P.: Runtime verification of LTL-based declarative process models. In: Khurshid, S., Sen, K. (eds.) RV 2011. LNCS, vol. 7186, pp. 131–146. Springer, Heidelberg (2012). https://doi.org/10.1007/978-3-642-29860-8_11
17. André, É., Liu, S., Liu, Y., Choppy, C., Sun, J., Dong, J.S.: Formalizing UML state machines for automated verification – a survey. ACM Comput. Surv. **55**(13s), 1–47 (2023)

Author Index